What I

LEAV

MOVING FOR

... HOPE AND COURAGE.

"*Leaving the Past Behind* touches the reader through the author's unself-conscious honesty and vulnerability. Glenda Alvord's focus on practical ways to change persistent thought patterns is a refreshing approach, as she points the wounded soul to the One who stands ready to heal."

Jennifer Garrity Author of *Reich Child: A Lebensborn Life*
Greater Europe Mission

"This is a very important work that every person involved in ministry should read. Child abuse colors and distorts every aspect of life and those who seek to minister need to be informed and prepared to deal with it. What courage it must have taken to share this story. Thank you!"

George Helton, Minister Retired, Counselor, Yakima, WA

"I had the pleasure of reading and re-reading the book during the editing process and it encouraged me to continue "moving forward" on my own healing path. Once in the reader's hands, may it accompany a host of men and women on a journey of delivery."

Dianne Mayse, MSMFT, retired Marriage and Family Therapist

"Glenda's personal struggles with childhood sexual abuse and her steps toward healing are the backdrop of this book. This is a good primer for anyone who is starting their own journey toward healing."

Mary Miller, Greater Europe Mission, Pastoral Care

"Glenda gives tremendous insight into a little child's mind and inability to communicate after an abusive situation, as well as the signals to watch for in children. She also walks through effective steps toward healing. A must read!"

Iva Morelli, Editing Consultant

"As the mother of two young sons who were abused repeatedly by a trusted family friend, I pray parents will read this book and cue into any signals their children are sending regarding unease around anyone. Children must be assured of their parent's love and desire to be told anytime they feel uncomfortable. They must know their bodies belong to them! No one else! May God bless this book, spread it far and wide and may it enlighten and help all who read it."

Kathy Parks, Portland, OR

"The courage that Glenda exemplifies by putting her story in writing assures survivors they are not alone in this healing journey and that Christ, the healer, is still at work today. Her well-grounded knowledge of Scripture and passion for Jesus radiate not only through her life, but also in the penned pages of her story. Glenda speaks personally of how the living words of God transform thoughts and heal wounds. She shows that the difficult healing journey is worth pursuing, especially when the God of Hosts is at the center of the journey and advocating for you."

Terri Smalley, LCSW, ACSW

"A sensitively told story of a journey from woundedness to wholeness during which the light of God's faithfulness shines through. The story is helpful, hopeful and encouraging for others on a similar quest. If you've not been there, it is altogether too easy to ignore. But we must not. Too many lives have been destroyed by our reluctance, even as people of faith, to confront the abuse."

Paul R. Smith, D.Min., Presbyterian pastor and author of several books including *Jesus, Meet Him Again for the First Time* and *God's Plan for Our Good.*

"Ever so often a book comes along that tells the story of how abuse shreds the soul—and how God restores. Leaving the Past Behind: Moving Forward with Hope and Courage will serve as a reliable guide in that journey. It is packed with insight that only a woman who has been there can offer. I recommend this book to every woman who needs the courage to heal."

Paula Rinehart, LCSW, author of *Strong Women , Soft Hearts.*

"Glenda has graduated from the school of hard knocks, and her willingness to share her life's lessons provides us with a treasure trove of lessons we can learn the easy way - by reading this book and applying its wisdom, before we find ourselves in similar circumstances. I, personally, would use this book in several arenas, including pre-marital counseling, grief recovery, leadership training, and more. It is a great, very Biblical tool."

Tom Eynon, Army combat officer; missionary to Taiwan, China, Hong Kong, and Russia.

LEAVING
THE PAST BEHIND:

moving forward with hope and courage

Glenda Platt Alvord

Entrust Source Publishers
For more information, please go to: www.entrustsource.com.

Leaving the Past Behind: Moving Forward with Hope and Courage

All Scripture quotations, unless otherwise indicated, are taken from the New International Version copyright 1984.
ISBN-978-1-942308-27-0

Cover created by Entrust Source LLC, Judy Buckert

Printed in the United States of America

Entrust Source Publishers
281 Camino la Pasida
Rio Rico, AZ 85648
www.entrustsourcepublishers.com

In Memory of Louis Platt,
a man without guile.
John 1:47
1941-2010

To my children and grandchildren:
Jeremy, Heather, Daniel and Abby Platt.
Lizzy, Scott, Mason, Oliver and Calvin Minaglia
who give me joy every day,
and to my husband
Herb Alvord
who encouraged my every step.

PREFACE

BURTIGNY, SWITZERLAND
OCTOBER 2016

The village below lies still in the quiet of the autumn afternoon. Beyond Lake Geneva, Eiger, Jungfrau and Mount Blanc stand sentinel over this peaceful valley as local farmers harvest corn and plant winter wheat in the fields that cover the surrounding hills. The air is rich with the smell of freshly plowed earth and cut hay. I am surrounded by fall's bounty. Fields of sunflowers turn their faces to the sun, cornstalks rustle in the light breeze. I am at peace.

But that was not so days before as I walked these hills questioning.

"Am I really to do this?"

The impression I received was a clear affirmative.

"I'm not sure I can," I argued.
"I will give you the words. It needs to be done."

And so, I write.

ACKNOWLEDGMENTS

Although it is the author who spends hours in solitude writing, rewriting, and wondering if the process will ever end, the inspiration to see it through comes from a cadre of family and friends.

Those who did the hard work of slogging through the first draft and pronounced it worth pursuing were dear friends Nancy Bringolf, Rachel Bucholtz, Mary Beth Holladay, Jay and Priscilla Maurer, Kathy Parks and my husband Herb Alvord. They were followed by George Helton, long time pastor and counselor, Rusty Rustenbach author of *Listening and Healing Prayer* as well as Karen Kotecki, Navigators, Europe and Africa.

Dianne Mayse a dear friend and counselor provided editing and invaluable suggestions as did Paula Rinehart, counselor, speaker, and author of *Sex and the Soul of a Woman.*

Friends in Germany Terri Smalley, Bev Brettenny and Marcy Pusey, of Teach Beyond and author of *Reclaiming Hope* also encouraged me through the process.

Jenny Garrity, Greater Europe Mission and author of *Reich Child: A Lebensborn Life* suggested Entrust Source Publishers where I was connected with Editor Iva Morelli and their wonderful publishing team without whom this endeavor would not have come to fruition. Thank you all!

Niece Nina and Will de Burgh made their lovely home Kilteelagh House available for rest and writing. I will not soon forget those peaceful productive days and Irish country walks. Thank you, Nina and Will.

Last but far from least is the 250 plus individuals who read my newsletters and prayed this publication into reality.

May God richly bless you all for accompanying me on this journey and may your prayers return a hundredfold fruit in the lives of many.

AUTHOR'S NOTE

When I began this writing, I was puzzled that I could not refer to my sister or to myself by name. Thus, I used the names "Sister" and "Li'l Sis," myself being the latter.

Neither could I write in first person although Part I is a first-person account. Initially, this was puzzling to me. It wasn't that I couldn't take ownership. It was my story. It was that I didn't want to make it their story as I realized if I referred to my sister and myself by name, I would be identifying them with all the sorrow that was to come, laying it all on their innocent young shoulders, and I couldn't do that. They were happy and untouched by that which lay ahead. I wanted to protect them as long as I could.

It was not until the end of Chapter 5 that I could finally write in first person. The worst had been revealed, and Li'l Sis had become me. Until that point, the chapters are written in third person. The Reflection, however, at the end of each chapter is written in first person.

INTRODUCTION

Some ask, "Why not forget the past and leave it behind? Isn't it better to live in the present?"

Others see it quite differently: "Buried hurts are buried alive only to resurface."

Most individuals who have experienced childhood trauma in the form of abuse or neglect default to the first approach. They desperately try to forget, often building walls of idyllic childhood memories around the abuse to minimize the effects, even as I did. Others totally block out their past, remembering nothing.

Unfortunately, the experience of many has shown that traumatic events, especially when they occur during childhood, can be life altering.

As I considered my own childhood experience, I saw that at an early age, I came to believe and base my life on assumptions that were untrue; assumptions such as:

I must be bad, or bad things wouldn't happen to me.

If I could show God and everyone else that I am worthy of protection, maybe they would protect me, and the abuse would stop.

No one cares about me. No one will protect me. I'm going to have to look out for myself.

Out of an attempt to "look out for myself," came the development of negative or dysfunctional coping mechanisms resulting in an unhealthy independence and attitude of distrust toward my parents and God.

Although these coping mechanisms provided a sense of security in the short term, over time they became a part of the problem as I came to depend on my ability to cope instead of turning to God and godly principles for dealing directly with difficulties. It is only as these and other negative defense mechanisms are recognized, traced to their roots and processed, that healing can occur. This "processing" often requires the guidance of a godly mentor or counselor. It can be very difficult to deal with these issues alone. As James writes: "Therefore confess your sins to each other and pray for each other so that you may be healed. The prayer of a righteous person is powerful and effective" (James 5:16).

As long as we live in this fallen world, children will sadly continue to experience trauma from abuse and neglect resulting in dysfunction that follows into adulthood. Although I am not a trained counselor or licensed therapist, it is my hope that my experience as reflected in this writing will bring comfort to victims and understanding to those who minister to them.

I have been bent and broken, but - I hope - into a better shape.
— Charles Dickens, *Great Expectations*

RESPONSE

I will never be that child again, but I have become something better. Scarred but becoming whole; weaker yet stronger; disillusioned yet hopeful, not only for myself but for others who have traveled the same path (see 2 Corinthians 4:8-9).

Coming to see one's life as a whole rather than only focusing on the incidents of abuse and neglect is an integral part of the healing process. For this reason, the discussion questions focus on many different aspects of life not just on the negative.

1 How would you personally define childhood abuse and neglect? Consider different kinds of abuse as well as neglect.

2 Some ask, "Why not forget the past and leave it behind? Isn't it better to live in the present?" Others see it quite differently: "Buried hurts are buried alive only to resurface."Where do you stand on this issue? Explain your position.

3 Why do you think many individuals who have experienced childhood abuse and neglect default to forgetting the past or blocking it out?

4 Can you recall traumatic events that occurred in your childhood that had the potential of being or actually were life altering?

5 Did you try to build "idyllic memories" around traumatic events from your childhood,minimize them, forget them, or block them out

6 Did you come to believe lies about yourself, God and others as a result of these traumatic events? Lies such as, "I must not be worth protecting or God—or someone—would protect me," "I'm damaged goods," or "God can't love me or He would protect me."

TABLE OF CONTENTS

PART ONE
THE STORY

The following chapters chronicle the story of a little girl's journey from serendipitous childhood to a very dark period of the soul. Over time this was followed by a gradual return to functional normalcy furthered by an encounter with Jesus Christ who would become her Savior and Lord.

Some chapters are bright and filled with light, others are sad and dark. Through the Reflection at the end of each chapter, the development of negative coping skills or defense mechanisms common to survivors of childhood trauma can be traced as can the gradual ascent out of the dark into the light of the grace of God.

Tracing the development of negative coping mechanisms is crucial as many survivors of childhood trauma are unaware of them. They simply view them as a part of their God-given personality that people just have to accept. Sadly these coping mechanisms developed to make the victims feel safe in a world gone awry can become barriers to spiritual growth and hinder the ability to work cooperatively with team members.

Additionally, it is crucial for a survivor of childhood abuse or neglect to look for the good, however small, that has occurred in one's life. To only concentrate on the negative will result in stoicism, a victim mentality or bitterness, none of which leads to healing.

As you read, I pray you will gain a clearer understanding of the source of your own struggles, or perhaps of the struggles of others in your life and ministry. And out of that understanding will come mutual support and growth, resulting in increased fruitfulness and a clearer understanding of who you are in Christ, His love for you and how He will redeem the past to grow you and open doors of healing ministry to others. "Praise be to the God and Father of our Lord Jesus Christ who comforts us in all our troubles, so that we can comfort those in any trouble with the comfort we ourselves received from God" (2 Corinthians 1:3-4; see also Ephesians 1:11; Romans 8:28).

RESPONSE

1. The author speaks of "negative coping mechanisms common to survivors of childhood abuse." What might some of those negative coping mechanisms rooted in childhood trauma be?

2. Can you identify negative coping skills in your own life that originated in childhood?

3. According to the text, it is crucial for a survivor of childhood abuse or neglect to look for the good, however small, that has occurred in one's life. For to only concentrate on the negative will result in stoicism, a victim mentality or bitterness, none of which leads to healing.

   ▸ How would you know if you have a victim mentality, are bitter or if you have become stoic regarding childhood abuse and/or neglect? What clues might there be? Begin by defining the terms.

CHAPTER 1
HAPPY DAYS

DECATUR, ALABAMA 1948

I remember her, but the memories come and go like a dream scene from a black and white movie with fog blowing across the set.

Sometimes I catch a glimpse of her, but then she steps out of view as I arrive on a scene that takes me back to my childhood.

At two years old, Li'l Sis was not a pretty child, but was rather a pale little girl with thin straight blond hair and green eyes when you were expecting blue. She was, however, a happy child, despite having little to be happy about, at least as seen from a materialistic point of view; however, of this she was blissfully unaware.

Her primary joy was time spent with her pretty mama. Li'l Sis loved snuggling in Mama's soft bosom and playing with her curly brown hair.

Each morning, after their breakfast of biscuits and gravy, mother and child washed and dried the dishes together in the sparsely furnished kitchen. They worked side by side; Li'l Sis standing on the seat of a straight back chair so that she could reach the flatware which she carefully dried. Peeling oilcloth covered the table which held the enamel dishpan and the inverted dishes drying on a sackcloth towel decorated in the corners with a bit of embroidery. Next to the table stood a kerosene stove for cooking. On hot summer days, the acrid smell of kerosene permeated the air.

In the middle of the kitchen stood an enamel table with four straight back chairs. It too had an oilcloth cover with a red checkered pattern. The table was a new acquisition from the secondhand store, and Mama was very proud of it. There was also a stand-alone kitchen cabinet with an enameled workspace. Above, sliding tin panels concealed shelves where dishes and staples were stored. Under the workspace were more shelves for pots and pans and several drawers; one of which was a huge bin where flour was kept.

After finishing their morning chores, Mama and Li'l Sis would sit on the front porch of their clapboard house which stood in a row of identical two-room houses behind the Decatur Cotton Mill. As Mama shelled beans for supper, Li'l Sis played at her feet or "helped" shell beans, most of which escaped her small hands and rolled around the porch floor at which Mama would say, "Be careful baby. That's our supper."

Sometimes they ate their noon meal of leftover biscuits and molasses there on the porch with the hollyhocks swaying in the light breeze, and the air abuzz with the sound of bees in the petunias.

On Monday mornings, they'd heat water on the stove and do the wash in the big zinc tub that sat on the back porch. Mama rubbed the dirty clothes on her washboard, and Li'l Sis washed her dolly clothes on her own miniature board.

With the laundry finished and hanging on the line across the backyard, they returned to the front porch and shared an orange soda as they watched the cotton lint from the mill dance in the hot summer sun. Hollyhocks, cannas and marigolds clustered around the porch steps where Li'l Sis played decorating her mud pies with smooth round stones or the flowers from dandelions.

Petunias spread their sweet fragrance as they cascaded down the sides of old buckets and chamber pots forming a border along the porch edge and on each end of the steps. These were Mama's favorite flowers, and they moved with her every time the family relocated which was not infrequently.

Li'l Sis was a treasured child, a gift from God when the doctors said there could be no more babies. From time to time, Mama would remind Li'l Sis of this which always made the little girl smile.

Mama sat in a cane bottom chair, and the little girl sat in another with her legs happily dangling as she sucked her soda through a hole in the bottle cap. Mama made that hole with a hammer and nail she kept in the kitchen drawer especially for the purpose.

Around four o'clock, the sound of the school bus could be heard approaching on the parallel street. Li'l Sis became all ears, listening for it to stop. Once it squeaked to a halt, she was on the alert, peering down the shady lane that ran between the row of houses and the back of the cotton mill.

"Mama," Li'l Sis squealed, "I see her coming." This was followed by a happy dance as she waved and hollered, "Sister's coming. I see her, I see her!"

Tired and sweaty from the long bus ride, Sister trudged up the steps with Li'l Sis at her heels. She plopped her heavy load of books down on the porch, then seeing the half-full soda bottle still cold from the icebox, she perked up as she asked, "Can I have some?" Sister finished the soda sip by sip making it last as long as she could as she told them about her day at school.

"I just don't understand mathematics, Mama. Teacher goes so fast, and it doesn't make sense."

"Maybe your daddy can help you when he gets home, Sister. There's no use in my trying." We knew it was true. Mama was smart enough, but she just couldn't see the numbers or read the story problems. Her eyesight was that bad.

SISTER'S FRIENDS

When Sister's friends came to the door calling for her to come out and play, Li'l Sis dropped whatever she was doing and in a flash was out the door after her sister. "Wait for me," Li'l Sis cried as the group of laughing ten-year-old's disappeared down the sandy alley behind the row of small white houses.

Next came Mama's voice from the house, "Sister, don't you leave that baby," and Sister would wait, torn between her disappearing friends and her approaching little sister flying after her as she ran through the tall dry weeds of the backyard.

When she reached her sister, with a tearful, "Don't go off and leave me," Sister would stoop down beside her, give her a hug and sympathize with her scratched legs, as she looked over her shoulder to see her friends turn the corner into the hedgerow of plum trees that lined the creek behind the house.

Later when they caught up, her friends would scold Sister, "Why you always have to bring that tagalong? You ought to just run off and leave her." At this, Li'l Sis hid her face in her silent sister's skirts, wondering at such a horrible possibility.

Sister and Li'l Sis sat on the sandy bank under the wild plum trees, pushing the cool wet sand around with their feet, feeling a bit left out as the others talked of forming a club and who could and couldn't be in it. The tension eased when one of the kids found an old tin can and they all joined in the search and capture of tadpoles and crayfish.

After a while, they heard Mama's voice calling them home. They hurried down the sandy alley making soft footprints with their bare feet as they called, "We're coming, Mama."

FAMILY LIFE

The girls each had daily chores. One of Sister's summer jobs was picking and washing lettuce and other veggies from the little garden behind the house. Li'l Sis dried the flatware when Mama washed dishes and she also set the table each day at suppertime. She loved that chore especially because of Mama's pretty dishes. There were golden colored cups and saucers that came out of oatmeal boxes as well as "flowery" plates from the filling station where Papa got gas for the car. Sweet iced tea was poured still warm over ice chips that Mama put in jelly glasses or small fruit jars and set at each place.

The dishes from the gas station had a wide blue border with pink roses in the middle. Li'l Sis loved those dishes and would trace their pattern with fingers that were grubby from playing in the dirt, that is, until Mama caught her and sent her off to wash her hands in the basin on the shelf by the back door.

Soon Papa would come home, tired and dirty from his job at Red Stone Arsenal where he decommissioned ordinance. Li'l Sis didn't know what those big words meant, but she knew her Papa was glad to have a job even if his back hurt. He was also happy to see his little girls who ran to take his shoes off, give him a hug and ask for a nickel for a Coca-Cola, which was what they called any soft drink in that day.

By then supper would be on the table; pinto beans, turnip greens with fatback, cornbread and wilted salad with green onions. The girls thought the dinner was grand, but Papa often said that he worried about the hot bacon grease that Mama poured over the salad greens. Mama would reply that a little fat never hurt anyone, and the girls would sigh in relief as they loved that wilted salad and were relieved it would appear again.

After supper, Papa sat on the porch stoop with the family, read the newspaper or played his guitar awhile, and then went to bed early as his back was sure to be sore and hurting. A cool breeze blew the curtains in a rhythmic dance as the frogs from the branch that ran behind the house lulled them all to sleep.

THE HOUSE NEAR THE TRACKS—FLINT, ALABAMA

Mama grew up in the country on a small farm and was never quite at home living in a town. In case Papa forgot, she reminded him regularly. One day he came home from work with the news that he had heard of a house for rent in a rural area several miles away near the town of Flint.

It was a big four-room house, each room half as big as the whole mill house. Best of all to Mama, there were no near neighbors. The house sat all alone in a field near the railroad tracks. Because Mama worried that the girls might get hurt on the tracks, she had a solemn talk with Sister and Li'l Sis about the dangers of railroad tracks and trains in general. Mama ended the conversation with the story of a little boy who got his foot caught between the railroad ties as a train was coming. After that talk, there was no danger of the girls going near those tracks. They happily stayed in their yard and waved to the engineer as he went past blowing the horn and waving to the little girls.

The only time they neared the tracks was when they walked along the rails with Papa to see if they could find coal (for the fireplace) that had fallen from the open cars as the train passed through.

On Sundays, the family went to the local Methodist church where they met their near neighbors. After church one Sunday, the Turners who lived about a mile away, invited them for Sunday dinner. Mama was glad because she was awfully shy and found it hard to meet folks. When they arrived, Mrs. Turner met Mama at the door and invited her into the kitchen to help dish up the dinner. Mama was always comfortable if she was given a job to do. "Makes getting to know people a lot easier," she'd say.

The Turners were farmers who raised cows, chickens and pigs, most of which made their appearance on the dinner table. There was fried chicken and leftover roast from the week before and all manner of vegetables, cornbread and sweet tea, which were staples on any country table unless there was no money in the house at all.

Everyone had a good time. Li'l Sis loved the fried chicken. Sister met a new friend, Francis. Papa, ever the farmer at heart, loved being on a farm again. Mama enjoyed it too, except for the flies which were everywhere. Papa said it was because the barn lot was so close to the house. Mama said it was because the window screens were full of holes.

Holey screens were common as were ramshackle houses like the one the family lived in set so far off the road that visitors rarely came. One afternoon while Papa was at work and Sister at school, there came a knock at the door. This happened so rarely that Mama hesitated answering the door. After peeking through the curtains and seeing that the visitor looked respectable, Mama opened the door and the next thing Li'l Sis knew, there was a new Electrolux in the house. Mama never had a vacuum cleaner before, but she had one now, and a coupon book for payments to go with it.

The girls took turns vacuuming the wooden floor and cleaning the dirt out of the wide cracks between the boards. Papa said they'd have trouble heating the house that winter cause the dirt between the boards served as chinks against the cold wind blowing up through the floor. Papa must have known what he was talking about because that winter when the cold wind blew, the linoleum rug would rise off the floor as though it had a mind of its own.

REFLECTION

I am amazed at how much I remember of that happy time prior to the abuse and the explosion of fallout in my life. What a happy, contented little girl I was basking in the love and devotion of my mother. A barefoot little sprite who marveled at spiderwebs sprinkled with dew and the strange insects hiding in Mama's flowers.

However, I wonder what it must have felt like for Sister, sitting in math class day after day, understanding little and knowing help was not to be had at home. Papa was good at math. He used it in his work, but he did it all in his head. He didn't know how to explain it to Sister.

Mama, dear pretty Mama, had her own problems as well. Because of her limited eyesight, she rarely left the house. There was also no reason to leave. Papa brought home any groceries that were needed. There was the garden out back and the canned goods that Mama and Papa had put up the summer before. We lived to ourselves, had no visitors and were content so. When necessity dictated that Mama go into town, she walked down the street keeping her eyes on the ground so as not to miss the curb, or she stared stoically ahead leaving puzzled neighbors wondering why she didn't acknowledge them in passing. The answer was simple, you didn't speak to folks you didn't know, and Mama didn't see anyone she knew. She saw that poorly. But she was happy. God had given her a child after the loss of her second baby girl, and Li'l Sis was the joy of her life.

Looking back on those family scenes, the overwhelming impression is that I was loved. I was loved by them all. Although in a very short time, I would come to doubt that I was loved by anyone.

Yet, as I write, memories flood back of happy innocent times of enjoyment that I had forgotten. Years buried in shame and hurt dominated my memories. What a loss. There was so much joy in those early years. Are those incidents of joy less worthy of memory than the sad ones that held sway for so many years? I think not. I also think there is healing in those happy memories, more healing yet to come.
And then there was the Electrolux. Mama finally had to give it up 40 years later when parts were no longer available. It proved to have been a very good investment, indeed.

RESPONSE

DECATUR, ALABAMA 1948

1 How would you describe Li'l Sis's relationship with her mama at age two? List phrases that support your answer.

2 How would you describe Li'l Sis's self-image at this age?

SISTER'S FRIENDS

3 From the perspective of yourself as a child, would you most identify with Sister or Li'l Sis in the following scenes from the text? Explain.

"Next came Mama's voice from the house, 'Sister, don't you leave that baby,' and Sister would wait, torn between her disappearing friends and her approaching little sister flying after her as she ran through the tall dry weeds of the backyard."

▸ What thoughts do you think might have gone through Sister's mind during the scene above?

▸ Do you think Mama was right in handling the situation as she did?

▸ What budding character traits do you see in Li'l Sis at this point?

4 "When Li'l Sis reached her sister, with a tearful, 'Don't go off and leave me,' Sister would stoop down beside her, give her a hug and sympathize with her scratched legs, as she looked over her shoulder to see her friends disappear into the hedgerow of plum trees that lined the creek behind the house."

▸ How might the above, if often repeated, affect Sister's view of herself and her world?

FAMILY LIFE

5 How would you describe their family life?

6 Were they concerned or even aware that they lived on or below the poverty level?

7 How does their family life compare to yours growing up?

8 "When there is abuse or neglect in the past, healing can come from remembering sources of past delight like the dinner plates and the joy their beauty brought to Li'l Sis."

▸ Can you recall "sources of delight" that ameliorate difficult things from your childhood? Not that they were equal, but simply something that gave you reprieve however great or small for a period of time.

9 Do you have an affinity for or collect anything that might be rooted in your childhood? Explain.

10 Sources of reprieve can also be attached to shame. Examples might be stealing, lying, masturbation, mistreating a weaker sibling or rebellion, all of which can provide a sense of control or power. Satan loves to use these secret practices to condemn and multiply guilt. Is there anything that you would like to share with the group in this area?

THE HOUSE NEAR THE TRACKS—FLINT, ALABAMA

11 How might living in a city have been difficult for Mama in light of her background and limited eyesight?

12 What does the visit to the Turners, the railroad story, the Electrolux vacuum tell you about Mama's personality?

13 How would you compare/contrast Mama to/with your own mother during your growing up years?

14 I was indeed strong willed, however "my strong-willed determination would prove to be a double-edged sword when as an adult I would face difficulties in my own strength instead of seeking the help of leadership or mature believers in the body of Christ."

- What shadow side of your own strengths do you battle?

CHAPTER 2
LIFE CHANGING

MAMA'S ILLNESS

At times Mama didn't feel well and she would ask Li'l Sis to play quietly with her crayons while she laid down for a spell. Li'l Sis would roll out an old roll of wallpaper and draw crayon landscapes on the back to her heart's content; green mountains and bright flowers and houses where happy, smiling mamas and papas and little children lived.

Saturdays meant long trips to doctor offices, sometimes to distant cities, ever in search of a doctor who could make Mama well. In those days, there were no appointments. You just showed up and waited for hours until your turn came. But, still, Mama didn't get better.

Rather than sit all afternoon in the doctor's office waiting with Mama, Papa would take the little girls to the picture show downtown. The only problem was Papa only liked war movies. Saturday afternoon became a torment for the little girls as they sat through World War II movie after movie: *The Bataan Death March, The Capture of Iwo Jima*. They were undoubtedly the only two little girls in the state of Alabama who knew well the history of the war in the Pacific, at least as told by Hollywood.

Mama had two things wrong with her. She could hardly see. "Unless you're up right close, I can't see who you are," she would say. Her other problem was something she called "female troubles." The not seeing, Li'l Sis could understand. The only thing she knew about "female troubles" was that they put Mama to bed and Li'l Sis had to play quietly.

One day Li'l Sis overheard Mama and Papa talking about paying one of the Turner girls to take care of Mama after she got home from the hospital.

"I can take care of Mama," Li'l Sis announced. "I set the table, I dry the dishes, vacuum the floors, and I can help Sister cook."

"But baby, when Mama is in the hospital you would be here all alone."

"I'll go with you to the hospital and take care of you there," Li'l Sis declared.

Mama smiled and patted her on the head as she explained that Li'l Sis would be going to stay with Cousin Josie and her family. There she could play with her cousin Amanda on the farm. As soon as Mama was better, they would come get her.

Li'l Sis was heartbroken. The decision had been made; nevertheless, she persisted.

"Please, Mama. I'm a big girl, and I will take care of you. Please, Mama. Please, Mama. Please!" She cried herself to sleep that night as did her mama.

THE STAY WITH COUSIN JOSIE AND HER FAMILY

Soon the day came. Sunday after church the family made the hour drive across the big Tennessee River bridge, through Huntsville, over Monte Sano Mountain down into the valley and up Jenkins Mountain where Cousin Josie and her husband Cousin Fred lived on a farm with their son Nick and his family.

Once they arrived, Li'l Sis was quiet and worried about being left there. She couldn't even bring herself to play with her cousin Amanda. After Sunday dinner when everything was washed up and cleared away, Cousin Janie played the guitar and everyone sang old hymns and funny songs. "When the Roll is Called Up Yonder," "Going Down Cripple Creek," and "Let the Circle Be Unbroken," but still Li'l Sis clung to Mama's skirt.

When the time came to leave, Li'l Sis screamed and pled with her tearful mama, "Take me with you, Mama. Take me with you." Cousin Josie scooped her up and held her fast, as she struggled to get away. Reaching toward her mother's retreating figure, she continued to beg, "Don't leave me. Please, Mama, please."

As the car drove away, Li'l Sis continued to hold out her arms begging to go with her mama. Sister's face sadly framed in the back window of the car was wet with tears as she waved goodbye until the little black coup disappeared down the dirt road.

I wonder, did Li'l Sis know her life was about to change forever? I don't know, but I think children sometimes know more than we give them credit for knowing. Grown-up Cousin Janie (Nick's wife) told her, "Stop that crying. You are a big girl and big girls didn't cry." Besides she had Cousin Amanda to play with. She had nothing to cry about! But still, she cried. Cousin Josie took her on her lap and comforted her a while until she quieted down, then gave her a vanilla wafer and some milk which made things better.

As the days went by, Li'l Sis gradually settled down. She played with her cousin under the big trees in the backyard making playhouses of boards set on old coffee cans where they fed their dollies and put them to bed. They took turns pushing each other in the tire swing, chasing the chickens, and watching the cows chew their cud in the barn lot.

Sometimes Li'l Sis cried for her mama, especially at night, or when she took her afternoon nap. Cousin Josie would comfort her saying, "Your Mama will come soon, child. She'll come soon."

After lunch each day, Li'l Sis took a nap on the big soft bed in the front bedroom. She would lie there watching the cool breeze blow the sheer curtains until she fell asleep. One afternoon she was wakened by heavy breathing and rough hands on her body. The hands probed and hurt her, but in fear, she froze, afraid to move.

Then Cousin Janie came into the room, saying in an angry voice, "Nick, what are you doing?" Her husband stooping over Li'l Sis, answered that he was checking to see if Li'l Sis had wet the bed. Angry words followed during which the child slid off the bed and ran wide-eyed with fright to Cousin Josie. More angry words followed as Cousin Josie put her in a tub of water and began to wash her with soap.

Li'l Sis was frightened and confused by all the shouting and anger. There was no warm water, and the soap stung her body as she shivered in the cold tub. Cousin Josie was short with her and seemed angry which made Li'l Sis wonder what she'd done to make them all angry and want to hurt her. All Li'l Sis wanted was to go home to her mama. No one seemed to like her anymore. Not even Amanda who had always played with her. What had she done?

Finally, the day came. A car could be heard on the gravel road that ran from the highway along the mountain's edge to Cousin Josie's house. It was Papa, Mama and Sister and they had come to get her. She ran and cried and laughed and danced. She could go home with her Mama.

HOME AGAIN

It wasn't long before Li'l Sis was herself again, running barefoot through the warm summer grass, watching the bees in the clover and hearing Papa talk about one of these days when they got settled on their own place, they'd have their own beehives and sweet honey. When Papa said, "One of these days," it seemed like a long way off, but it didn't matter. Li'l Sis was just happy to be home again.

Autumn followed summer and Sister went back to school. Li'l Sis counted the hours till Sister came home as she sat in front of the fireplace with her roll of old wallpaper drawing beautiful green mountains and flowers with roads going off in the distance. Sometimes she'd take a toy car and push it along the road she had drawn, wondering where it led. Other times she'd play with her baby doll or sit before the fire snug in her flannel pajamas and robe "reading" her Little Golden books and eating her lunch of pinto beans and cornbread from supper the night before. (When it was really cold, you stayed in your pajamas and housecoat because they were warmer than your clothes; sometimes you wore both.)

When Mama felt well enough, and oft times when she didn't, every few months she spent a day making lye soap from rendered bacon grease and lye which she processed from fireplace ashes. This she used to wash the family laundry in a big black cast-iron washpot in the backyard. When Mama felt especially bad, Papa filled the washpot with water from the well the night before. Then he'd pile kindling and firewood around the pot so Mama just had to start the fire with a stick of kindling soaked in kerosene to heat the water for washing the clothes. In the coldest months, the laundry was done in a washtub on the back porch or in the kitchen with water heated on the stove.

Each day Mama did the housework and cooked their meals on the kerosene stove, even though she was scared to death of that stove. She told Papa frequently, "That thing is going to blow up one of these days and burn us all up."

It never did, but Mama's fear was not unfounded as confirmed by periodic black smoke on the horizon and the news of disaster in the neighborhood. Mama's response was always the same. First, she went to the smokehouse to find a wooden crate or a sturdy box that she would line with newspaper, then she filled it with canned beans, soup, pickles and peaches that she and Papa had put up the summer before. Next, she would go through her quilt box and agonize over which one of her lovely old quilts she would give away. Most of them were worn like the ones on their beds, but Mama reasoned that if the family who got burned out, had nothing, "worn" wouldn't matter. When Papa got home from work, he would make the delivery.

In the afternoon, when Sister came home from school, the two girls would go outside and play with the Turner kids. Francis had an old bike that she let Sister ride. Li'l Sis, who never wanted to be left out of anything, begged to go for a ride until Sister finally let her sit on the back fender and off they went. Everything was just fine until Li'l Sis got her bare foot too close to the spokes. Her ankle was bruised and cut. Li'l Sis yelled and cried as Sister comforted her. Her ankle hurt awfully bad. But having been warned to stay away from the bike, she was afraid to tell Mama what she had done. Even so she was glad she had gone for the ride. Until she got her foot caught in the spokes, it was splendid, and she couldn't wait to learn to ride herself.

Every day around 4 o'clock the freight train from Memphis came through. The girls and neighborhood kids playing in the front yard waved and made signs for the engineer to blow the horn which he always did. In response they danced around, laughing as they made the sound, "Choo chooooo." Afterward, they returned to their games of Kick the Can, Hide and Seek or Throw the Ball Over the Roof. Mama didn't like the bounce, bounce, bounce of the ball on the tin roof, so that game didn't last long.

REFLECTION

I look back with a great deal of admiration for Papa, dedicating each Saturday to finding a doctor who might be able to help Mama get well. He refused to accept that there wasn't a doctor somewhere in north Alabama who could find a solution to Mama's problem. Thus, our regular Saturday journeys to first one doctor and then another continued, sadly, all to no avail.

Decades later that same determination passed down would drive me to find medical care for our small daughter suffering from chronic allergies when treatment was not available in the area of Germany where we lived. When there was a sick family member, you simply didn't give up until all possibilities had been explored.

I cannot help smiling as I remember that strong-willed little girl making clear to all that she did not want to leave her Mama, and furthermore, she was quite capable of caring for Mama herself. I was indeed a strong-willed child who made my opinions known. Yet at the same time, I am saddened as later I would learn that this stay with Cousin Josie wasn't my first extended visit with her family. I cannot but wonder if my aversion to going there was rooted in prior abuse at the hands of Nick which instilled fear in my soul at going there again.

Sister and I both were strong-willed and determined. Most of the time it served us well. Sister would be the first one in the family to graduate high school and go on for further training at a business college. I would be the first in the immediate family to graduate from a university. I'm not sure either of us would have reached those educational milestones without a great deal of determination. Even though, it didn't always serve us well, as we found out that cold winter, when the winds blew through the vacuumed out cracks in the floor as Papa predicted they would.

I thank God for those traits as I fear I would have been destroyed by the events that were to follow had my temperament been otherwise. However being strong willed would not serve me well when as an adult I would face difficulties in my own strength instead of seeking the help of leadership or mature believers in the body of Christ. I mistakenly thought that if God allowed a trial in my life, it was my responsibility to deal with it on my own. This independent spirit would cost me dearly on the mission field. That being said, on the positive side, I never gave up. If a problem arose or a roadblock was thrown in my way, with God's help I would do my best to overcome it.

Medical personnel who work with small children comment on the differences in personality that are observable in newborn nurseries. Throughout my life, I have had a sense of adventure and a love of challenge. In elementary school, I read a biography of Livingston and decided I wanted to travel to Africa as a medical missionary. At sixteen, I left home to live with a relative in another town to receive a better education. After college, I took jobs that others would avoid at all cost: working with drug addicted patients in a county hospital, and a decade later teaching juvenile offenders in a maximum security lock-up facility for a period of 10 years. This followed by seven years teaching in alternative schools. There was also 14 years with my late husband, Louis, in university ministry in Germany. Then at age 70, I returned to Europe to teach in an international school and mentor young missionary families across Europe with my husband, Herb.

It is no wonder that at age 3, I was sure I was equal to the task of caring for my Mama.

However, I was not equal to the task of dealing with the abuse. When the shouting began, thankfully the paralysis of fear was broken, and I ran looking for Cousin Josie. In my confused state, I thought the angry voices were directed at me. Being put in a tub of cold water and washed with stinging soap only added to my confusion. This all contributed toward a feeling of overpowering abandonment and shame which led to the conviction that I had done something terribly wrong. As I look back on that time, I realize it was the reaction of those around me which I interpreted as anger toward me that caused the most pain. If children are surrounded by love, understanding and the reassurance that they have done nothing wrong, much damage can be prevented. Suffering alone is difficult for anyone but for a child it is devastating.

When a child asks the question, "What did I do to cause this?" the follow-up question is: "What can I do to make it right?" This, however, opens a veritable Pandora's Box of dysfunctional behaviors which can include perfectionism, workaholism and people pleasing, all of which are destructive for the victim as well as their relationships.

It is easy to look back and blame Nick who obviously was to blame, but Cousins Josie and Janie knew of the incident, yet they did nothing to protect me from further contact with Nick nor did they inform my parents. At the very least, knowing of the incident would have kept my parents from allowing me to visit them again and prevented future abuse.

The joy of being back in the safety and security of my family largely dispelled the effects of the visit to Cousin Josie and the abuse at the hands of Nick. Soon, all was right again in my world, and I was content and confident in the embrace of my family. Had the encounter with Nick not been repeated, I believe I would have escaped relatively unscathed.

RESPONSE

MAMA'S ILLNESS

1 Illness, work, stress and other worries can distract parents from the care and protection of their children. Was this the case in your family of origin? Explain.

2 Drawing on the back of an old roll of wallpaper became a much loved distraction especially when Mama didn't feel well. Did you have a favorite distraction with which you busied yourself when your parents were occupied or absent?

3 Were there child inappropriate activities in which you participated by default that shaped your personality such as the WW II matinées that became a Saturday staple during Mama's doctor's office visits?

THE STAY WITH COUSIN JOSIE AND HER FAMILY

4 Was there a pivotal event in your childhood that shaped your personality or were there multiple events? Who were the players? Explain.

5 How were you affected by this event(s)? Did you come to believe things about yourself that were untrue? Can you share them with the group?

HOME AGAIN

6 A child exposed to abuse or neglect will often ask the question, "What did I do to cause this?" Was this your experience? Explain.

7 The above question is often followed by, "Since I caused this, what can I do to make it right?" This can open a veritable Pandora's Box of dysfunctional behaviors leading to perfectionism, workaholism, and people pleasing. Does this describe your experience or that of someone you know? If so, explain.

8 When difficult things happen in one's life, they are often followed by a period of respite. Can you recall happy childhood events that followed specific difficult times?

9 Parents or other significant players in your life, who may have failed to provide protection because of illness or simply not being aware, often have redeeming qualities. Can you recall any of those qualities? Have they been passed down to you?

10 As you look back over these questions, is there any new insight?

CHAPTER 3
JOY AND SORROW

THE HOLIDAYS 1948

About the first of November, the Christmas edition of the Sears, Roebuck & Company catalog came in the mail. The girls were delighted and sat for hours before the coal fire choosing "their doll." There was a moment of calamity when Li'l Sis realized that Sister wanted the same doll for Christmas that she had chosen; a beautiful doll with long curly hair and a suitcase full of clothes. Sister told Li'l Sis it didn't matter because there were lots of those dolls in Santa's workshop. "But there is only one in the catalog," Li'l Sis wailed. "Looky here, there is only one." She was heartbroken.

Thanksgiving came cold and wet but inside, everything was warm and toasty with good smells coming from the kitchen. Papa chopped the head off one of Mama's chickens that wasn't laying anymore. Mama said it would probably be tough as the hen was so old, but with cornbread stuffing and gravy, no one was complaining. There was also the sweet, spicy smell of sweet potatoes and pecan pie made from little bitty pecans that Mama and Papa had found under a tree in a deserted pasture. Of course, they had to ask before taking them. You never went onto someone else's property without first asking. Each night for most of a week, they sat before the fire picking the kernels out of the tiny, hard shells. It was worth the effort though. Everyone loved pecan pie.

December 3 was Li'l Sis's third birthday. Mama made her a birthday cake with coconut frosting. After supper, they cut the cake enjoying every morsel. It wasn't every day that you had cake.

As Christmas neared, Papa asked a neighbor if he could cut a Christmas tree out of his fence row for the girls. After Sunday dinner, Papa set out in the drizzle with a bow saw under his arm. About an hour later he came back with a pretty, little cedar tree that he put in an old gallon bucket of rock and sand. Mama and the girls centered it in front of the window in the girl's bedroom which also served as the sitting room and decorated it with silver tinsel and glass balls from the five and dime store. The girls thought it was the most beautiful sight they had ever seen as they nodded off to sleep each night with the light from the fire dancing in the branches and sparkling off the tinsel.

The girls hoped for snow, but only rain fell on the tin roof when they woke on Christmas morning. The rain, however, was soon forgotten as they clamored out of bed to see what Santy Claus had brought them. Squeals of laughter filled the house as they found celluloid Kewpie dolls and new warm pajamas under the tree. There was also a Little Golden Book called Santy's Workshop nestled in the branches for Li'l Sis.

Then came a moment of disappointment as Li'l Sis wondered aloud why they didn't get their dolls from the Sears Roebuck Christmas Catalog. Sister thought maybe Santy Claus ran out after all and brought them the Kewpie dolls instead.

In the end, it didn't matter so very much. Kewpie dolls were nice too, and they spent the rest of the morning playing with them while Mama and Papa baked their Christmas chicken with sage dressing, gravy and the second pecan pie they'd had in a month. Life was good.

THE HOUSE IN THE FIELD,
OWENS CROSS ROADS, ALABAMA 1949

In early spring, Papa began to talk of moving again. Mama wanted to move closer to her family and Papa wanted to live in the area where he hoped to buy a farm someday. After several Sunday afternoon drives looking for a rental house, Papa found a small deserted house at the end of a lane, surrounded by cotton fields. After inquiring at a neighboring house, Papa located the landlord, found the rent reasonable and the rooms smaller which meant they would be easier to heat.

On the Saturday after school let out for the summer, Cousin Fred and Cousin Josie arrived in their pickup truck to help pack for the move. Li'l Sis was not nearly as excited to see Cousin Josie as Cousin Josie appeared to see Li'l Sis. Never one to appreciate smothering hugs, Li'l

Sis wiggled out of her motherly embrace as soon as she could and kept her distance. Cousin Josie scolded Li'l Sis for her cool response reminding her that she had taken care of Li'l Sis many times while her Mama was sick. Unmoved, Li'l Sis kept her distance.

Packing the truck didn't take long as there wasn't much to pack; just the few boxes of Mama's dishes, the iron bedsteads, bedding and feather beds, a half dozen straight back chairs, the enamel table, kitchen cabinet and an ice box that had been a recent addition to Mama's kitchen. There was also a small box of books containing a medical encyclopedia, a Bible and a large, burnt orange, clothbound edition of Webster's Dictionary. It was a splendid book with watercolor illustrations of plants, animals and insects that were all the colors of the rainbow. Even though she couldn't read because of her failing eyesight, Mama was proud of those books and had written Papa's name in large scrawling letters in the front of each book.

Finally, everything was packed from the clothes to the chickens and they were on their way. At the end of the forty-mile drive, they came to a short overgrown lane which cut across a cotton field and ended in front of a small weather-beaten house with a rusted tin roof. If the house had ever been painted, all evidence to that effect was long since gone. That, however, mattered not one whit to the little girls. They were out of the car in a flash, exploring every nook and cranny of the house, the outbuildings and the overgrown yard. They found the yellow berries of the chinaberry trees especially fun as they squished them with their bare feet.

Out back, there was an old plum tree, just the right size for climbing. There was also a branch behind the house where they were sure to find tadpoles and crayfish. The place was grand.

Soon the whole family, including the chickens, were settled in. Like the other houses where the family had lived, this one also had two bedrooms and a kitchen. Farmhouses in those days were heated by an open fireplace where wood or coal was burned for heat. The girl's bedroom was always the room with the fireplace as Mama and Papa didn't want their girls to be cold on long winter nights. It was also the sitting room, with the straight back, cane bottom chairs standing in a half circle in front of the hearth.

With summer approaching, every spare moment went into readying a plot of ground next to the house for a vegetable garden. Each day after work, Papa drove the "push plow" ahead of him, while the girls and Mama broke up the turned over clods of earth with a hoe and a rake.

During the following weeks, Mama and the girls spent part of each day working in the garden. When Papa came home from work, he joined them making straight rows of shallow trenches where the girls carefully dropped seeds, spacing them according to Papa's directions. Then came the waiting and daily trips to the garden to see if any of the seeds were pushing up between the clods of dirt.

There were also other chores. Sister and Li'l Sis were in charge of feeding the chickens and gathering the eggs each afternoon. Because there were snakes in the area with a fondness for eggs, the chicken coop and nests were raised off the ground about five feet; high enough to be out of reach for an enterprising snake but too high for little girls to see where they were reaching their hands. One afternoon Mama heard a bloodcurdling scream from the direction of the chicken coop. Almost simultaneously, she was met by two white faced little girls stampeding through the door. The girls had interrupted a three-foot black racer helping himself to a clutch of eggs.

Mama knew what to do. With garden hoe in hand, she soon dispatched the snake whose dead body, the girls were sure, was lumpy with eggs.

When the cotton pickers came to the fields near their house, Mama and the girls would pick for the day. Mama had a big, long sack, but, despite her limited vision, she made little sacks from feed sacks on her treadle sewing machine for the girls. They were about as long as the girls were tall. One day when Li'l Sis and Sister were picking without Mama, Li'l Sis was just a few ounces short of earning a dime. Seeing the sadness on her face, a tall black man took a handful of cotton from his sack and put it in hers, telling the farmer that should just about do it, and it did. A happy Li'l Sis went home with a shiny dime to show Papa when he came home.

All that summer they worked in the garden behind the house, hoeing and weeding. There were rows and rows of corn and peas, green beans, potatoes, onions and tomatoes but especially corn and field peas. That summer the family ate so many field peas that Sister would be a grown woman before she could eat them again.

One day toward the end of summer, Papa came home with an electric freezer from Montgomery Ward's Department Store. He and Mama hauled it inside, put it under the window in their bedroom and placed an embroidered scarf and lamp on top and plugged it in. That weekend the whole family picked corn and shelled peas. Papa read the directions on how to "put up" vegetables in the freezer and the whole family worked together blanching and bagging vegetables. By Saturday night, the freezer was half full of vegetables which Mama said would get them through the winter. Papa said if his job held out, maybe they could buy a quarter beef before long. Papa's job did hold out, and one Friday night he brought home two big boxes of frozen meat wrapped in shiny white paper with black writing.

The girls felt extremely rich, it seemed like they had a whole grocery store in that big shiny white chest freezer not to mention all the rows of canned vegetables, fruits, jellies and jams that lined the walls on the pantry shelves by the back door

.

CHRISTMAS 1949

While working as a carpenter's helper on a construction job at Red Stone Arsenal, Papa met a man named Kirkpatrick who said he could get Papa in the pipefitter's union if he were interested.

Papa was interested, and Mr. Kirk, as he was called, walked Papa through the process of getting on with the union. He also helped Papa get a job with a construction company in Tuskegee, Alabama, about four hours south of where we lived, and the only place hiring at the time.

Unsure how long the job would last, Papa found a room where he could stay near the construction site and came home on weekends. The weekend before Christmas, Papa brought home a big box of chocolates, a bag of peppermint sticks and a large bag of oranges that the foreman had passed out to all the men on the job. The only chocolates the girls had seen before were chocolate covered cherries which were a Christmas staple, but these chocolates were different. Each one was nestled in a tiny pleated paper cup, and many of them were wrapped in colored foil as well. Inside were different kinds of creams, caramels and nougats. They had never seen anything like it and could not believe their good fortune.

Papa told the girls that when he was a boy, he sometimes only got an orange and a peppermint stick for Christmas. The little girls felt sorry for Papa that he had gotten so little. But Papa didn't feel sorry for himself. He said, "Many others had gotten less."

After supper, they all sat in front of the fireplace eating oranges. Papa showed the girls how to make a hole in an orange, fill it with broken pieces of candy cane and then suck the sweet juice from the orange. They went through orange after orange, pulling them apart when they were dry and eating the candy and pulp down to the peel. Li'l Sis even tried some of the peel, but only once.

Christmas morning came, and Sister got her long wished-for basketball. Girls had to play basketball in Physical Education at school and Sister was miserable at it; couldn't dribble, couldn't make a basket, and was always the last one chosen when the captains picked their teams. If she just had a ball, maybe she could practice and get better.

For Li'l Sis there was a blue tin high chair under the tree. The girls spent the morning taking turns feeding bits of biscuit from their Christmas breakfast to their Kewpie dolls as they sat perched in the new blue high chair. They would have to wait until the rain stopped before they could go outside to play with the basketball as the ground was sodden and the weeds knee high and wet.

Mama who had always had tin flatware, got a silver-plated set from the Sears Roebuck catalog. She never had anything nice like that before, and she was very pleased. It also came with silver-plated salt and pepper shakers.

After opening their presents, they sat in front of the fire eating oranges and tossing the peeling on the coals. Li'l Sis loved the sizzle and smell of the orange rinds in the fire, but after a while, restlessness set in and she decided to put water in one of the silver-plated salt and pepper shakers to see what would happen if she sprinkled the fire with water. What happened was that the top flew off in the hot coals. Mama and Li'l Sis were both horrified. Mama's beautiful salt and pepper set was ruined, and Li'l Sis's heart was broken. She had done it. She had ruined the only nice thing Mama had ever owned. She cried and cried.

Some Christmases you remember because they were happy. Some you remember because they weren't.

ADVENTURES 1950

On milder days, after the spring rains were passed, Li'l Sis and Sister would play outside. There was only one problem; the tall dry grass that surrounded the house. It tripped them up when they ran. It also made dribbling the basketball impossible, so one day they decided to get rid of it. They tried using the swing blade from the shed as there was no lawnmower, not that any mower under the sun could have cut those knee-high weeds. Then they remembered that they had seen the neighbors burn off their dead grass. Why couldn't they do the same thing? It never occurred to them to ask Mama's advice. They just did it. They made a little pile of dry grass, got matches from the kitchen and set it on fire. Unfortunately, the fire just took off in every direction including straight for the house. In no time, Mama was out the door with a bucket of water and a broom beating out the fire which got all the way up to the house and what was worse, burned the basketball before Mama got it out.

They were sorry about the fire and sorry that they had almost burned the house down, but they were devastated about the basketball. They felt even worse when Mama said there was no money for another one.

Every day Li'l Sis waited expectantly for Sister to come home from school. She wanted to hear all about school and pretended to do her homework while Sister did hers. She kept begging Mama to let her go to school with Sister, but Mama kept saying she was too young. One afternoon after hearing Li'l Sis ask for the hundredth time if she couldn't go to school with Sister, Mama said, "Yes."

Next morning Li'l Sis got on the bus with Sister, and off they went to school. When they walked into Sister's classroom, all Sister's friends came running over to meet Li'l Sis. The pretty young teacher was not so welcoming and told Sister, Li'l Sis would have to go home. However, until the bus could come around to return her home, she would have to sit quietly. With that, she handed Li'l Sis a box of crayons and some drawing paper.

Li'l Sis didn't understand why she had to go home but decided to enjoy herself while she was there and colored away, as it turned out, for the whole day as the bus never came to pick her up. At the end of the day, the teacher complimented Li'l Sis on her behavior and her "artwork" but then reminded Sister that Li'l Sis could not come again until she entered first grade.

SISTER'S BRUSH WITH DEATH

The closest neighbors, the Whites, lived down the lane and across the county road. The first time Mama and the girls went visiting, the girls were amazed at all the stuffed animals that covered the top of the chest freezer in the sitting room, also known as the front room. Li'l Sis asked if they had children. "No," Mrs. White said. The toys belonged to Elaine, their little granddaughter who was in the hospital in Birmingham in an iron lung.

"What's an iron lung?" Li'l Sis asked. What an iron lung was and why the little girl was in it, other than that the little girl would die if they took her out, Li'l Sis never understood. But from then on, every time she got the sniffles or a sore throat, she was sure she was going to die of polio as that was how Mrs. White said polio began.

On Sunday afternoons Papa, Mama and the girls would sometimes walk over to the White's house to visit, exchange recipes and get the latest farm news. One afternoon when the air was heavy with humidity and thunderheads mounted on the horizon, they paid a visit to the Whites. Papa stopped on the front porch to talk crops with Mr. White while Mama went inside to visit with Mrs. White. The girls sat on the porch swing, enjoying the cool wind from the coming storm until rain began blowing across the porch and lightning grew closer.

Papa, feeling uneasy, told the girls to go inside. As Sister reached for the screen door handle, a loud clap of thunder broke and a flash of lightning went between Sister and the door. Sister screamed and fell in front of the screen door. Papa scooped her up and carried her into the house yelling for Li'l Sis to get inside, "Now!"

Mrs. White cleared a place on the bed in the front room for Papa to lay Sister down. Smoke that smelled like spent shotgun shells was coming out of Sister's clothes. She was limp, and it seemed like she was half asleep. Mama quickly pulled Sister's clothes off and put cold cloths on her head and on her red and white striped body. Papa used the White's phone to call Dr. Carpenter at home. The doctor said if Sister was awake and could talk, she would be all right, but it was a wonder that she was alive.

After Sister had rested for a while, she asked for water and said she wanted to go home. Papa carried her the short distance down the lane to our house. No one spoke. We were all thinking about Dr. Carpenter's words, "It was a wonder she was alive."

REFLECTION

As I write, I vacillate between euphoria and an urge to get this done as reflected in the rapid sequence of events covered. Euphoria that until the age of three, my childhood was largely happy. Our parents loved us and provided for us as best they could. At the same time, there is a compulsion to get this written, to get past the sadness and betrayal that is to come, to just get it over with.

Nevertheless, I can clearly see that in the core of my being, I am who I always was. Granted a bit dysfunctional and codependent from the experiences I had and the choices I made, but I still bear the original blueprint that makes me uniquely me: adventurous, determined, kindhearted and creative with a love of beautiful things.

I do wonder though, if my collection of vintage toys and the playroom I have in my attic where I play with the grandchildren, isn't in some way connected to those Christmases long ago? Perhaps the connection is to a little girl's disappointment that Santa ran out of "those dolls" and the other things we chose from the catalog. However, the connection could also be to the pure unmitigated joy two little girls experienced when they woke on Christmas morning and saw something new and shiny under the tree meant just for them.

Even though I believe I had largely recovered from the experience at the hands of Nick, I did not want to be around Cousin Josie. In response to my lack of warmth toward her, she kept reminding me she had cared for me while Mother was ill. Unmoved, I just wanted to get away from her.

Cousin Josie's behavior toward me after the visit during which I was molested, makes me think she carried a great deal of guilt, as well she should. Not to tell my parents about the incident was unconscionable. How much I could have been spared if only she had communicated honestly. Children often communicate more honestly than adults as I did by avoiding Cousin Josie. I wanted nothing to do with her. She had abandoned me during that traumatic time when I was under her protection. Then rather than inform my parents, Cousin Josie tried to mask it all over, acting as though nothing had happened. Even as a young child, I recognized her hypocrisy and avoided her whenever possible.

To this day, it is hard to recall that I was responsible for the loss of one of Mama's few nice things. In years to come, I would save diligently all year long to buy gifts for Mother on her birthday, Mother's Day and Christmas. The loss of something nice today isn't so tragic. It would simply be replaced, but to someone who has little, it was a real loss. I felt deeply, not only my sorrow but Mama's as well.

After that day with Sister at school, I had school stories of my own to share. I had spent the whole day coloring with a brand-new box of crayons. Of course, I had to leave them at school. I knew they weren't for me to keep but just having a new box and all the paper I could use was something to remember. Sister's friends had included me in their play during recess as well as at lunch. It had been a memorable day. I was a bit sad the teacher hadn't wanted me there at first, but when the bus never came and I just kept on working quietly on my art, the teacher seemed fine, even complimented me on my behavior. Mama couldn't understand why the teacher was upset. She would never have let me go if she hadn't known I would be just fine.

Having taught school for many years, I understand the young teacher's misgivings. There are pressures and distractions enough in a classroom without bringing a young child into the mix. Nevertheless, almost six decades later, I still remember the joy of sitting there next to Sister coloring page after beautiful page of brightly colored pictures.

As much as I enjoy writing about the good and not so good times, sometimes when I stop, I have this feeling of unquiet that I must get back to it, I must get it done. There is a compulsion to get this down on paper. When it is done, maybe it will stay there. Perhaps it will all stick to the pages like flies on flypaper. At times, it's hard to stay focused on the pleasant memories because of what looms on the horizon. Other times, I feel euphoric with the joy of those happy days when life was good and joy was an old roll of wallpaper and a shoebox of broken crayons.

Each time I finished one of those childhood drawings, I would survey my work with the road wandering across the scroll of paper before me and wonder where the road went from the edge of the scroll. There have been many twists and turns, surprises and sometimes disappointments and sorrow, but it has all worked together to make a whole; a whole allowed and redeemed by God.

RESPONSE

THE HOLIDAYS 1948

1 Can you share holiday delights and disappointments that brightened or saddened your childhood?

THE HOUSE IN THE FIELD, OWENS CROSS ROADS, ALABAMA 1949

2 The whole family was proud of their Webster's dictionary. Was there a similar possession in which everyone took pride when you were growing up? Explain.

3 Did your family relocate often? What do you remember about those moves and how they affected your life and the life of your family?

CHRISTMAS 1949

4 "Just before Christmas, Papa brought home a big box of

chocolates, a bag of peppermint sticks and a box of oranges that the foreman had passed out to all the men on the job. Each chocolate was nestled in a tiny pleated paper cup, and many of them were wrapped in colored foil. We had never seen anything like it and could not believe our good fortune."

▸ Can you share a time when you or your family received a gift so special that you could "not believe your good fortune"? Explain.

5 Some Christmases you remember because they were happy. Some you remember because they weren't.

▸ Can you recall an event made memorable because something very good or very bad happened? Did you, like Li'l Sis, cause or play a part in the event?

ADVENTURES 1950

6 Did you, as a child, cause a near catastrophe as the girls did trying to get rid of the tall dry grass in their yard? Explain.

SISTER'S NEAR BRUSH WITH DEATH

7 Can you recall when you first became aware of death or of the danger of dying? Explain.

8 How did that experience affect you?

CHAPTER 4
A DREAM COME TRUE

THE LITTLE WHITE HOUSE IN THE PINEY WOODS 1951

As the school year drew to a close, Papa decided it was time to move the family closer to his job near Tuskegee and started looking for a house. He soon found one to rent owned by the Kirkpatrick family and before long, another moving day was upon them. Cousin Fred came with his truck bringing Cousin Josie to help pack. She said Mama had moved so many times that when the chickens saw her coming with string in her hands, they just laid down and crossed their legs to be tied up. Mama wished that were true as she and Papa chased the chickens around the yard, bound their legs and put them in a makeshift chicken coop for transport.

Driving through a small town somewhere south of Gadsden, a low hanging limb swept the washtub full of Mama's pretty dishes off the top of the loaded truck bed and smashed them to smithereens in the street. Mama got out of the car following along behind and helped pick up the pieces. Sad though she was at the loss, she brightened when she found a few unbroken pieces. Among them was the brown Depression Era glass cake plate that one of Papa's town relatives had given Mama for a wedding present many years before.

About an hour later near Tuskegee, they came to a Y in the road. Papa took the right fork and soon pointed off to the right where a big white house stood surrounded by spreading oak trees. Papa told Mama that was where the Kirkpatricks lived.

Just to the left, they took a dirt road down toward piney woods where they saw the little white house which was to be their home. As soon as Papa stopped the car, the girls jumped out of the back seat of the little black '37 Chevy. Well, not exactly the back seat, because there wasn't a back seat. The girls sat on two old apple crates, hanging onto the back of the seat in front to steady themselves as Papa took the curves. On this trip, there hadn't been much danger of falling off their seats because they were wedged in on all sides by boxes of household goods.

Once out of the car, the girls ran to the house which was relatively new and still had the smell of freshly cut wood and new paint. There were three rooms, a kitchen and two bedrooms which meant the girls would again have a bedroom of their own. But it was different from the other houses. It was new and tightly built, and instead of being heated by a fireplace, there was a coal burning stove to keep them warm in the winter.

Cousin Fred and Papa began unloading the truck, bringing in the big iron bedsteads and black and white stripped mattresses. The open bed springs were dangerous as Li'l Sis found out when she tried to jump on them, fell through and got her foot caught in a spring. As usual, Sister pulled Li'l Sis out and comforted her. Then they were off to explore the piney woods that spread out in front of the house as Mama called, "Don't you go far!" And they didn't as on the edge of the pine thicket was a clearing where a big oak tree stood on a bank leading down to a ravine. Someone had hung an old tire on one of the lower hanging limbs positioning it so you could swing out over the gully that ran through the clearing. There were also large Muscadine grape vines entwined around the tree limbs. One was big enough for the children to use for a swing. Soon the girls were joined by the Kirkpatrick children from up the hill. Shy at first, it wasn't long before they were pushing each other on the swing and playing on the vines.

In no time, the black and white enamel table and cane chairs were set up in the kitchen along with the kerosene stove, and Mama was calling the girls to come to supper. As the girls ran through the door, they were met by the smell of biscuits baking, scrambled eggs, and sizzling bacon. They knew they were home.

Every day after school, the Kirkpatrick kids came over to play. Together they built "hideouts" in the woods using fallen limbs to make a frame and covering it with pine straw. They watched falling stars and picked up cinders from the fields where they landed. They found a pit dug in the sandy soil where they smoked rabbit weed tobacco rolled in brown paper from a grocery sack and ate picnic lunches of cornbread and onions.

One Saturday night, the Kirkpatrick children went to Opelika to the picture show with their older brothers and asked Sis and Li'l Sis to join them. The girls were so excited. "Pinocchio" was playing.

Things got off to an interesting start when Li'l Sis wanted to sit upstairs in the balcony. The Kirkpatrick girls looked at her in amazement telling her only the Coloreds sat up there. She was genuinely puzzled as she wondered why they could not sit there as well.

Unfortunately, the movie was almost as scary as the war movies they'd seen with Papa. Pinocchio was in terrible danger, and he didn't even know it. Li'l Sis could not understand why he didn't just behave himself, do the right thing and go home with Jiminy Cricket to his papa. Even though, in the end, he did just that, the movie was still upsetting, and Li'l Sis was not at all sure she wanted to go to the picture show again.

Sunday mornings the family went to the Tabernacle Methodist Church near Opelika. where Li'l Sis escaped the hot sultry service by falling asleep with her head on Mama's lap.

Once during a revival meeting, there was a "Dinner on the Ground." Mama was hoping to meet some new folks in the community and had Papa kill one of her hens that she fried up on the kerosene stove. After church, everyone went outside and spread oil tablecloths on the ground where they sat down with their family and unpacked a picnic lunch. Mama did the same only all she had brought was chicken, thinking it was a potluck. The girls looked longingly at the bowls of potato salad and pies that folks around them pulled out of their baskets. A few folks also looked with curiosity at the new family in church who had just brought a fried chicken for dinner, but no one offered to share. Mama said that was the last "Dinner on the Ground" she was going to, and it was.

One night after supper, Mr. Kirkpatrick came down to the house to tell Papa that an Army truck had run off the road over at the river bridge. All the neighbors had gone down to the river to fish clothes and blankets and dishes out of the river. Papa ought to go down and see what he could get as well. Papa didn't see it that way. All that stuff belonged to the Army, he said, and they'd be back in a day or two to get the truck and fish the boxes out of the river. Sure enough, the next day they came and hauled the truck away but made no attempt to retrieve the military clothes, bedding, and dishes from the river. Seeing as how they had abandoned their property, Papa went down to see what he could find. For years afterward, he wore drab olive undershirts, and we ate off of Army stoneware; a poor substitute for Mama's beautiful blue rimmed flowery plates lost during the move.

Along in the summer Mrs. Kirkpatrick invited Mama and the girls to pick beans and corn from their garden. The girls helped pick, then played in the cool of the shade trees with the Kirkpatrick girls while Mama and Mrs. Kirkpatrick sat on the front porch shelling peas and beans.

When Li'l Sis asked if someone would go to the outhouse with her, she was amazed to be told that she could "go" in the house. Other than at the Saturday picture show, she had never seen an indoor toilet. After going potty, Li'l Sis was tempted to push the handle down again and again, but Sister said they'd hear and get mad, so she resisted the temptation. She did, however, run her hand over the pretty pink tile that lined the walls. It was beautifully smooth and cool to the touch. There were even pictures of black tropical fish painted under the glaze. It was a fine bathroom indeed, a far cry from the smelly outhouse and chamber pot under their bed at home in the little white house.

When Papa came home from work, the girls told him about the visit to the Kirkpatrick's and their indoor plumbing. These new things were all very exciting, but the girls were happy with their little house in the woods and especially glad that the family was all together again.

PAPA'S DREAM COMES TRUE

From the time the girls could remember, Papa talked about, "When we get our own place." Sister and Li'l Sis wondered about that. Why was Papa always talking about having a farm of their own? One day Papa told them why.

Papa had grown up on a small forty-acre farm co-owned by his father, whom the girls called Papaw and his grandfather, who was known as

Grandpa. Together the extended family had run the farm. While they were not wealthy by any means, they weren't hungry either unlike many others who lived near starvation during the Depression Era.

From the age of six, Papa was sent to the field to follow along behind the plow. His mother, Mamaw, worried about him because the corn he plowed was much taller than Papa as a young boy. The only way she could keep up with where he was in the field was to look for the mule's ears which she could glimpse now and then just above the top of the cornrows.

When the girls marveled at how Papa could have "followed the plow" when he was so young, Papa smiled and said, "All I had to do was keep the plow upright, the mule did the rest." He did admit, however, turning the plow at the end of the row was hard because it was so heavy, but he somehow managed.

Papa loved the land and would often tell the girls that everyone needed to own land free and clear, because land would always be worth something.

Papa was sixteen when the Great Depression hit, closing banks and sending the economic world into a tailspin. Wall Street seemed so far away that the family felt removed from it all until the run on the banks. That was when Papaw, Papa's father, realized he had to get their money out of the bank. It was their mortgage payment, the yearly payment for which they saved all year long. When Papaw got to the bank, it was closed, and when it reopened, their money was gone.

Nevertheless, some months later when the mortgage was due, Papaw, bank book in hand, went to the bank and wrote a check for the mortgage only to be told again he had no money in the bank. Later on, the same bank foreclosed on the farm and the family had to move away, becoming sharecroppers on another farm.

Before he left, Papa went up in the barn loft and carved his initials on a rafter. He was laying claim to that farm, even if they took it away. He wanted someone to know that at one time, it had been theirs. Seventy years later when the old barn fell down, the current owner found

Papa's initials carved in the rafter, cut the length of wood out and gave it to Sister as a memorial to the family farm.

The loss of the farm meant not only that Papaw and Grandpa became sharecroppers, but it also meant that Papa, then 18 years old, had to join the C. C. Corps (Civilian Conservation Corps) to help support the family. At the time, the Corps was widening the highway over Monte Sano Mountain about twenty miles away.

The Army Corps of Engineers used dynamite to blast huge boulders out of the right of way, but that left a lot of large stones that were too big for the rock crushers which provided gravel for the road. The job of the C.C. Corps was to break the larger stones sometimes weighing hundreds of pounds into smaller pieces that the rock crushers could handle. They did this with a sledgehammer.

At the time, Papa was 6 feet tall and weighed 160 pounds. The work was too hard for such a thin young man, but Papa persisted knowing how desperately his parents needed the income. The cost to himself, however, he would bear for the rest of his life. The impact of sledgehammer on rock damaged several discs in his back. A few years later, Papa's already injured back would be further damaged through his work as a pipefitter lifting heavy steel pipe. Chronic pain would lead to emotional instability and severe depression.

Losing the family farm became the driving force in Papa's life. He was determined to own a farm of his own and to that end, had been saving for years.

By the early 50s, Papa and Mama had saved a $500.00 down payment, and Papa began looking for a farm near Little Cove, the site of the old family farm. Before long, he found a forty-acre place with a farmhouse, a barn and a rental house. Papa also found a local businessman who would lend him the rest of the money. He was not about to borrow money from a bank.

Moving day was always exciting but this one especially so, as they were moving to their own place. Cousin Fred came again with his truck, and Cousin Josie came to help pack. Mama was glad to be moving back to north Alabama because she would be living within a few miles of Cousin Josie as well as her mother, Big Mama, who sadly was no longer in good health.

Sister and Li'l Sis were excited and sad all at the same time; excited at the thought of the new adventure and sad to leave their little white house in the piney woods, the Kirkpatrick kids and all their adventures there.

THE FARM 1952

As they drove down the gravel lane leading to the little red house in the field, the girls looked out the window with excitement. It was their farm. As long as they made the yearly payment of $500 to Mr. Reed, it was theirs. The girls were thrilled that Papa's dream of owning their own farm had finally come true.

As soon as the car stopped, they squeezed out of the back seat and ran into the house. There were worn linoleum rugs on all the floors and a limestone fireplace in one of the rooms. Papa said he'd have to keep a fire going all night in the winter, but it should keep them from freezing. When winter came, they would see that Papa was partially right. They didn't freeze, but the water in the wash basin by the back door and in the tea kettle on the stove froze solid. However, that mattered little. They had their own farm.

One of the first things the girls always did when they moved into a new house was to look through the different layers of linoleum area rugs on the floors. Sometimes a rug several layers down was prettier or in better shape than the one on top and Papa would switch it out. Li'l Sis found a rug a couple of layers down that had beautiful roses all over a dark brown background. They ran to Mama with the news of the lovely linoleum. Mama looked but said it was too dried out and thin to move to the top. It would break apart.

Seeing the disappointment in Li'l Sis's eyes, Mama added, "Maybe we can get a new one later on." Sadly, when they did look for a new linoleum, the only patterns available were geometric designs. From time to time when no one was around, Li'l Sis would lift the corner of the stack of linoleum and look longingly at the pretty rose pattern below.

There were four rooms in the new house including the kitchen, but unfortunately, the roof over the room in the back leaked as they could see from the watermarks on the floor. Although this rendered the room unusable, it didn't matter as they had three dry rooms.

Mama said they could use the room with the leaky roof for storage. "Just make sure you don't put any boxes under the leaks," Mama said. The result was a basically empty room with various stacks of boxes strategically placed here and there in a maze-like fashion with buckets under the leaks.

"I'll get up on the roof," Papa said, "as soon as I can, and try to find the leaks. Maybe a piece of tin blew loose. They've had some bad winds here lately. There could be old nail holes that need to be patched with hot tar. But that will have to wait until the weather gets hotter. Can't work with tar till the hottest part of the summer."

There were boxes in the room left by the last folks who had lived there. Inside Li'l Sis found several rolls of old wallpaper that she excitedly claimed for drawing. "That's fine," Mama said, "as long as it doesn't match any of the paper on the walls." Soon Li'l Sis reported back, "None of it matches, Mama." Then she was off to find her box of crayons.

She would spend hours in the days and weeks ahead drawing her mountains scattered with flowers and valleys crisscrossed by flowing rivers. As always there would be a brown dirt road bordered with flowers and tufts of grass, running from east to west across the middle of the drawing. When Li'l Sis finished her drawing, she would always wonder where the road led.

Like the other houses where they had lived, there was electricity but no running water. A single light bulb hung from the middle of each room with a pull string switch. Even though the house wasn't plumbed, there was a well on the back porch. Papa said, "I'll put a pump in the well and run water into the kitchen. At least we'll have cold water in the house." There was also room for a wringer washer on the open back porch. Maybe he could find a used one, Papa said. Meanwhile, they would use a bucket to draw water from the well and continue to use the black cast iron washpot in which Mama did the wash. For washing hands, there was the usual wash basin on a shelf by the back door.

Moving in didn't take long, although there was a new addition to the family's furniture; a chifforobe with a mirrored door in the center and drawers below for underwear and socks. To the left and right were also mirrored doors behind which clothes could be hung. Until that time, clothes were hung on hooks or nails on the back of bedroom doors. Once the boxes of books, linens and kitchenware were brought in, Papa began setting up the kerosene stove and before long, smells from the kitchen told the girls that supper would soon be on the table. There would be home canned pinto beans, cornbread and a jar of Georgia peaches that Mama had put up the summer before.

By that time, the girls had explored the orchard and every nook and cranny of the old slanty-roofed garage, soon to be a pigsty that stood near the house. The chickens, already recovered from the ordeal of being moved yet again, were happily foraging for bugs in the yard.

There was also a rental house which Papa would be able to rent for $15.00 a month. It too was without plumbing, but it was dry and sturdy.

On the property, next to the rental house, out near the main road, was a big barn where Papa soon had a milk cow, a calf and a couple of pigs. Every day before he went to work, he milked the cow and fed all the animals. As soon as he got home from work, he did it all again.

Papa was proud of the farm, but it was a lot of work with animals to care for, fences to mend and repairs on the house and barn. He was already exhausted when he got home, and the stress of the farm began to take its toll. The depression that Papa had struggled with off and on for years returned and the little girls would sometimes come into the house and find Papa sitting at the kitchen table with his head on his arms quietly crying.

This frightened the girls especially when Mama would get mad and tell Papa she'd never known a man to cry so much. This made both him and the little girls cry even more. But after a while, the girls began to wonder if Mama was right as Papa seemed to cry at any and everything. But the girls also knew his back hurt terribly as some mornings he couldn't even sit up on the side of the bed to stand up. Rather he would have to slide off the bed and crawl to the chair where his back brace hung, pull himself up on the chair and strap the brace on before he could stand up. Then he would go to work where he fit together heavy metal pipe.

It was awful seeing Papa so terribly sad and Mama mad at him. The little girls didn't know what to think or do. They just felt scared and alone.

A few weeks after the move to the little red house, Papa set up another iron bedstead in the girl's room where the fireplace was and Big Mama (Mama's mama) moved in with the family. She was a sweet little old lady who lived on a farm a short distance away, but from time to time, as she got older, would spend a few weeks with first one and then another of her children. Big Mama always wore dark printed dresses and black lace-up shoes with square heels. Any time she went to the doctor or to church, she wore a broad-brimmed hat with a black band around the crown. Sis and Li'l Sis thought that hat was grand. If they were very careful, from time to time, they were allowed to try the hat on in front of one of the mirrored doors of the chifforobe.

Afternoons on warm summer days, Big Mama would ask the girls to fetch an old tin can to be used as a spittoon, then she would go to the willow tree out back to get a twig to be used as a dipping stick in her snuffbox. Once everything was assembled, she would sit on the front porch and have a dip of snuff. The girls could never understand how anyone as sweet as Big Mama could dip snuff. It seemed so out of place for such a nice gentle lady who wore such a pretty hat.

REFLECTION

I sometimes wonder if that childhood curiosity about what lay ahead wasn't used by God to direct my life even to this day. Fourteen years in university ministry in Europe from my late twenties through to my forties, then a return to the field in my sixties after 17 years of teaching at-risk teens in Seattle, would not be predictable for someone who started out the daughter of an Alabama sharecropper, but God has His own ways and means.

Although I am proud of Papa's selfless commitment to support his parents, brothers and sisters through his work in the C.C. Corps, it saddens me deeply that this commitment cost him and our immediate family dearly in the years to come. There are times in life when the only choices available are bad choices.

When I think of my parents, I am reminded of Jesus' words, "In this world you will have trouble [or difficulties]" (John 16:33b). Life is often cruel, robbing parents of the stability and resources they need to nourish and protect their children. Mama and Papa used the tools they had to parent as best they knew how. There was just a lot they didn't know. There was also a lot they didn't know about supporting each other.

Mama was raised by a rageaholic father who beat his children unmercifully and abused and disrespected his wife relentlessly. Whereas Mama was undoubtedly attracted to my soft-spoken father by his gentle manner, she did not understand his emotional instability or know how to support him.

Over sixty years later, it saddens me still that the fulfillment of Papa's long sought-after dream of owning his own farm would result in so much sadness for us all. Although Papa would own his farm, he would lose his health and emotional stability as the stress of his job coupled with running the farm and the pressure to make the yearly payments in a terribly depressed economy, would push him deeper and deeper into depression.

Whereas before, if anyone asked about my childhood, I would talk of growing up in the country, running barefoot in the summer sun, chasing cows and then quickly steer the conversation in another direction. Invariably my listeners responded with, "What an ideal childhood you had." It wasn't until I began this writing that I really had anything positive to share. My memories were so dominated by harm at the hands of my relatives I could not see beyond the negative.

Ill health and emotional instability would also play a role in my life on the mission field many years later. Sadly those young formative years spent observing our parents struggle often reappear in our adult years, in my case when the stress of cultural adjustment, family responsibilities and ministry seemed insurmountable.

RESPONSE

THE LITTLE HOUSE IN THE PINEY WOODS 1951

1 Can you recall a memorable event like Li'l Sis's first trip to a children's movie? Was it a delight or a disappointment?

2 Did you have an older sibling who took care of you or were you the caretaker for a younger sibling? Was the experience positive?

PAPA'S DREAM COME TRUE

3 Mama's dream was to have a second child which would be Li'l Sis. Papa's dream was to own his own farm. This dream was deeply rooted in the loss of his own family's farm.

▸ Did either of your parents have a dream rooted in an earlier family loss or disappointment? Explain.

THE FARM 1952

4 Did you or your family have the experience of "A Dream Come True" that turned out very differently than expected? Explain.

5 Did you have a relative who visited your family when you were young? Did she/he have a possession that you admired?

6 Was there a favorite childhood occupation that indicated the direction your life would take as an adult? Explain.

7 Were there parental struggles that disrupted family life during your childhood?

8 The author writes, "It saddens me still, that...Papa's... dream of owning his own farm would result in so much sadness for the family."

▸ How can a believer reconcile the sovereignty of God and deep disappointment from loss and illness? Do any verses come to mind that might relate? Consider Ephesians 1:11; Romans 8:28, Isaiah 43:2, 2 Corinthians 1:8-10.

CHAPTER 5
GRIEF AND SADNESS

A DEATH IN THE FAMILY

A short time after the family moved into the little red house, panel trucks with Southern Bell Telephone Company appeared on the county road at the end of our lane and workmen began stringing telephone lines along the length of the road that ran past the farm. It was a big event, and soon there was a shiny black rotary phone sitting on a three-legged table just inside our front door.

Each morning Mama would talk to Cousin Josie who lived a few miles away in a white farmhouse on the side of Jenkins Mountain. They would share recipes, talk about what they were going to do that day or had already done, and complain, "Somebody was listening on the party line." One morning the phone rang, and a short time later, Mama began to cry. The girls who had never seen their Mama cry, gathered around asking, "Mama, what's wrong? Why you crying, Mama?"

Through her tears, Mama answered in a hoarse voice, "Big Mama died."

The girls were sad Big Mama was dead, that they would never see her again, but they were deeply shaken by Mama's tears. Mama was the strong one who never cried. Mama was the one who comforted them when they cried. Seeing Mama sitting there sobbing, weak and helpless left the girls feeling abandoned and alone.

A few days later, the family drove to Big Mama's house around the big curve next to the mountain. Mama picked Li'l Sis up to say good-bye to Big Mama who looked peaceful and pretty but very still lying in her coffin in the front room. There were a lot of people there and a lot of food. The girls perked up when they saw the food but felt strange that everyone laughed and talked and seemed to have a good time except Mama, her sisters and cousins who cried softly in the other room and talked about what a good woman Big Mama had been and what a hard life she'd had.

As they talked, Cousin Nick approached the group of women and suggested it might be best if he took the kids swimming rather than have them sit through the long hot funeral service the next day. Mama thought it was a good idea and the following afternoon just before all the adults left for the funeral, Nick came to pick up the girls.

THE DAY OF THE FUNERAL

Sister and Li'l Sis watched as Nick turned off the road onto the lane leading to the house. As the pickup came to a stop, they climbed in the back, their bare feet burning on the hot metal truck bed as they made their way to Nick's children sitting with their back to the cab.

The girls were excited but also anxious. Swimming was a rare treat in this farming community of sharecroppers and manual laborers, and it would have been just that, a rare treat, if Nick hadn't been a serial pedophile. Li'l Sis knew this but Mama didn't, and Li'l Sis didn't have the words to tell Mama she was afraid of Nick and would rather go to the funeral with her because of what Nick did that time when she was two and sent to live with Cousin Josie and her family.

Turning off the main road onto the lane leading to the river, Nick gunned the motor throwing the children against the sides of the truck bed as they bounced along the rutted road.

Climbing down from the tailgate rubbing bumps and bruises, they saw several large cows from the adjacent pastures watering in the shallows. The cows raised their heads looking in the direction of the children as they flicked flies from their backs with their long swishing tails. The girls watched anxiously as they picked their way through the cow piles to the river's edge. The water was cold. The rocks were slippery. Skittering water bugs and dragonflies frightened Li'l Sis as she clung to her sister. *I need to stay close to Sister. I have got to stay close to Sister. I am safe if I stay close to Sister.*

Approaching unseen from behind the girls, Nick grabbed Li'l Sis and slung her onto his back heading for deep water.

“Gonna show you the sinkhole,” he said in his coarse, nasal voice.

“No,” she screamed soundlessly, her paralyzed limbs reaching for her sister but there was no movement. She was captured prey—a mouse dangling from the claws of a raptor.

Clinging to his back, Li'l Sis froze as Nick approached the vortex, stopping only when he came to the edge. She trembled at the sight of the swirling dark water, then stiffened as Nick’s fingers cupping her bottom begin to move assaulting her soul with evil indifference. Shaking with cold, her body burning, she struggled to get free as she looked back toward Sister who was trying to reach her over the slick rocks. Nick shouted for Sister to stay where she was or drown.

He then walked further away into deeper water, his hands on Li’l Sis’s body under the waterline. Warning his children to stay away, he continued to probe that sacred part of her soul with rough callused hands as her body stung and her soul cried out as she pleadingly reached in Sister’s direction.

Finally Nick made his way back into the shallow water, put Li’l Sis down and walked away to play with his children in the river as though nothing had happened. Wide-eyed with fear, Li’l Sis ran to Sister as best she could over the slippery stones dissolving wordlessly into her arms as she comforted her.

DESTRUCTIVE GENERATIONAL THEMES

During a period of depression, Mama told the girls about a family history of suicidal ideations that a much-loved relative, Papa’s mama (Mammaw), had struggled with for years. Mama gave a vivid description which haunted Li’l Sis with mental flashes of knives and death by suicide for years to come.

Papa’s mama and papa weren’t the only ones in the family who struggled emotionally. Li’l Sis once asked Papa why Papaw, his daddy, seemed to be so gruff at times. Papa answered that Papaw was an unloved son. Papaw’s brother, Walter, was the golden boy in the family; Papaw was the outcast.

Papa then went on to say that he too had been rejected by his father, Papaw, because instead of looking like the paternal line of the family, he had the dark hair and blue eyes from his Mama's line. Little Sis could not imagine how anyone could not love Papa's blue eyes and dark hair. She loved her daddy.

In one of Mama's many talks with the girls, she also said she was afraid Papa was going to kill himself "one of these days," and that Sister and Li'l Sis had to play very quietly and not upset Papa or he might do it.

It was hard to run and play when you were afraid you might upset your Papa so badly he would kill himself. Then they really would be all alone.

Li'l Sis also remembered this when Mama and Papa would argue. She was alternately torn between love and resentment toward her parents. Their arguments almost always began with Papa looking for an important bill that had to be paid or paper that had to be found. He knew right where he had left it and it wasn't there, so, SOMEBODY, meaning Mama or one of the girls, had moved it. Papa would tear through his papers working himself into a frenzy until he finally burst into tears, then leave the house with his gun saying he was going to the barn to shoot rats.

When this happened, Mama, Sister and Li'l Sis would huddle together in bed waiting for the first shot, then the second which meant Papa hadn't killed himself with the first. He was still alive. Finally, the little girls and Mama would fall asleep from exhaustion, listening for the next shot.

IF I SHOULD DIE BEFORE I WAKE..."

The only prayer that Li'l Sis knew, besides the one Papa prayed over their meals each day, ended with, "If I should die before I wake, I pray the Lord my soul to take." She knew that children died. A neighbor's granddaughter had died of polio. Each night she prayed that prayer and each night she was afraid to go to sleep; afraid that she would die and that she would go straight to hell because of the bad things she had "let" Cousin Nick do to her.

That possibility had to exist she reasoned, why else would she need to pray that God would take her soul to heaven. If it were a given, she wouldn't need to ask, and if you need to ask for something, the possibility exists the answer will be, "No."

When Papa was working away from home, Li'l Sis slept with Mama. Because she was afraid she and Mama might die in their sleep, she stayed awake until she could tell by Mama's regular breathing she was sleeping. Then Li'l Sis would fall asleep holding onto Mama's gown tail as tightly as she could, hoping if she and Mama died in their sleep, she would get drug along to heaven with Mama, if she only held on tightly enough. She would sometimes wake with a start, realizing she had lost her grip on Mama's gown, grab it in her tight little fist and try harder to hold on as she again drifted off to sleep.

At best, she didn't sleep well. She was worried about so many things. The happy carefree child she had been began to recede further and further into the darkness of abandonment, even as her parents sunk deeper and deeper into their own abyss of illness and depression.

As the change occurred gradually, Mama and Papa barely noticed the difference in Li'l Sis, but it was more evident to those who only saw her occasionally.

One Saturday afternoon, Cousin Josie and Cousin Fred stopped by for a visit. Mama met them at the door with Li'l Sis hiding behind her skirts. Cousin Josie greeted Mama, then took one look at Li'l Sis and said, "What is wrong with that child? Why is she so backward?"

Li'l Sis could have told them "why," but she didn't have the words. She just shrank back and hid her face in her mama's skirts as Mama looked at her in embarrassment and said, "I don't know what's gotten into her."

Whereas before there had been a faint flicker, a faint hope, someone would understand and help her, now that was gone. Even her mother was embarrassed by her. She would never again be the happy carefree child she had been. Something inside her died, and she became me.

A LOST LITTLE GIRL

I was a lost little girl who lived in her head, a head filled with sexual ideations that almost drove me mad at times.

Sundays after church, we often went to my grandfather Papaw's house for Sunday dinner. Papaw subscribed to the Sunday edition of the Huntsville Times, and after dinner, we would sit on the front porch in the swing and read the comics which we called the "funny papers." Whereas "reading the funnies" had always been something that I looked forward to, suddenly it was a nightmare. The characters were sexualized as were all their actions.

But there was also respite amidst the chaos in my mind. I loved Aunt Effie, my grandfather's second wife, who would always sit by me at the dinner table and talk with me, asking me what I had been doing and what I was learning at school. Somehow I think she sensed when the others didn't that something had gone sadly awry in my life.

Granny Anne, Papaw's mother who lived with him and Aunt Effie, had a red satin heart-shaped box filled with old valentines, cards and letters that her soldier sons had sent from Europe during the war. If we promised to handle them very carefully, she would let Sister and I sit in the middle of a big feather bed and look at the treasured cards. Years later, I would collect antique reproduction valentines in memory of those happy times that provided diversion from the raging thoughts careening though my mind.

REFLECTION

Nick's offer to babysit during the funeral took advantage of a perfect storm. Mama distracted by her own grief was undoubtedly glad that Sister and I would not have to sit through the long hot service. Nick, a serial pedophile, recognized his opportunity, moved in and took advantage of the distraction of the funeral.

Decades later, I would discover that there were family members who were aware that Nick was a pedophile, even at that time, but they told no one assuming that the children who went with Nick were complicit and found the experience pleasurable; otherwise, they would have stayed away from him. I was speechless when I heard these comments remembering the terror I experienced at the hands of Nick.

Knowing first hand a pedophile's skill at grooming small vulnerable children and the anguish it had brought into my life, I wanted to scream, "You knew and you remained silent!!!"

I don't know what happened when we got home from the river. I know I wanted to tell Mama but was sure she would be angry with me, especially when a few days later she told Sister and me about what she called the "facts of life."

Following a description of what men "do to women," Mama concluded with, "some men like to do things to little girls, too." Then Mama said in a very stern voice, "Don't you ever let a man touch you."

I froze inside. I had "LET" NICK TOUCH ME! My grief and guilt knew no end. I felt utterly forsaken and damned, hope drained from my soul.

When bad things happen to small children, they often conclude that it must be because they are bad; they must deserve what happened to them. My six-year-old world was falling apart and my parents, drowning in their own pain, were oblivious to the sense of abandonment tearing their little girl apart. Abuse is difficult enough, but when a child is left to deal with it alone, despair will often follow.

Other than Sister, the only person who ever had time for me was Nick who hurt and frightened me. Although I somehow knew what he did was wrong, in my thinking his guilt spilled over onto me making me afraid to "tell," afraid that I would be blamed because after Nick hurt me, he'd tell me I couldn't tell anyone or I would be in a lot of trouble. What was worse, after hurting me, when we were around other family members, Nick would ignore me, acting as though I wasn't there, as though he wanted to have nothing to do with me. This convinced me even more that I was bad, unworthy of anyone's love and support. I felt totally alone.

This aloneness only deepened when mother told Sister and me of grandmother's suicidal struggles. Not having the skills to process them as my grandmother's struggles not mine or my father's, they were stored in my memory as images that would come back to haunt me with visions of knives and death by suicide for decades to come. Gradually realizing that this reaction is understandable given the circumstances helped diffuse the impact.[1] However, it would be years, before I would finally make the connection between my uneasiness around large knives and the family history of suicidal ideations which my mother being unaware of the effect of her words, had related to me as a young child.

Although I had grown up in a family of hunters and owned a shotgun since my twelfth birthday, I could never kill anything. Instead, I would aim, close my eyes and pray I hit nothing. I usually did.

It would also be years before I would connect my disappointing skills as a hunter to my fear that my father would kill himself with a gun. It is no wonder that I never wanted to hunt, this also to my father's disappointment.

Sadly, by age six I was increasingly moving toward isolation, feeling I could trust no one. Whether in truth my parents abandoned me emotionally as they drowned in their own pain and suffering, or whether it was simply the perception of a hurting six-year-old, I am unsure, but I do know that it was then the realization began to form that I was alone in the world and if I wanted to survive, I would have to do it on my own. Of that, I was sure.

Although I have little memory of my sister during this time, I'm sure she was there, taking care of me as best she could, but I was becoming more and more distant and depressed. To what extent the abuse continued during these years, I don't know. Except for isolated events, I remember little. From time to time, I would again try to win my parents' approval, however, eventually that too would fall away.

I have no words to describe the mental agony that I suffered during this period of my childhood as I teetered on the edge of losing touch with reality. Even though Nick was not present, he was ever present through the sexualized imaginative world in which I lived. I was miserable. I even wondered if my parents knew and approved of Nick's abusive treatment of me; if it were some sort of rite of passage that prepared me for the adult experience of Mama's description of "what men did to women."

In my muddled way of childish thinking, I am not even sure I understood Nick was the problem. I felt confused by his behavior. He was nice to other children, played with them but not with me. He spoke kindly to me when he hurt me. Other than Aunt Effie and Sister and occasionally Mama and Papa, no one else spoke kindly to me, or if they did, I didn't recognize it as kindness.

Kindness from an abuser can introduce a veritable firestorm of conflicting emotions that further contribute to dysfunction, guilt and shame. Believing what the perpetrator is doing is evil yet being attracted to him as the only source of recognized attention, results in guilt and shame few victims can sort through on their own.

Even more complications arise when a child is stimulated sexually. The following is shared with permission from a dear friend who has been a counselor of abuse victims for 43 years.

> "When a child is abused sexually, that child will often experience an orgasm or at least pleasant physical sensations. While the child knows that this type of touching is "bad" the pleasant sensations cannot be denied. In addition, the abuser will often manipulate the child by withdrawing attention and acting indifferent as a means to more securely bind the child psychologically. It doesn't take long for the child to learn that to get the pleasurable feelings and missing emotional nurture, they will have to allow the physical touching which they know to be wrong.
>
> "As the grooming process continues, it reinforces the emotional/pleasure cycle while setting up major cognitive dissonance because the child knows that the behavior is unacceptable. This sets up what I call 'the dreaded desire.' The child wants and often craves the attention/pleasure while knowing that it is 'bad' to take part in it. Additionally the victim will often be lacking the nurture and attention that they need from family. This further sets the stage for a terrible situation from which a child cannot see a way forward.
>
> "When being ignored by the abuser, it is not uncommon for the child to reinitiate contact and allow the abuse in order to fulfill their desire for emotional support and physical pleas-

ure. I have had clients who tearfully shared that as children they often approached adults and did things that they knew would cause the behavior that they needed. Lacking the insight and maturity to know that they were conditioned and groomed to behave this way, they internalized that they were evil and that no one would ever love or take care of them.

"I wish that I could say that this is rare; it is not. I have seen it over and over and each time my heart aches for the individual. The reason that this is so hard to treat is that even as adults, individuals do not understand that children are not responsible for their actions. Victims are like every other child that wants and needs nurture, love, closeness, support and understanding. If it is withheld at home, then children look for it anywhere they can find it. They are not 'bad' for having normal nurturing needs. Rather, the adults around them fail them miserably and the children suffer for it; often for a lifetime.

"However, here is the cruelest part. As adults, victims are often not able to separate their actions as abused children from their own sense of self as an adult. They will share everything else with a counselor but withhold this one terrible secret because, 'If I admit that I sometimes sought the abuse, then even this person will reject me.' Because they cannot share openly and allow the counselor to help them through it, they carry it for the rest of their lives. They truly believe that they are evil at their core and no amount of prayer and penance will free them from it. The secret remains within and poisons every aspect of their lives. Even as I write, I can remember many individuals who were set free because they had the courage to admit that they were victims of this most terrible affliction.

"Abused children survive the best way they can. They have the tools that every child has, but ONLY those tools. It is completely unreasonable to believe that a child should or could have adult values and coping skills with which to resist the grooming process. But abuse victims often assume just that and, it destroys their sense of well-being."

George Helton, Counselor, Yakima, WA

Thirty years after the events of abuse in my life when I finally shared my story with a Christian counselor, his response was, "You had to prostitute yourself for every bit of affection you received as a child." Although I am not sure he was correct in reference to my life, that statement would certainly have been true in reference to the clients described above by my counselor friend George.

After having written at length about my childhood, I would come to see that deep inside, in the core of my being, there are still vestiges of the carefree winsome child full of spunk and vinegar. However, at age five that child was becoming increasingly shrouded under layers of hurt and defensive behavior that would take years to peel away. Nonetheless, peel away they would under the gentle healing that comes with being loved, first by my Creator and then by those He put into my life.

I will never be that child again, but I have become something better. Scarred but becoming whole; weaker yet stronger; disillusioned yet hopeful, not only for myself but for others who have or will travel the same path (2 Corinthians 4:8-9).

RESPONSE

A DEATH IN THE FAMILY

1 Can you recall a childhood experience of death that left one of your parents devastated? Were you affected more by the death or by your parent's reaction?

2 Have you been to a funeral home or someone's home after the death of a loved one and wondered why some laughed and enjoyed themselves while others were deeply saddened? How do you account for the dichotomy?

THE DAY OF THE FUNERAL

3 Can you recall a time when you "didn't have the words" to tell your parents about a disturbing event? Can you describe your feelings during that time? Where do your

thoughts and emotions go when you read the story of abuse that occurred at the river?

4 How do you reconcile the love of God with, "Where is God when bad things happen?"

DESTRUCTIVE GENERATIONAL THEMES

5 Did your family struggle with destructive generational themes of abuse, neglect, suicidal or homicidal ideations?

‣ If you have experienced the above, please for the sake and safety of yourself and your family, seek help from a competent Christian counselor, pastor or mentor.

6 Did your parents have favorites? How did this affect the other children in the family?

7 How was Li'l Sis affected by Mama's warning that the girls could so upset their papa with their noisy play that he might kill himself?

8 Describe Li'l Sis's emotional response when Mama told the girls, "Don't you ever let a man touch you." Why did Mama's words impact Li'l Sis so deeply?

9 Does the author's statement that Li'l Sis was torn between love and resentment toward her parents resonate with you?

10 Did you struggle with fear that one of your parents would cause physical harm to themselves or another family member? Explain.

"IF I SHOULD DIE BEFORE I WAKE..."

11 Did you fear death as a child? Was that fear in some way connected to guilt related to trauma or neglect?

12 Did you go through a period when you felt you were damned to hell because of the abuse you had experienced

or something you had done? How did you cope with those feelings? Explain.

A LOST LITTLE GIRL

13 After the experience at the river, Li'l Sis was haunted by intrusive thoughts and sexual ideations. Yet she could tell no one. Nick had told her she would be in big trouble if she told and after Mama's talk, she was convinced he was right. She felt damned if she told and damned if she didn't. Can you relate to this maelstrom of condemnation?

14 Were you able to tell your parents of any abuse or mistreatment?

15 Despite the chaos in my mind, there were two relatives (a step grandmother and a great grandmother) who provided diversion. One talked with me about school and seemed genuinely interested. The other let me play with her box of antique valentines.

‣ Did you have anyone who provided respite or diversion from the troubles in your life?

CHAPTER 6
HARDSHIP AND HAPPINESS

LIFE ON THE FARM WITH PAPA AWAY

In order to provide for the family and make the yearly mortgage payments, Papa had to continue working as a pipefitter. As there was little construction in north Alabama at the time, local jobs were almost impossible to find. It also meant Papa was gone a lot either looking for work, sitting at the union office waiting for work, or working away from home, wherever jobs were to be found. Often, he was gone all week only coming home after work on Friday night, then leaving again Sunday afternoon. The focus of the family was work.

By the autumn of the first year, there were pigs, cows and of course, Mama's chickens to care for. The girls helped by shelling corn for the animals in an old hand crank corn sheller that Papa bought from a relative who made his living buying and selling random farm equipment he came across. His storefront was his front yard which looked like the back lot of a 19th century farm implement store. The girls were delighted when Papa came home with the corn sheller as they no longer had to shell the corn by hand, rubbing the dried ear of corn with a corn cob to break the kernels loose.

Late one cold rainy night when Papa was on a job in Tennessee and Mama and the girls were home alone, the phone rang. A late night call never brought good news. The girls listened intently trying to catch a word as Mama's face became grave.

It was a neighboring farmer, "Ma'am, your pigs are in my field tearing my corn up. If you don't get them out right now, I'm going to shoot them dead."

Mama calmly told him she would take care of it and then went to the shed with a flashlight looking for fencing staples and a hammer. These she put in her clothespin apron. After quickly dressing in Papa's old clothes and boots, Mama tied a headscarf on her head, her staple filled clothespin apron around her waist, and out she went into the dark wet night, a flashlight in her hand.

She had to find the hole in the fence where the pigs had gotten out, drive them back through and repair the fence. That would be hard enough for anyone, but it was night and Mama had very limited eyesight.

The little girls kept the fire going in the fireplace and prayed Mama would be able to get the pigs taken care of and get back soon, although they couldn't see how anybody who saw as badly as Mama would be able to do all that in the cold driving rain.

About an hour later, Mama came in the door, tired, wet through and amazed it had gone so well. After locating the hole in the fence, she found the pigs in the neighbor's field and drove them back along the fence line. When they came to the hole in the fence, Mama said, "Those pigs walked right though that hole into our pasture as though they were glad to be home." The girls thought maybe something told those pigs there would be a farmer gunning for them if they didn't. Whatever the reason, the girls were sure of one thing: God had answered their prayers. Li'l Sis just wished He would answer hers, by keeping her safe and bringing Papa home.

PRIMARY SCHOOL YEARS 1952-1956

First grade with Mrs. Howell should have been a happy time as she was a wonderfully kind teacher. But she was also very strict, especially about not wetting your pants. What she didn't know was that there was a big scary kid who sometimes hung out in front of the girl's bathroom. One day he and a group of his friends cornered me and told me that he was going to kill me, then threatened me further if I told anyone. What he could possibly have done that was worse than killing me, I don't know, but then I was six years old and convinced some horrible doom worse than death would be inflicted if "I told." The result was, if he was in view, I avoided the restroom, wet my pants and was totally humiliated when Mrs. Howell chastised me in front of the class making me clean up the floor as everyone snickered.

The big kid always kept an eye out for me and would often find me on the playground threatening and bullying me as his friends looked on. He made my life miserable, but I was afraid to tell anyone not even Sister; a reflection of Nick's, "You had better not tell."

Despite the bully, there was one thing that I loved about first grade. It was the Dick and Jane reading series. Their lives were very different from mine. They had parents who were affectionate towards them, took care of them and took them on train trips to the country to visit their grandparents on the family farm. It was a beautiful farm with a warm clean farmhouse and well-equipped barn. They drove nice cars and had nice clothes. Young though I was, I realized other people lived lives that were very different from mine. If their lives were different, perhaps someday mine would be different too. I believe hope that things could be different, enabled me to get through those difficult years.

Second grade was even more traumatic because my teacher, Mrs. Jackson, hadn't the faintest idea about how to teach children who had difficulty reading. I could not distinguish between the words: this, that, these, those, them, they, there, their, they're, and landed squarely in the Yellow Bird Reading Group which we all knew was really the Buzzard Reading Group.

Mrs. Jackson's solution to my reading problems was to keep me in during recess each day and have me write the missed words ten times each. Of course, even after writing the words hundreds of times, I still hadn't a clue as to how to pronounce them.

Each day when I didn't show up for recess, Sister would appear at my classroom door and wait there until she caught my eye, giving me a sad reassuring smile as she was not allowed to enter the classroom when I was being detained.

Mama couldn't help me with reading because she couldn't see well enough to correct my mistakes or read the words to me. She would ask me to spell the words when I couldn't pronounce them, but unfortunately, that wasn't possible as I didn't know the alphabet. Sister tried to help me as well, but I was so terror-stricken by all those "th" words that it seemed hopeless. I struggled with them all day at school and could not face them again when I got home.

I'm not sure I would have ever learned to read had it not been for Carol Ann Snead, a fellow student from the Blue Bird Reading Group, whom the teacher asked to help me. Away from the glaring spotlight of knowing "I would have to read next," I was able to learn to read those words within a short time. However, I would not stop there.

It was about this time that Papa joined the People's Book Club and began getting a new book each month, sometimes more than one. We didn't have plumbing, but we had books, and I was determined to read those books. I labored over them word by word and soon was reading the autobiographical works of Ralph Moody who grew up poor on a ranch in the Midwest. I loved reading about how his close-knit family helped each other during hard times, and I wished desperately that my family could help me as I struggled to make sense of all that had happened to me.

TRYING TO COMPENSATE

Feeling that I must be horribly bad or my parents would love and support me, I set about being as good as I possibly could be in order to "earn" their affection. Ironically, at the same time, I began to lie. If my parents asked if I had done something, assuming I was in trouble, I automatically lied. I also made up fanciful tales about things I had said, done or experienced, in a vain attempt to sound interesting and catch the attention of others. In conversation, I was very careful to say what I thought people wanted to hear. My goal was to become a person that people liked and respected. Not achieving the desired results, I became increasingly angry and resentful. At about the age of seven, I acted out these feelings through sexual play with a younger cousin who in her innocence promptly told her mom that we had been playing "doctor." Sadly, this is a common occurrence among children who are abused.[2]

By this time lying came easily, and I denied what I had just done. My aunt being more concerned about my lack of truthfulness than my actions, told me that when my cousin was a very little girl, her dad had taken her on his lap and explained to her the importance of always telling the truth after which, she had never lied again.

Missing the message entirely, I only remember thinking, "How I wish my daddy would take me on his lap." I especially wanted my father's affection and trailed him like a shadow.

The one time I had my father's undivided attention was when I was sick. To that end, I was often blessed with tonsillitis that sent my temperature soaring, several times resulting in delirium. When Papa came home from work, he would sit on my bedside and talk with Mama about what should be done. For that reason, I loved being sick except when it meant a house call from the doctor. That always resulted in a penicillin shot which I hated, but concluded you had to take the good with the bad. At least I had my father's attention.

I heard my younger cousins being praised for their accomplishments in school, so I made sure every good grade was brought to my father's attention. When I asked Papa what he thought about my grades, his stock reply whether it was an "A" or a "B" was, "It's alright." One day I asked why he never praised me for my good grades like Aunt Mary did her kids. He replied, "If I did, it would go to your head." Dear Papa, I don't think there was ever any danger of that.

Since there was no praise to be had from grades, I found a book on needlework and taught myself to embroider, knit and crochet presenting the finished products to my father. The response to my question of, "What do you think of this, Papa?" was always the same. "It's alright."

As none of my efforts produced the desired result, each interest gradually fell by the wayside only to be replaced by a new attempt to gain recognition from my parents.

I played piano for eight years. Each year during recital, poor Papa exhausted from overwork would sit through an hour of "Row, Row, Row Your Boat" and other little ditties from Thompson's First, and Second Grade Piano Books, waiting for my sister and I to take our turns along with the more advanced students. Afterwards when we asked how we had done, he would say, "Alright."

Finally, in 9th grade, I quit piano lessons much to my teacher's dismay. She pled with me not to quit, telling me that I played with more expression than some of her more advanced students. Whereas I appreciated her praise, money was tight at home and I couldn't see wasting anymore as music was getting me nowhere with my father whose praise I sought more than anything else.

HAPPY TIMES ON THE FARM

Despite my emotional struggles, all was not bleak. During the summer, my favorite pastime was soaring on the swing my father hung for my sister and me in the peach tree behind the little red house. I swung so high that the lower limbs swept the ground. Although I was probably in danger of breaking my neck had I fallen, I felt safe and unfettered as I soared through the air.

I also loved running through the grass barefoot on a warm summer's day across the yard and through the orchard, running as fast as I could, the dry weeds switching my legs. The pain of the scratches from the dry grass and weeds made me feel alive. I ran until I could run no further, then did it again. The higher I swung, the faster I ran, the less I felt the heaviness in my heart.

I sometimes climbed through the fence of the cow pasture and chased the cows until Mama spotted me and told me I'd ruin their milk if I didn't stop. I also picked tiny periwinkle blue flowers in the pasture that Mama called bluets. Those tiny bouquets of blue somehow satisfied my love of beauty and I looked forward to their appearance each spring.

Much to my sister's dismay, for an afternoon snack, I picked wild onions in the pasture and ate them with cornbread. I loved their sweet sharp flavor. My poor sister hated my onion breath. I also loved the attention I received from her complaining to Mama.

We "built" playhouses by outlining the perimeters with old boards from the shed. Once the boards were set up on discarded coffee cans, we had benches, tables, chairs and beds for our dollies. Then came the grand moment of serving dinner: mud pies decorated with wildflowers from the pasture.

Mama had a red silk rose with black highlights and a clear plastic dew drop she pinned on her good Sunday dress. Sometimes she would let me pin that beautiful rose on a scarf around my neck and play with her costume jewelry. We also had pink snap beads we made into necklaces and bracelets. Like all little girls, I would painstakingly dress in Mama's clothes, apply makeup and all of her costume jewelry along with my pink snap bead necklace. The final touch was Mama's scarf with the beautiful red silk rose pinned in place. I was sure I was beautiful and perhaps I was.

Each fall, Papa bought a load of scrap wood from the local sawmill to use as kindling. It was all odd shapes and impossible to stack, so it was simply unloaded in a huge pile which we would hollow out for a playhouse.

There were also baby pigs and calves that brightened our lives in the spring. Each year Mama would order baby chicks that Papa picked up at the post office. They felt like soft powder puffs when we held them to our cheeks. We kept them under the bed to protect them from getting chilled until the weather was warm enough for them to be outside.

On cold winter afternoons, Mama would have our housecoats warming by the fire when we arrived home from school. Hot steaming bowls of pinto beans and yellow cornbread would be waiting for us on the stove as we peeled off our clothes and shoes, wet from the rainy walk home down the graveled lane. After dressing quickly in our pajamas and housecoats, we'd wrap ourselves in a quilt and sit before the fire eating our supper as our shoes stuffed with newspaper steamed on the hearth.

After finishing our homework, sometimes we'd eat hickory nuts on cracked on the stone fireplace, read from the latest publication of People's Book Club then go to bed early, burrowing deep into the thick feather bed that covered our mattress in the winter.

REFLECTION

Mama's willingness to do whatever it took to care for and provide for her family whether it meant repairing a fence in the middle of a downpour or straining to read the Bible to her young girls, made her a guiding light in my life. However the incident with the pigs and fence posed a theological conundrum for me. I remember wondering afterwards why God had clearly answered our prayers that Mama would be able to take care of the pigs, but He didn't seem to be taking care of me. This wondering whether God was aware of my plight and cared about what was happening to me would shape my view of God for years to come.

Although I remember a great deal about my life prior to the age of seven, I remember little from age seven through eleven. This makes sense to me as stress affects short-term memory and I was a very stressed little girl.[3]

I do, however, clearly recall the bully and my genuinely believing he would kill me if I told anyone of his threats. I also recall the haven that books afforded—precious escape from a world that felt unsafe. There was also the world of my dolls whom I loved and for whom I cared. Their care was so important to me that if I forgot to tuck them in bed on a cold winter's night, I would climb out of bed, find a towel or doll blanket and make sure they were warmly tucked in before I could fall asleep.

That escape into the world of play appeals to me even today as I take particular joy in collecting toys from the era of my childhood. Fortunately, moving frequently and limited space keeps my collection within bounds, but there are always special toys that delight the grandchildren.

Although Mrs. Jackson did little to help me learn to read, that experience planted a desire in my heart to help others who had difficulty reading. In 1998 when I was teaching reading to incarcerated youth for Seattle Public Schools, I put together a reading program that was adopted and successfully used in juvenile detention centers across the U.S. I was motivated to do this not only by my own reading struggles as a child but through research that indicated a direct proportion between increased reading levels and decreased recidivism.

When the "Seattle Post Intelligencer," one of our local newspapers, ran an article on my student's progress, the AP picked it up and carried it across the U.S. For months afterwards, I fielded calls from schools and detention centers nationwide, many of whom adopted the reading methods I used.

Thank you, Carol Ann Snead, for teaching me to read in second grade!

Although my parents were unable to help with our academic struggles, there is no doubt in my mind that my parents loved us and had they been informed, would have done anything in their power to protect me. However, they were both struggling with physical and emotional issues of their own and were simply unaware.

Sadly, an emotionally unsupported child who has experienced abuse will sometimes act out his/her feelings of powerlessness by abusing other children. Overwhelmed by a sense of helplessness, they attempt to gain some semblance of control by taking away the power of those more helpless than they.[4]

Whether trying to gain my father's attention or concluding I had to depend on myself and myself alone, nothing took away the feeling of powerlessness. The only solution is to turn to God and follow biblical principles of dealing with the trauma from abuse (i.e. speaking truth, confronting the abuser, then moving on to forgiveness and healing to become a healing healer). Anything else will eventually result in more pain. However, at age 6, I was without the support or understanding needed to access this avenue of God's grace. God did, however, provide the diversion of escape through books, the farm and a temperament that enabled me to survive.

One of the unfortunate side effects of keeping terrible secrets is frequent illness as the immune system is depleted by stress related to the undisclosed trauma. I cannot recall being sick at all until the abuse began and the emotional turmoil escalated.

Dr. James W. Pennebaker has done extensive research at Stanford, Southern Methodist University and the University of Texas related to writing therapy and the link between illness and hidden trauma. He is recognized by the American Psychological Association for his work related to trauma disclosure and health. His books on the topic of "Writing to Heal" have been used to help many to heal from childhood as well as other forms of abuse and trauma.[5]

Although I often struggled with insecurity, there were times when I felt safe and in control. Within the board outline of my makeshift playhouse, my world was in order. I was productive and surrounded by the beauty of nature with my flower decorated mud pie dinners and my babies safely asleep on their board beds.

Running alone in the pasture and orchard, stopping to examine a tiny flower, watching the birds soar, wondering at tadpoles and other water creatures in the creek that ran through the farm, the books that I read, these diversions from the chaos in my young mind were my escape. I believe they preserved my sanity until as an adult I was finally able to begin to understand the effects of what had happened to me and turn to those biblical guidelines for healing.

RESPONSE

LIFE ON THE FARM WITH PAPA AWAY

1 Were either or both of your parents absent from the family because of work? How did this affect your family life? How did you cope?

2 Was unemployment and financial stress an issue in your family? What affect did it have on family life?

3 Does the late night adventure of pigs in the neighbor's corn field remind you of any late night emergency that your family experienced?

4 Li'l Sis was puzzled that God seemed to answer her prayers and take care of the pigs but He didn't seem to be taking care of her.

‣ Can you identify with her puzzlement? How might such confusion distort a child's view of God? Can you recall a childhood event that shaped your view of God?

PRIMARY SCHOOL YEARS 1952-1956

5 Were you bullied as a child? Were you a bully or an abuser? What self-beliefs fueled these behaviors?

6 Li'l Sis wanted a family like Dick and Jane's in her first-grade reader. Was there a family that you wished yours was like?

TRYING TO COMPENSATE

7 Did you attempt to gain your family's recognition through your words or actions as Li'l Sis did by teaching herself to do needlework?

▸ How did your parents respond? Did you gain their attention?

8 Why do you think Li'l Sis did not recognize her father's love for her?

9 Growing up, were you the "good kid," "bad kid," "clown, "lost child" "hero," "scape goat"or a combination of two or more?

10 Did you have a book series through which you escaped as a child?

▸ What about that series appealed to you?

11 Did you struggle with honesty as a child? As an adult?

HAPPY TIMES ON THE FARM

12 What were your favorite summer pastimes?

13 Li'l Sis loved the attention she received from her sister's complaints of her oniony breath.

▸ Did you have childhood habits that irritated your older siblings, much to your delight?

14 "The higher I swung, the faster I ran, the less I felt the heaviness in my heart."

▸ Was there a childhood activity that helped you forget "the heaviness in your heart?"

15 "On cold winter afternoons, Mama would have our housecoats warming by the fire when we arrived home from school. Hot steaming bowls of pinto beans and yellow cornbread would be waiting for us on the stove as we peeled off our clothes and shoes, wet from the rainy walk home down the graveled lane. After dressing quickly in our pajamas and housecoats, we'd wrap ourselves in a quilt and sit before the fire eating our supper as our shoes stuffed with newspaper steamed on the hearth."

▸ Were there after-school rituals that welcomed you home?

16 Did you have favorite dress-up clothes as a child?

▸ Did your mother/father have a favorite accessory that he/she allowed you to use for dress up?

17 When considering Mama and Papa, can you identify character traits that remind you of your own parents? How are they different?

18 Was there a childhood experience that influenced your career choice such as not being able to read influenced Li'l Sis as an adult? Explain.

18 One of the guiding rules in the family was, "Protect the honor of the family. Be careful what you say in front of other people." This involved secrecy and pretending things were fine when they weren't which played right into the scenario with Nick.

▸ Were there guiding rules in your family that made abuse easy or communication difficult?

20 The author writes, "There is no doubt in my mind that our parents loved us."

◂ Looking back, can you see evidence that they were loved. Can you see evidence that your parents loved you?

21 Were there times in your childhood when you felt especially safe and in control as Li'l Sis did "within the confines of her board and coffee can playhouse?" Explain.

CHAPTER 7
THE GOOD AND THE BAD

THE ABUSE CONTINUED

One summer night, our family was invited to Cousin Nick and Janie's house for supper. Afterward, we kids ran through the grass in a neighboring field catching fireflies that we put in glass fruit jars. The cousins smeared the fireflies on balls and threw them up glowing into the night sky sending me crying to my mother screaming, "They're killing them, Mama. They're killing them." Mama, not understanding at all what the ruckus was about dismissed my tears with the words, "There are fireflies to spare. Go back out and play." I still cried.

Later there were games of Hide and Seek and Red Rover Come Over while the adults sat on the porch talking. After a while, Nick joined the children and began swinging his children around in circles by their arms. Seeing the fun my cousins were having, I ran to Papa and asked him to please swing me around. When he refused, probably because he knew it would hurt his back, I asked Nick to swing me. Starved for attention, which I sought even from the man who abused me, I remember begging him to swing me too as I jumped up and down, dancing in front of him, "Please, please, please."

At first, he ignored me, then he grabbed my arms and swung me around so hard that I screamed in pain as I whirled through the air. When he finally stopped, I remember the strange look on his face as he grinned at me through clenched teeth, breathing heavily. I also remember my unsmiling father watching as he leaned against the porch rail. When I stumbled toward him dizzy and disoriented seeking his comfort, he said, "Don't come crying to me. You asked for it." To an extent, Papa was right. I did not want the abuse, but I so wanted to be included in the fun, I was willing to take a risk, even with Nick.

Another hot summer's day, Nick came to the house to drive Mama, Sister and me over for another visit with his family. Shortly before lunch, I needed to go potty and not wanting to go to the hot, smelly outhouse, I went to the barn. Suddenly Nick was there, squatting down over me. His hands on my body. I froze.

It was always the same. I was like a small cornered animal, prey in the clutches of a predator. I felt powerless, paralyzed, unable to move. Then he did something he had never done before. He asked, "Do you want me to keep on?" Being offered a choice brought me out of my paralyzed state. "No," I yelled, pulled up my pants and fled to the house where Mama and Nick's wife, Cousin Janie, were working in the kitchen. I so wanted to tell Mama what had just happened, but I couldn't because I had again "let" Cousin Nick touch me, something Mama had said a little girl should never do.

A short time later Nick presided at the dinner table when we all sat down to eat. He told animated stories and jokes entertaining everyone with tall tales while I sat there shaken to the core. I believe I was able to stay out of his reach for some time, but the damage was done. I knew I was worthless and unfit to be loved; otherwise, my parents, God or someone would protect me. Nick was the only person who paid any attention to me and that "attention" involved secrecy, pain and shame.

There were other times when Nick would go out of his way to cause me pain even in front of my father. On one occasion, he encouraged me to grab an electric fence, even demonstrated that it would not hurt me, grabbing the fence wearing rubber boots as I stood in front of him in the morning dew barefoot. Another time he talked me into touching live battery wires. The shock was substantial for a six-year-old, and I again went to my father who was standing by watching, but he offered no comfort again saying, "You asked for it."

DAY-TO-DAY LIFE ON THE FARM

In the early days when Mama washed our clothes in a black cast iron washpot in the backyard, Sister and I had the job of keeping the fire going under the pot. It was our favorite winter chore. We'd throw wood on the fire, then turn first one way and then the other to warm ourselves; one side burning,, the other side freezing.

However, this all changed when we moved into the little red house in the field and Papa bought Mama a used wringer washer, which he put on the back porch next to the well.

After the washing was done, Sister and I took turns running the clean laundry through the wringer, stacking it in a basket, emptying the washer and refilling it with water from the well to rinse the clothes. This was followed by wringing the clothes out again and hanging them up to dry.

One day Papa brought home a submersion heater so that Mama no longer had to heat wash water on the stove but could easily heat it directly in the washer. Having the well on the back porch was a great improvement over the days when Papa had to haul all our water from a spring in the mountain.

Unlike the days before we had electricity when Sister was a baby, Mama no longer had to heat her iron on the wood cook stove as she had an electric iron that plugged into an outlet screwed into the light socket hanging from the ceiling. She also had a nice padded ironing board which replaced the old quilt on the kitchen table that she previously used. In those days, almost everything was ironed: Papa's work shirts, all our clothes and the sheets and pillowcases, which Sister and I ironed.

There was also sewing to be done on Mama's treadle sewing machine. Dish towels and bath towels were made from hemmed feed sacks as were some of our sleeveless summer dresses. I don't know how she managed with her limited eyesight, but Mama did all of the sewing until Sister and I were old enough to sew hems ourselves.

That is not to say that Sister and I didn't have store bought dresses. At least once a year, perhaps more often, we would go into town and buy a dress around Easter or for a special event at school. In addition each fall, a school dress or two was ordered from the Sears Roebuck catalog.

There was also a distant cousin of Papa's who brought Sister and me her daughter's hand-me-down dresses. Her husband was a car salesman in Guntersville, and she always drove a big black Buick. I can still remember the thrill of seeing that big black car coming down our graveled lane and knowing new clothes were headed our way.

Despite her limited eyesight, Mama never assumed she couldn't do anything until she had tried. Papa found a used sofa somewhere and brought it home. As it was pretty much worn out, Mama decided to reupholster it.

Later that morning, Cousin Josie called and asked Mama, "Whatcha doing today?"

"Covering a couch."

"I didn't know you could do that."

"Well, I don't know if I can or not," Mama answered, "but I'm gonna find out." And she did find out. Not all the seams were straight. Nor were the tacks in a straight line, but it was covered with a nice clean cover and we used it for years.

I can only recall one cooking mishap which was related to Mama's eyesight. One cold winter's night, we sat down to a delicious dinner of cornbread and lima bean soup that Mama had made from dried beans stored in a flour sack from the summer before. With only a single light bulb hanging from the ceiling, lighting wasn't that good, but Sister noticed something unusual.

"Papa," she asked, "what are those little half circles floating on top of the soup?"

"Oh, it's just little weevils, but you needn't worry as all they've eaten their whole lives is beans."

And so we ate our soup without another thought.

In addition to the housework and the animals, the garden, canning and freezing also had to be done.

In late February, the garden was plowed and potatoes planted. Next came the planting of peas, beans and corn. Tender tomato plants started inside couldn't be planted until after the last frost, along with squash and cucumbers. By that time, the peach and apple trees were in bloom. We'd pray there'd be no frost after they bloomed. Otherwise there would be no summer fruit or fall apples.

In the spring when the calves and piglets were born, Papa often had to stay up all night to make sure they had a safe arrival. The smallest baby pigs would inevitably end up in a box in the kitchen next to the stove. They would be raised on the bottle until they were big enough to stay with their mother and fend for themselves against their stronger siblings.

Papa and I would also make our spring circuit of the local dairies to buy calves to raise on the bucket. Morning and evening we would mix powdered formula with warm water and feed the calves, scratching their ears as they sucked the nursing buckets.

Beehives had to be checked to see how they had fared during the winter, the hives repaired, and new supers added. I helped Papa by nailing bee frames together as well as following along the fence row behind him with a bucket of fencing staples as he reattached loose strands of wire. I wanted to be "Papa's girl" and much preferred being outside "helping" him, to being inside with Sister and Mama.

The first spring produce came in late April when Papa would pick "poke salat" along the side of the road. One time I asked Papa why it was called that. He said it was because you picked it and put it in a poke (another name for a bag or sack) as you walked down the road going into town.

The last fall harvest came just after the first frost when sassafras roots were dug in the mountain for tea. In between, there was the continual cycle of weeding, harvesting, freezing, canning and pickling. From the garden came lettuce, greens, tomatoes, beans, peas, okra, squash and corn. The orchard produced peaches, pears, apples, damson plums, walnuts and pecans. The fence rows and woods gave us wild greens, blackberries, wild plums, Muscadine grapes and hickory nuts a

In late summer, Papa and I cut and stacked wood from the river bottoms for winter. While he felled the trees, I gathered hickory nuts in an old flour sack. Afterward, we worked together to strip the trees of their limbs, cut the trunk into manageable lengths and loaded them in the back of the pickup truck which Papa bought following the move to the farm. After the corn harvest, which in the early days was done by hand, there was the trip to the grist mill on the river to have it ground into cornmeal. While the corn was being ground, Papa and I climbed the stairs to the loft from which we watched the gears and grinding stones do their work powered as the water wheel turned.

Although there was a lot of work involved, it was a happy time of working together toward a common goal; providing food, clothing and winter fuel for the family. Periodically mother would look around the dinner table with pride and comment that everything on the table had been "raised on the farm."

THE MOVE TO THE BIG HOUSE 1953

From time to time during the summer, Mama, Sister and I walked to the next farm to visit our neighbors the Jenkins. Mr. Jenkins farmed full time and his wife Ruth stayed home with their little girl Sissy.

We loved going there as the house had high ceilings and was always cool in the summer. Also, Miss Ruth, who was young and pretty, was sure to have iced tea and cake left from Sunday dinner that she would offer us.

Sissy, her three-year-old daughter, was an only child and had lots of playthings which we found fascinating.

Going around to the back door Mama would knock and call, "Ruth, you home? It's Mae and the girls."

Miss Ruth would come from the kitchen wiping her hands on her apron as she came.

"Why, y'all come in. Just don't look at this house. I'm in the middle of canning peaches. Jim brought some home from the roadside stand, and I'm up to my ears."

"Give me a pan full and a knife, Ruth, and we'll knock these out in no time," Mama would respond, and they did while Sister and I played with Sissy, whom her mama was delighted to have out from underfoot.

"Let's go play dolls, Sissy," and off we three went for an afternoon of playing with the beautiful dolls that sat in a row across Sissy's bed.

Shortly after harvest, we were outside bringing wood in when we heard a blood-curdling scream coming from the Jenkin's place.

As Mama headed across the field in the direction of the scream, she told us girls to go in the house and stay there until she got back. White-faced and scared, we watched at the window as a black car that we knew to be Dr. Carpenter's drove up to the Jenkin's house and stopped. Soon afterward, Mama returned.

In response to our questions, she said, "Jim died of a heart attack. Ruth heard him fall and found him lying on the floor unable to move. It was her scream that we heard."

"Her sister has come, and the doctor is there, so they will be all right," Mama said.

Several days later, we all went to the funeral. It was what you did. We also took a coconut cake to the house afterward and had cake and coffee with the family. That was also what you did. Sissy at age three didn't understand what had happened but told us her Daddy had "gone to Jesus."

Sometime later, Miss Ruth came to the house and asked Papa if he'd be interested in buying her farm.

"Mr. Louis, I can't run the farm by myself, so I'm going to have to sell out, but first, I want to know if you're interested. Since our farms border, you ought to have the first right of refusal."

"Well, Miss Ruth, Papa responded, I don't rightly know, but I'll think on it if you can give me a few days."

After talking it over with Mama, Papa went to see Mr. Reed to ask if he would back a second loan, which he agreed to do.

Although we were sad for Miss Ruth and Sissy losing Mr. Jim and now having to sell their farm, at the same time, Sister and I were really excited. Papa was going to buy the Jenkins's farm. That meant living in that big old house with the tall ceiling that made it so cool in the summer. What we didn't yet know was that it was freezing cold in the winter. But we would know soon enough.

Shortly after Mr. Reed agreed to the loan, we moved into the big house. There were two huge bedrooms, a living room, kitchen, front hall, and front and back porch. I begged Papa to put a bed in the front hall so I could have a room of my own and he did; a big iron bedstead that he found in the barn. Mama let me have a small square mirror and an old washstand where I could store my clothes. Patchwork quilts and an old white chenille bedspread completed the furnishings. With my dolls on my bed and my books standing in a straight row on the washstand, it was a grand room—that is until winter came and blew through the cracks so hard that the bedspread fluttered in the breeze. At that point, I moved into Sister's bed with her and wintered very well until spring when I happily moved back into my own bedroom.

We had a huge garden that summer in the field next to the house. It was especially hot and dry which produced a bumper watermelon crop. Some were deep green in color. Others were oblong with green and white stripes. They were so plentiful that Papa brought them in from the field still warm from the sun, dropped them on the ground and cut the heart out with his pocket knife. After we had eaten the center from each one, the rest would go to the pigs. With such extravagance, we felt like kings.

Autumn meant the apple harvest and cider making. One Saturday afternoon we all piled into the pickup truck, my sister and I in the back, and off we went to the orchard. Sitting on the tailgate, the weeds whipping our legs as we bumped through the pasture, rates right up there with running barefoot through the warm summer grass and swinging in the peach tree swing. I loved the wind in my hair and sun on my face as we sped along with Mama shouting to Papa, "Slow down before you bump the girls off."

Nothing compares with the smell of an orchard on a hot summer's day. The air is heavy with the fragrance of ripe tart apples and pears. The buzz of bees and wasps feeding on the ripe fruit fills the air.

As our parents sampled the different trees, they talked about which apples would be best for applesauce, pies or cider.

"Winesap mixed with Goldens to cut the tartness for cider," Papa said.

"Winesap will also make good pies, keep them from being too sweet," Mama added.

Sister and I bit into apples from each tree trying to decide which one was our favorite as we carefully stepped between bees feasting on the fallen fruit around our bare feet.

Returning to the house with washtubs of apples in the back of the truck, we quickly unloaded, gave the apples a quick rinse and threw them in the hopper. Taking turns at the crank, we soon had juice pouring out of the press into the gathering pan below.

By day's end, the refrigerator was filled with gallon jugs of apple juice waiting to be canned the next day.

THE BIRTHDAY PARTY 1957

Quiet, shy and terribly desperate for friends, when I turned twelve, I somehow talked Mama into letting me have a birthday party, a first for our family. I was thrilled. We bought invitations at the five and dime in Huntsville and I passed them out to several of the students at my school who I hoped would come. Mama made a cake and bought premade icing candle holders in pink and white that we stuck in the cake in a circle of twelve candles.

Cousin Janie asked how we would entertain the kids I had invited. Never having been to a birthday party, we didn't know we were supposed to entertain them. The only thing I knew was that friends came, brought presents and ate cake and ice cream. Cousin Janie offered to bring Pin the Tail on the Donkey and lead the kids in other games like Blind Man's Bluff. She then asked what prizes we had bought and was amused that we were planning a party but were totally unprepared which made us feel even more insecure. I don't remember what we did about the game prizes or even if we had any, but finally, the day came.

Several of my friends from sixth grade arrived and indeed brought gifts. I was so nervous about everything that it was hard for me to enjoy myself, but after they all left, I very much enjoyed their presents. There was a picture album which I filled with valentines from school and a diary in which I would record some of my first attempts at writing.

A shocking birthday "present" came a few days after the event. As I was walking out the door, probably after some smart retort to my Mother, she replied, "One thing you need to know is that once you turn twelve, all your sins are recorded and counted against you."

Stopping in my tracks, I said nothing but looked at her in utter disbelief as I thought, "Couldn't you have given me a bit more warning?"

Having feared I was condemned to hell from the time I was a small child, now I had evidence. But I would not accept defeat lightly. Having always been a goal-oriented child, I would do all I could to avoid damnation. From then on, every time there was a revival at our small country church, I would go forward to be "saved." Finally, Mama, embarrassed by my frequent trips to the altar, told me that I really didn't need to "go forward" every time. Mama, however, was unaware to the depth of guilt with which I was dealing, nor would she know for years to come.

It was also during this time that I was given an opportunity through the small country church that we attended to sign up for a pen pal in Africa. In the mid-50s and 60s, the Methodist Conference supported mission schools in southern Rhodesia and asked their churches, small and large, to encourage their youth to correspond with Rhodesian school children.

As it was a church activity and I was trying to please God, I gladly signed up. I was also intrigued by the fact that I could write letters to someone who lived on the continent where Livingston had lived and worked. After reading his biography, I was interested in becoming a scientist researching cures for exotic diseases, that is, until I came to

Pre-Algebra which convinced me that math and science were not my fields.

I looked forward to the first letter from my Rhodesian pen pal as I was sure she lived in a mud hut and cut paths through the jungle dodging venomous snakes as Livingston did. However, I was to be disappointed as when the letter came, she lived in a large city, nowhere near the jungle. The content of her letter was equally disappointing as it contained numerous Bible passages followed by a lengthy description of her love for Jesus. Despite my disappointment, I continued to write until she immigrated to America. Unaware of the dangerous conditions in her country, I was baffled by anyone's decision to leave Africa to move to New York City.

The only other person I knew who was interested in the Bible and God was my mother who watched Billy Graham on TV. Not only did she watch the Graham crusades, she expected me to as well and at Dr. Graham's suggestion, made me sit on her lap so that she could "dedicate me to the Lord."

At the time, Papa was totally unimpressed with television and radio preachers and tended to make fun of them. He may also have resented the crumpled dollar bill that Mama would smooth out from time to time and put in an envelope addressed to the Billy Graham Association. As Papa was my idol, I thought as he did.

FINAL ENCOUNTER

The only other incident of abuse at Nick's hands that I remember occurred when I was around twelve or thirteen. While the adults were picking corn and beans for freezing and canning, Nick's daughter Amanda and I, who were not considered skilled enough to determine which ears of corn were mature for picking, spent the afternoon reading Amanda's comic book collection.

Lying across Amanda's bed with a stack of comic books between us, we were having a reading marathon. Engrossed in a storyline, I didn't notice Amanda leave but the next thing I knew, Nick was hovering over me with his hands on my body. My initial reaction was to freeze when I felt his hands, but when he once again asked if I wanted him to continue, I found my voice, said, "No," and fled the room.

Only a short time later, I would have to again endure the charade of sitting through dinner with Nick presiding as he entertained all present with his animated stories and tales as though nothing had just happened.

Years later during my freshman year, the damage would be compounded when Amanda told a young man of whom I was very fond that I had been her father's lover, thus ending that relationship and causing me to wonder if I would ever be free of the specter of Nick.

REFLECTION

Interesting question, "Will I ever be free of the specter of Nick?" Probably not, at least not totally in this life. So much of my life has been influenced by those encounters; my view of God, of myself, as well as my relationships with others (see Chapter 11). Yet through the process of facing the effects of the abuse, I have been able to understand and help others in ways that would not have been possible otherwise. Am I glad that I had those experiences? No! But I am ever so grateful that God has redeemed them into something useful for His kingdom; a tender heart toward the hurting and a sensitivity that recognizes suffering and pain in others.

I have also come to the point where I can accept that God is God and He is not accountable to me regarding what He allows into my life. However, He only allows difficulty for the purpose of bringing me to a place in my relationship with Him that would otherwise not have been attainable.

God is a loving father who has my best interests at heart whether I understand the circumstances or not. Life's dark events are teaching me to seek God for who He is, not for what I want from Him. No, I have not "arrived" but I am ever so gradually moving out of Martha's kitchen expecting Jesus to do my bidding to join Mary at His feet (Luke 10:38-42; James 1:2-4; Romans 5:3-4).

From the dysfunctional coping skills developed as a child to deal with the trauma of abuse, I have learned that any time we rely on anything other than God and His truth to save us from our woundedness, we only compound our misery. Make no mistake. "Relying on God" doesn't mean humbly submitting to abuse whether as a child or as an adult. It means following the biblical guidelines of speaking truth, seeking help, forgiving our abuser and working through the past with a skilled mentor or counselor. It also means taking personal discipleship seriously which includes the practice of spiritual disciplines. If it sounds easy, it isn't, but it is the only way to move forward (see Chapter 12 Dysfunctional Coping Mechanisms and Chapter 13 Effective Strategies for Healing).

I grew up in an age in which children were anything but coddled. We were never told that we could be or do anything that we set our minds to, nor were we told that we were loved. When as a teenager, I asked my father what he thought I would contribute to society, his laughing response was, "Probably a couple of squalling kids." Ironically, years later, when my husband and I wanted to have children, it was discovered that I was infertile.

Papa was a product of his age, convinced that the best upbringing for children living in a hostile world was "to toughen them up." However, for a child in emotional crisis who desperately needed support, his seeming indifference strengthened my conviction that I wasn't worth protecting. At the time, I was unable to recognize that Papa was showing his love and support by providing piano lessons, books and even a tv when no on else in the neighborhood had one.

Although I know that children carry no guilt in these situations, to an extent, Papa was right, when he said, "I had asked for it" when I came staggering to him after being swung around violently by Nick. As a child, I clearly had no understanding of boundaries and may have made it easy for Nick to groom and abuse me, starved as I was for affection.

During this period, I was in a swirl of conflicting emotions. Hemmed in by Nick's power over me as the only adult who gave me attention and the shame I felt that kept me from telling my mother, I remained silent. The absolute importance of assuring children that they can communicate anything to their parents without fear of an angry response is crucial if they are to report instances in which they feel uncomfortable or endangered.

Equally important is the need to communicate to children that they have choices. Dr. J.D. Bremner, Harvard trained psychologist and pro-

fessor at Emory University, cites National Institute of Health brain studies related to early childhood trauma which indicate an almost complete shutdown of the left hemisphere of the brain during traumatic events resulting in a frozen state as opposed to a state of "fight or flight."[6] This was my response. I froze.

That began to change when cornered in the barn by Nick. It finally occurred to me that I had a choice. In response to his question of should he continue, I yelled, "No," and fled. Up until that point, I didn't know I had a choice.

From these experiences, I have seen the importance of teaching children to say, "No," and to flee when things don't feel right. A helpful resource is, "It's My Body: A Book to Teach Young Children to Resist Uncomfortable Touch."[7] Choice can be taught early on by giving children simple tasks such as choosing which outfit they will wear or game they would like to play—"This one or this one?"

Prior to writing this manuscript, my childhood memories centered primarily around the abuse and the effect that it had on my life. Purposely looking back has uncovered a world of joyful memories and lessons learned from parents who did the best they could considering the resources they had. Writing with the goal of remembering and recording positive as well as negative events can be a powerful beginning for redeeming a lost childhood. There is restoration and an awareness of God's providing respite in those happy times (see Chapter 15).

As I consider my spiritual journey, I find it interesting that the first person to share the gospel with me was a young African teenager living in war-torn Rhodesia. How unlikely is that? A preteen living in poverty in north Alabama first hears the gospel from a young Christian woman in Africa? The sovereignty of God is not limited by geography or what we can imagine, yet the thread of His sovereignty runs through our lives from beginning to end.

Later in college when I met two Catholic students who also took their faith in God seriously, I would remember that African pen pal whose name has long since been lost to time. Unfortunately, at that juncture, I was too preoccupied with having a good time to pursue an interest in God.

RESPONSE

THE ABUSE CONTINUED

1 Why would Li'l Sis approach Nick asking him to swing her around?

2 Why do you think Nick ignored Li'l Sis's pleas to be swung around, "then grabbed her arms and swung her around so fiercely that she screamed in pain as she whirled through the air"?

3 Do you identify with fight, flight or freeze when you recall your reaction to childhood trauma?

4 Were you offered a choice by your abuser?

5 How did your abuser treat you when others were around? How did that make you feel?

DAY-TO-DAY LIFE ON THE FARM

6 Was there a family member with special needs or addictions when you were growing up? How did this affect your family life?

7 Even though you probably didn't grow up on a farm where you worked together as a family to raise your own food, were there projects that you worked on together for the benefit of the family?

THE MOVE TO THE BIG HOUSE 1953

8 Can you recall a move during your childhood that was particularly significant for you? Explain why.

9 Were there family events from your childhood that you recall with particular pleasure?

THE BIRTHDAY PARTY 1957

10 Can you recall anything significant about any birthday party that you can remember?

11 When did you first grapple with the question of heaven and hell? What spurred those thoughts?

12 Did you grow up thinking good works would get you into heaven and bad ones would send you to hell? How might such opinions affect your view of God?

FINAL ENCOUNTER

13 Do you sometimes wonder if you will ever be free of the specter of the person who abused or neglected you? How would you answer that question?

14 Why is it important to teach young children they have a choice? Did you know that you had a choice when you were being abused or mistreated? If you had known, do you think it would have made a difference? Or did you feel you had a choice?

15 Explain why you agree or disagree with the following quote, "Writing with the goal of remembering and recording positive as well as negative events can be a powerful beginning for redeeming a lost childhood. There is restoration and an awareness of God's providing respite in those happy times."

16 "The author first heard the gospel message from a pen pal living in war-torn Rhodesia in the 50s."

▸ When did you first hear the gospel message of salvation through faith in Christ's sacrificial death? How did you respond?" Did you commit your life to Christ at that point? Was it late, or have you yet to make that decision?

CHAPTER 8
EXPANDING HORIZONS

MIDDLE SCHOOL 1956-1959

My sister played a very important role in my life throughout middle school and early high school. Although quiet and shy like Mama, Sister was a beautiful blue-eyed blond who played the piano and had a clear singing voice. She also had a gentle quiet spirit, whereas, I was short-tempered and had a critical outlook on life.

Sister was not only beautiful, she was happy and loved by all. I was miserable and insecure.

This wasn't helped by the comparisons from relatives. There was an uncle who each time he saw me would ask, "Now, why can't you be pretty like your sister with her long curly hair and blue eyes?" This, to a skinny middle schooler who was all elbows and knees, with thin straight hair and green eyes!

My sullenness and negativity only increased as I progressed through middle school. My mother said I was like my grandfather who always said what he thought whether he should or not. My father gave me the book *How to Win Friends and Influence People* and told me to read it. He also told me if I didn't stop arguing with my sister, we were going to grow up hating each other just like my grandfather hated and was hated by his own brother.

Although Papa was prone to exaggeration, there were times when I was not at all kind to my sister. She was so beautiful and gentle, and I was such an ugly duckling: tall, awkward and terribly insecure outside of our home.

However, the negative aspects of our relations were more than balanced by the positive. Being six years older than I, by the time I entered seventh grade, Sister had graduated high school, attended business college and had a secretarial job.

Her first purchase was a 1957 Buick Century. It was a beautiful car, mauve and gray, and made even more beautiful by the fact our family car had been a green Chevy pickup truck for the last seven years.

Up until that point, we had lived a relatively isolated life living almost 20 miles from the nearest town. Other than attending school, grocery shopping on Saturday mornings and Sunday church, we rarely left the farm. Car ownership changed all that. Sister and I signed up for swim lessons at the YMCA; two different times as neither of us could master the American Crawl. We didn't mind signing up twice as after swim lessons every Thursday night, we would stop by the Dough Nut Shop and pick up a dozen glazed doughnuts. They were always fresh and so hot they sizzled in your mouth.

Saturdays we would go to a dress shop that advertised dresses "as seen in Cosmopolitan Magazine," then to a bookstore where we gradually collected and read every book written by Victoria Holt and Daphne Du Maurier. The bookstore owner let us know when a new book was coming out and we'd mark the calendar, waiting for the date.

This was the era of the Rogers and Hammerstein musicals and we saw them all as soon as they were released in our area: *Oklahoma, South Pacific, Show Boat, The King and I, The Sound of Music,* and the list goes on. Sister bought the soundtracks on LP records as well as the sheet music, which we played on the piano and sang to our heart's content.

In addition to being a member of the People's Book Club, Papa had a weekly subscription to *Life magazine* and *The Saturday Evening Post.* Each Thursday afternoon, I'd sit on the concrete porch steps enjoying the coolness as I waited for Mr. Kraft, the postman, to arrive with the weekly editions. As soon as his car pulled away, I'd sprint across the hot melting asphalt road barefoot, grab the mail and spend the next few days lying on my belly on the cool wood floor of the front room, reading the magazines cover to cover, advertisements and all.

I marveled at all that went on in the world, and in 1956 wept over the story of Jim Elliot and his fellow missionaries killed in Ecuador by the tribal people whom they sought to reach with the gospel. My horizons were expanding.

A NEW SCHOOL 1960-1964

The high school Sunday school teacher at our little country church was also an English teacher at a neighboring high school. One Sunday she approached me after church and asked about my plans after graduation. During the conversation, she emphasized the importance of writing skills in college and suggested that I consider transferring to the school where she taught so that she could help me prepare for college.

I was intrigued by her suggestion for several reasons. I was keenly aware of the cold hard fact that I was basically a social failure at my current school and such a move would give me an opportunity to start over. I also realized I would be better equipped for college under her tutelage.

If there was anything my parents were committed to, it was education. Having had to drop out of school in their mid-teens to work in the fields, they wanted "better" for their girls. When I spoke to them, they agreed that it could be a good move and contacted a great aunt who lived in the community where Mrs. Brownly taught.

Soon it was arranged. I would live with my aunt and in the fall, I would enroll at Lewis High School as a sophomore.

Miracle of miracles, almost immediately I caught the eye of the captain of the football team and although still a bit of an outsider, I was soon hanging out with the cool crowd.

Mrs. Brownly, true to her word, provided a rigorous comprehensive writing program with strict guidelines. I worked hard and honed my developing skills. Near the end of my junior year, she returned a graded short story with the comment, "You know, you could be a writer someday."

Unfortunately, things were not going as well in my social life. I soon discovered all the captain of the football team could think of was having bragging rights in the locker room. There was constant pressure to "give it up." He tried first one approach and then another, even at one point threatening suicide.

Over Christmas break, he invited me to a Christmas party given by his best friend in a nearby town. When he picked me up for the party, I asked why he was driving out into the country instead of into town where the party was to be held. "Oh, the party has been canceled," he answered, "we're going to another place."

"Where?" I persisted. No answer came. He drove on in silence, finally turning into a deserted parking lot near a lake. Here he attempted to force himself upon me. I was saved from the inevitable when a local sheriff drove his patrol car into the parking lot and headed in our direction.

The boyfriend wasted no time pulling himself together, starting the car and heading toward the parking lot exit; direction back home. The sheriff having achieved his goal went on his way.

From then on, every date was a fight to keep him off. Although he never had his way, I was sickened and sullied by it all. Yet I did not want to be the lone wallflower again. For a time, I continued to endure his advances which never went far enough for him.

Finally, he asked, "What is wrong with you? All your friends have gone all the way."

"How would you know?" I countered.

"Because that's all the guys talk about in the locker room."

Silence followed as I thought to myself, "And you have nothing to brag about."

The real death of our relationship came a short time later when his last tactic was followed up with a proposal of marriage. I declined explaining that I planned to go to college.

His incredulous response was, "You? You? Go to college?"

For that response, I will forever be grateful to that young man. From that point on, I was even more determined to attend college and succeed.

Spring came and my soon-to-be-former boyfriend graduated and moved on to a series of jobs at various fast food chains working weekends, which meant we rarely saw each other and gradually drifted apart.

It wasn't easy going from always having a date and someone to hang out with at school, to sitting home on Saturday night, but it was a huge relief to no longer have the pressure to compromise. At the same time, I felt at loose ends. Something was missing, something more than a Saturday night date. It was also at a time when I again began to think about God.

One afternoon as I sat at my desk studying, a terrible storm blew up, whipping the limbs of the oak trees surrounding the house and flinging acorns against the windows. I loved storms, seeing in them the power of the God I didn't understand. Leaving my homework undone, I went out into the yard, looked up into the boiling sky and prayed, "God if you are really there, reveal yourself to me." I don't know what I expected, but nothing happened, at least not immediately.

I missed an opportunity during my freshman year in college when two Christian girls in the dorm invited me to join their youth group. I declined. Two more years would pass before I met Rusty, a female Campus Crusade for Christ (CRU) staff member who shared with me how I could know Christ as my Savior.

LAST CONTACT WITH NICK 1963

The only other contact with Nick I can remember was the summer before my senior year.

I was backing down the drive to leave when Nick approached the car motioning for me to stop. In a solicitous manner, he said, "You wouldn't believe the lies a neighborhood girl has been spreading about me."

Stunned he was seeking my support against these charges, I responded, "I rather suspect, I would," and quickly drove away.

Such hypocrisy was beyond the pale. Did Nick actually expect sympathy from me or was he merely fishing to see if I would accuse him as well? Whatever he wanted, I would have none of it.

My only regret is I didn't immediately drive to the home of the girl accusing Nick of inappropriate behavior and join her in making his actions known to the authorities for the sake of other children who were likely to be his victims. At that time, it would have been possible to have brought charges. However, 15 years later when I finally sought counseling and at the prompting of my counselor reported the abuse to the authorities, I was told the statute of limitations had expired, and I could do nothing. This sickened me as I had recently learned that Nick continued his work as a children's program volunteer. I pled with the officer with whom I had spoken to at least take Nick's name and investigate whether he was supervised, but there was nothing she could do unless current charges of abuse were brought against him. I felt ill knowing Nick was very likely continuing his abusive behavior and there was nothing I could do.

After that last encounter with Nick, I finally told my mother. One thing that made it very hard "to tell" was my mother's admiration for Nick. She would often mention his service in the community and children's work in the church.

Mother and I were standing at the kitchen sink finishing up the dinner dishes when she again mentioned Nick's church work with youth. I finally found my tongue and responded in anger, "I don't know about his church work, but I do know he couldn't keep his hands off of me." At that point, I left my startled mother standing at the sink, staring in disbelief.

Nothing more was said until several days later when she told me Nick's wife, Cousin Janie, upon being told had said, "I don't know why he does things like that," a clear testimony I was not the first or only victim of whom she was aware.

My father's response to mother's news was he would kill Nick if he knew it was true. "Knew it was true?" "Knew it was true?!!!" I was shocked and hurt by my Father's words. Finally, I had the courage to speak up, and he didn't know if it was true?

JUNIOR COLLEGE YEARS 1964-1966

My first two years of college were spent at a small denominational school in central Alabama. On the fashion scene, things were changing. This was the age of "Twiggy," a tall thin model with straight blond hair, and I was suddenly "in."

My first semester in college, I met a young engineering student who totally captured my heart. He played guitar, we sang folksong duets, strolled around campus hand in hand, went to church, the movies and did our homework together. He was hilarious and kept me in stitches. We dated for several months before he abruptly left school to join the military. I never heard from him again. I was heartbroken. However, I soon learned that a broken heart can be a great asset, for now, I was free to date without danger of becoming emotionally involved.

There was Sam the comedian, Howard the gentleman, Jeff from the military academy, Bill just out of the military, Lee the ROTC guy who was just a little too outspoken about the Vietnam War which cost him his rank but may have saved his life as he was later deemed unfit to lead a platoon in Vietnam and sent to Germany.

There was Doug, the cowboy, who invited me to spend Thanksgiving with his family on a ranch atop Look Out Mountain near the Georgia, Alabama state line. It was beautiful there, snowy riding trails, a home in the woods; the closest I ever came to my dream of a remote cabin in the woods raising horses. Doug asked me to marry him, but, of course, if he was interested in me, my interest would begin to wane.

There was also Woody, the future Pentecostal minister who played the guitar and drove a convertible. We had a lot of fun hanging out, playing rock 'n' roll and folk music, singing and being good, a rarity in the sixties.

The one dark shadow on my first two years of college was a terribly sweet, terribly troubled friend named Jane. Away from home for the first time, she fell madly in love with the first guy she dated. Much too sophisticated for Jane, all John wanted was a one-night stand.

Naive Jane thought John loved her and was stunned by his sudden disinterest. I walked with her through the aftershock and recovery from two suicide attempts, after which she decided she could never trust another man and promptly fell in love with me. I thought I had died and gone to hell. I could not deal with a girl looking longingly at me.

Later Jane would follow me to Auburn where I tried in vain to persuade her to seek counseling, fearing she might again attempt suicide. She would hear nothing of the sort insisting that she was no longer suicidal.

Since we were from the same area, one weekend she offered to give me a ride home. About a mile north of Auburn, she stopped at a liquor store and bought a six pack which she quickly finished off as she drove erratically through the countryside. I began to genuinely fear for my life as she careened around one corner after another.

Jane, on the other hand, appeared to be enjoying herself immensely, glancing in my direction to see if I was sufficiently impressed by her screeching wheels. At first, I managed to keep calm and told her if she wanted to kill herself, she could, but I needed to get home and finish a research paper that was due the following Monday. The only thing that kept me from exiting the car at the first stop sign was the stack of library books on the back seat I knew I'd never see again.

As her erratic driving continued, along with her alcohol consumption, I did try to exit the car at a stop sign, after which she simply blew straight through, no longer stopping. It grew dark as she took unfamiliar roads generally heading north but definitely not the route home.

I began to panic, asking where she was taking us and insisting she stop the car and let me call my parents who would be worried as we were long overdue. This seemed to energize her even more. Ignoring my pleas, she kept asking if I hated her yet; saying I needed to see she couldn't be helped and I needed to HATE her! I felt no hatred for her, just resentment that after my supporting her through all that had transpired, she would amuse herself by tormenting me in this way. I believe it was her own self-loathing that inspired her desire to have me hate her as well.

Hours later she turned off a county road onto a series of dirt roads, into a driveway and up to a house where she exited the car without a word. Taking the car keys with her, she knocked on the door.

A man in his thirties came to the door followed by his wife. Jane's cousins were surprised by the late-night visit but seeing Jane's state of inebriation said nothing. When Jane fell asleep where she was sitting, I explained what had happened and called my parents who eventually found the location. After having feared for my life, I teared up when I saw my mother who said under her breath, "Don't cry, they'll think you're drunk like Jane."

We drove home in silence.

A few weeks later, Jane again attempted suicide and was forced to leave Auburn. After that, I only heard from her once—she had found healing through traveling with the Jesus People ministry which provided the close support and guidance she needed during recovery. Marriage to a fellow traveler followed and the last I heard, she was happily raising a family in north Alabama.

AUBURN UNIVERSITY JANUARY 1967-MARCH 1968

If an Alabama farm kid dreamed of attending a university in the sixties, it was Auburn. That dream came true for me in January of 1967, but not knowing anyone and not having the money or the motivation to join a sorority, I was one lonely kid.

Although I had a few dates, Auburn men were very different from the guys I had known at the small denominational college I had attended. They had one thing, and one thing only on their minds, and I wasn't interested. I finally gave up the dating scene entirely. It was just as well, as it soon became apparent Auburn was a step up academically, and I needed to concentrate on my studies.

Toward the end of my first quarter at Auburn, I noticed a sign on the dorm bulletin board announcing Wednesday night dorm devotionals being held in the commons area. Although I had attended church since infancy, it was there at that meeting I first heard and understood the message of salvation through faith in Christ. The presenter was Rusty Armstrong, former CRU staff member, whose husband Joe was head of the Equine Science Department on campus. While Joe taught at the university, Rusty spent her days getting to know students on campus and sharing the good news of salvation in Jesus. One of her venues was weekly dorm devotionals.

That Wednesday night, Rusty told us about King Solomon from the book of Ecclesiastes. He was the wisest, wealthiest man who had ever lived, and yet, he concluded apart from God, everything was "meaningless, a chasing after the wind" (Ecclesiastes 1:14; 2:11, 17, 26; 4:4, 15; 6:9).

At that point in my life, I had four loves: literature, music, the great outdoors and horses. Solomon had pursued those four areas of interest to an extent I could only imagine. He had built libraries and stables housing thousands of horses in strategic cities across Israel. He had choirs and musicians. He had beautiful gardens and parks constructed in the city of Jerusalem. He had pursued all I desired to a degree I could never possibly achieve, yet he concluded without a relationship with God, all is meaningless!

"So," I thought, "I want to find out where he did find meaning, and how?"

At the end of the meeting, Rusty passed out three by five cards and asked all the girls attending to write down their names and phone numbers if interested in further discussion. So many girls responded it took Rusty weeks to get to me.

When she called, I was delighted and made an appointment to meet with her right away even though it was final's week. After explaining all of mankind through thought or deed had fallen short of God's perfect standard, Rusty explained according to that standard, everyone deserved to be banned from God's presence forever. She then showed me from Scripture that Jesus through His substitutionary death had paid the price required by the law of God for my sin. All I had to do was receive His proffered free gift of salvation, and eternal life with Christ would be mine. That, however, was just the beginning. From then on, Christ Himself through the person of the Holy Spirit would be with me, guiding me, comforting me, directing me. That which I had sought from childhood was being offered to me. I would no longer be alone.

Toward the end of our conversation, Rusty asked if there was any reason why I wouldn't want to receive Christ as my Savior right then and there. I was ready to commit my life to Jesus, no holds barred.

How often had I sat in church and wondered at the minister's words as he proclaimed, "God gave His only begotten Son to die for our sins!" only to question, "How different is that from fathers who have to give up their sons every day to go off to war and die?"

I just hadn't understood. This was Jesus voluntarily leaving the splendor of heaven, coming to earth to be rejected by His own people and die a criminal's death to pay for my sins so I could not only have peace with God but could become a daughter of God, a member of the family of God. Once I understood, I gladly gave my life to Christ.

There wasn't a great change immediately other than a sense of calm I hadn't known before. However, a few days later I realized something was missing. It was the burden of guilt I had carried since I was a child; the feeling I was irreparably damaged by the abuse of my childhood. That guilt was gone and I was amazed. I kept thinking it would return, but it never did.

I remember memorizing John 14:27 and quoting it to myself as I walked across campus: "Peace, I leave with you; my peace I give you. I do not give to you as the world gives. Do not let your hearts be troubled and do not be afraid."

Unschooled as I was in theology, I knew that the peace that the world gives was dependent on everything going my way. Christ was saying He would give me peace even when things went badly.

Soon afterward, a Bible study was organized, and I began to learn about my new life in Christ, read the Scripture and learn to pray. As more girls came to Christ, there was a need for someone to take over the girls' ministry. Since I had been a Christian longer than anyone else, the job fell to me. Soon I was helping organize Bible studies, evangelistic outreach and fellowship meetings as well as meeting with the new campus director for planning.

The summer of 1967, I flew to CRU Headquarters in San Bernardino, California where I joined other students from across the U.S. for a summer of Bible study and lectures from various theologians. Hal Lindsey taught the book of Revelation during the Six Day War between Egypt, Jordan, Syria and Israel. We felt we were experiencing prophesy first hand as he gave reports received directly from Israeli contacts inside the country.

I returned to Auburn at the end of the summer, full of enthusiasm and seriously considering returning to CRU Headquarters for staff training after graduation the next summer.

That fall our group continued to grow, and soon we were having Sunday night meetings in fraternity and sorority houses. I, along with other students, gave my testimony to packed audiences and shared the gospel one on one with student contacts. Many came to Christ.

It was during this time that several students from Columbus, Georgia joined our group. Periodically on weekends, we would drive over to Columbus for conferences or fellowship meetings. It was there I met Tom and Carolyn Eynon and their young son, Brent. Tom was a major in the Army between tours in Vietnam. He and Carolyn had both been Young Life leaders and knew how to entertain as well as disciple students. We looked forward to our weekends with them.

On a weekend in February 1968, we attended a Christian Discipleship Conference in Columbus, Georgia where I sat in on a workshop on Time Management taught by a young man who led a military ministry in Florida. It was interesting and informative, and the workshop leader was obviously someone who was very committed to the Lord, but then, so were most of the attendees whom I met at that conference. However, Louis and I would meet again.

To graduate on time, I had to cut back on my ministry responsibilities and double up on coursework. Although that meant less involvement with the group, when I graduated in March, it was with the intent of returning to California the following summer for staff training. My life was coming together, and I was excited about the future.

REFLECTION

When a child or young person feels rejected and without support, the result is often depression or desperation which can lead to angry outbursts, frequently against individuals deemed "safe." I would never have lashed out at my parents, but Sister loved me, and I knew intuitively would tolerate my sullenness and anger.

She was the picture, not only of beauty but of sweetness of spirit and generosity. Papa need not have feared for we became the best of friends. As adults, we traveled widely together and remained devoted to each other until her untimely death from a rare form of cancer in her mid-sixties.

How grateful I am to God for putting her in my life. She was my stay.

Although I was stung by my father's response, in retrospect I believe Papa overcome with anger, was expressing his care and concern for me. He clearly couldn't kill Nick and he may have had doubts I was telling the truth as I had become a liar in my pursuit of trying to say things I thought would get people's attention. He may have simply seen it as grandstanding.

Nick never spoke to me or touched me again but strangely, expected to be greeted with a hug anytime I returned home, even as an adult. It would be years before I had the courage to stop the charade of greeting him as "a dear relative:" a positive step in the direction of no longer keeping silent and pretending nothing had happened.

For a sexual predator, keeping up the masquerade they have done nothing wrong is crucial. Nick could relate to family members whom he had just abused as though nothing was amiss. He was in such denial that in his mind, there wasn't. Furthermore, he was extremely offended, even self-righteous when called out, as in the case of the neighborhood girl. That Nick's response to her accusation was to come to me, one of his victims, seeking support, illustrates the depth of his narcissism.

My mother's embarrassment that I teared up when she and my father finally arrived to take me home after the harrowing ride with Jane, cut to the quick. However, as much as I resented her fear of what people might think, it was a flaw I learned well as it kept me from asking for help when Jane began floundering emotionally. Although I realized I needed to speak with someone in authority about Jane's emotional instability and abuse of alcohol, I did not. Out of embarrassment I had not asked for help, but had remained silent, afraid "to tell." This was another dysfunction carried over from my childhood. Sadly, the result was Jane attempted suicide again, an attempt which could have been deadly. Silence is not always "golden."

Having suffered myself, I was often drawn to help those like Jane who suffered. Upon several occasions, that desire landed me in the middle of a sticky situation. It would be years before I learned recognizing a need does not mean that I am to meet that need. Eventually I learned to pray specifically for guidance before getting involved in "helping" someone, and not move forward until I knew God was clearly directing me.

My rescue attempts at helping Jane were undoubtedly a reflection of years spent trying to protect my father who also struggled with suicidal ideations. However by the time I reached college, I had moved on from focusing on my father and seeking his attention. It hadn't worked. I gave up. Having reached a stage where I finally caught the attention of the opposite sex, I began dating two or three fellows at a time. This, I believe was simply transference of my pursuit of my father to other men.

It was always the aloof young men, especially those on a mission, kind but not really interested that attracted me, even from the time I was in elementary school. After having sought my father's affection without success, I wasn't really comfortable unless I had the challenge of pursuing someone who was just out of reach.

Somewhere deep in my psyche lay the conviction I was worthless, therefore anyone interested in me could not be worth consideration. I had been hurt by Nick and neglected by my father. The pursuit was familiar. I had pursued my father my whole life. But as soon as a young man was interested in getting to know me, I became distant and continued my pursuit of the disinterested ones. This pattern would follow me into my twenties.

However, I didn't become rebellious or immoral. I had learned too much from the captain of the football team whose only interest was bragging rights in the locker room, to go in that direction. No, I merely wanted to have a good time, enjoy life while I waited for my flame, the engineer who had joined the military.

It is interesting to me today to look back and see how my relationships with four men who hurt me deeply also were largely used to shape me into the person I am today. First and foremost, my father, whose approval I desperately sought turned me into a hardworking overachiever by the example that he set. Nick's abuse left me determined to see those wounds redeemed into a life of helping others. The captain of the football team who wanted to use me for bragging rights, did me a favor by scorning my dream of attending college, spurring me on to prove him wrong. Lastly, there was the engineering student who pursued me, talking of marriage, only to suddenly disappear from my life never to return. That experience left me with a determination not to seek a serious relationship until my husband to be knew I was the one and initiated the relationship without any encouragement from me. And so it would be.

Although it was decades ago that I chose to accept Christ's free gift of salvation through His substitutionary death for my sins, I clearly remember several days later realizing the burden of guilt for the wrong things I had done was gone. It felt like a load had been lifted from my shoulders. It was a burden I hadn't even realized was there until it was gone.

Yes, the guilt was gone, but not the low self-esteem or the dysfunctional coping mechanisms I had learned over the years, however, I didn't know that then. I didn't even know I had them. Those coping mechanisms based on lies that I was damaged goods would continue to varying degrees for decades to come, but at least I no longer felt the abuse was somehow my fault. That was gone (see Chapters 12 and 13).

RESPONSE

MIDDLE SCHOOL 1956-1959

1. Was there anyone in your life who played an important role during your middle school years other than your parents? Explain.

2. Was there anyone who played a negative role? In what way?

3. Was there an "ugly duckling" in your family? A caretaker? A scapegoat? How did they cope?

4. Li'l Sis's and Sister's horizons were expanded through the purchase of Sister's car, stylish clothes, and publications like Life Magazine, movies and books.

   ▸ Do you remember a time when you became aware of how the rest of the world lived? Was the effect positive or negative? In what way?

5. Give possible reasons why Li'l Sis was sullen and negative by the time she reached middle school. Was middle school also a difficult time for you?

6. Can you identify negative coping mechanisms that could have developed out of these years?

7. Li'l Sis first became aware of missionaries living and dying for the Lord when she read the story of the massacre of Jim Elliott and his four companions. The story of their massacre by the Huaorani tribe in eastern Ecuador recorded in Life Magazine affected her deeply.

   ▸ How did you first learn of the life of sacrifice to which some missionaries are called? Did it impact your life?

A NEW SCHOOL 1954-1960

8 Was there a teacher or coach who went out of their way to help you succeed? Explain.

9 Was your social life in high school affected by abuse and neglect from your childhood? If so, how?

10 When did you begin to seek God? Did you have a "storm in the oak trees" experience where you cried out to God to reveal Himself?

11 What were the factors that led you to Christ as your Savior and Lord?

LAST CONTACT WITH NICK 1963

12 Did you talk with your parents about events of abuse or neglect in your life? How did you feel going into the conversation? How did you feel afterwards? What was their response?

JUNIOR COLLEGE YEARS 1964-1966

13 How would you describe your social life in your college age years?

14 Were you at all interested in God?

15 Did the abuse and or neglect from your childhood manifest in your relationships?

16 What challenges did you face related to your friendship relationships? Did you seem to attract dysfunctional friends like Jane?

17 Was there "one who got away" who affected your dating relationships?

AUBURN UNIVERSITY JANUARY 1967-MARCH 1968

18 Did your parents or someone else influence your educational goals?

19 Was there a time in your childhood when you felt "rejected and without support?"

If so how did you respond? How else might a child respond if their temperament were different from yours?

20 Did you have a sibling against whom you were measured?
"For a sexual predator, keeping up the masquerade they
have done nothing wrong is crucial. Nick could relate to
21 family members whom he had just abused as though nothing was amiss."

▸ Can you explain Nick's behavior toward Li'l Sis after abusing her? Can you understand her devastation?

22 The author writes: "My mother's embarrassment that I teared up when she and my father finally arrived to take me home after the harrowing ride with Joan, cut to the quick. However, as much as I resented her fear of what people might think, it was a flaw I learned well as it kept me from asking for help when Jane began floundering emotionally and when I floundered emotionally as an adult on the mission field."

▸ In what way do you think Li'l Sis's relationship with Jane was influenced by her relationship with her parents and Nick?

23 Were you, like Li'l Sis a "rescuer" in your family? Did that carry over into your adult relationships?

24 Was there someone in your family whose affection you pursued, and later transferred to your dating relationships as Li'l Sis did her dad?

25 The author writes regarding her conversion to faith in Christ: "Yes, the guilt (related to the abuse) was gone, but not the low self-esteem or the dysfunctional coping mechanisms I had developed in an attempt to feel safe in a world gone awry."

▸ What dysfunctional coping mechanisms can you identify in the life of the author up to this point? Can you identify with any of these?

CHAPTER 9
CAREER, LOVE AND MARRIAGE

LIFE AFTER GRADUATION

After graduation in March of '68, I returned to the farm in north Alabama where I joined the children's leadership team in our small country church. Although I enjoyed the children, going from campus life back to rural life required a monumental adjustment. That summer I did the music program at the church's Vacation Bible School, cut grass, cleaned out barn stalls and worked in the garden.

It was also during this time, I received a call from the CRU director at Auburn offering a scholarship for staff training in California. It made me heartsick to decline, but I no longer felt I was ready for that step. Not knowing what I should do, I began applying for teaching jobs in local schools.

When nothing turned up by mid-summer, I was really discouraged. Also, I missed my friends and the camaraderie of campus ministry.

About that time, a call came from Tom and Carolyn Eynon, friends with the military ministry in Columbus, Georgia, asking if I would consider coming to Columbus, living with them and looking for a teaching job there. I was thrilled and began packing. My parents were also happy for me, as try though I might to reacclimate to farm life, they knew I missed my friends and needed a job which I found within days of arriving in Columbus.

After a month of substitute teaching high schoolers, some of whom were six inches taller than I and outweighed me by a hundred pounds, I was offered and gratefully accepted a job teaching middle school language arts.

It was no easy task. Even in middle school, I didn't look a lot older than my students. This was further complicated by the veteran teachers who had earned the right to choose whom they would teach. Thus all the rowdy students were bequeathed to me. I finally came up with a plan that worked. I would teach grammar two days a week, then have the students take notes as we read Tom Sawyer followed by watching excerpts from the Hollywood version of the book on alternate days. Thus, I survived the first semester without bleeding, letting blood or getting fired.

I learned a lot about classroom management and thanked heaven things were going as well as they were when one afternoon a new recruit in the science department turned in her grade book and said she would not be coming back. At least I was still there.

Tom and Carolyn, with whom I lived, were like family. We worked together, studied the Scriptures, went to Bible Study and worshiped at base chapel together each Sunday. We also played together, shooting skeet, playing board games and listening to Tom's hilarious stories of his growing up years in a house full of boys in Pennsylvania. Carolyn was a local girl, and I was included in her family gatherings as well.

Several girls from the CRU ministry at Auburn continued to come over for visits and before long I had a roommate at the Eynon's home when my friend, Becky, was offered a mid-year position at Columbus High teaching Spanish. As Becky would later learn from her students, her predecessor, a gentleman also in his first year of teaching, had resigned after his students bodily picked him up and threatened to drop him from an upstairs window. Fortunately, he was saved when a school administrator passing by in the hall, heard the commotion and came to investigate. Becky too, had her challenges in her first year of teaching.

The camaraderie, friendship and support I enjoyed during those stressful, yet halcyon days that marked my passage into adulthood, are treasured memories to this day.

Happy though those days were, from time to time, I would experience periods of depression and insecurity. At one point, I asked a mentor if she would advise my seeing a counselor given the abuse I had experienced as a child. She quoted 2 Corinthians 5:17 (NKJV) saying, "Therefore, if anyone is in Christ, he is a new creation; old things have passed away; behold, all things have become new." She concluded, "If you want, you can pay a counselor to listen to your story, or you can tell God and be done with it." I accepted her advice but wouldn't know how wrong we both were until years later.[8]

ENTER LOUIS PLATT 1969

In January 1969, I attended a New Year's discipleship conference with several of my girlfriends from the Auburn University ministry. We were driven to Montgomery by a missionary couple who recently returned from Germany. The Sherwoods were looking forward to seeing a young man, Louis Platt, who had been a part of their ministry in Germany during his Army deployment there.

Louis was driving to Montgomery from Florida where he was leading a ministry to young airmen at Eglin Air Force Base. The Sherwoods talked about his commitment to Christ and work among servicemen.

They continued that he spoke fluent German and planned to return to Germany to work with university students. My friends and I listened and nodded politely and wondered when the conversation would turn to something more interesting than their protégé.

At the opening meeting of the conference, Ron York, the minister in charge, asked my roommate Becky and I if we would sing a duet as their special music hadn't arrived and they needed a quick stand-in. We chose a hymn and sang "Trust and Obey," one we both knew from the Methodist hymnal growing up.

The conference went as most do, reconnecting with friends from past retreats, inspirational speakers, informative workshops on various topics, and then it was time to leave.

After fetching our coats and getting halfway to the car, I realized I had left my umbrella and returned to the cloakroom to retrieve it. Several young men helped me locate it, and I was soon back in the car on the way to Columbus. Again, the Sherwood's topic of conversation was Louis Platt; how wonderful it was to see him again and hear of his ministry at the Air Force base in Florida. We still hadn't a clue as to who they were talking about as none of us had met him, although I would later discover he had helped me locate my umbrella. After a while, conversation drifted to other topics and the elusive Louis Platt was soon forgotten.

Life continued as usual at the Eynon's with Tom off to work at the base each morning, Carolyn looking after Brent and involved in various community and ministry activities, and Becky and I teaching school. Weekends we had family picnics at a nearby lake, Sunday lunch at the officer's club after chapel, an occasional movie with one of Carolyn's brothers or an afternoon at the community pool.

Each week I attended Bible Study with other singles connected to the Ft. Benning military ministry. How refreshing it was to be around young men with no agenda other than to learn about the Lord and enjoy the camaraderie.

Life was good and predictable until one afternoon I received a call from the local mission's director. He asked if I could drop by his office for a chat. When I arrived, he went straight to the point. There was a young man at the conference in Montgomery who would like to meet me. He continued that he was leading a military ministry on a base in Florida, and had been involved in ministry for a number of years while stationed in Germany.

Finally finding my voice, I responded, "Can you tell me his name?" It was the elusive Louis Platt.

"What is he like?" I queried.

"After a pause," Ron replied. "Do you know the story of when Jesus met Nathaniel?"

"Yes."

"Louis is like Nathaniel, a man without guile."

Although I knew the story, I wasn't sure of the meaning of the word "guile." However, I would waste no time in finding out as I immediately located a dictionary upon returning home. There I read, "Without deceit or evil intent." *Yes, I wanted to meet this man.*

A DIFFERENT KIND OF RELATIONSHIP

Soon a letter came from Louis. After writing back and forth for several weeks, sharing how we came to know Christ and what we were learning from our devotionals and Bible study, we talked on the phone and made plans to meet. Louis would drive up from Florida.

The Eynons, wanting to help us break the ice, invited Louis to join us for an afternoon picnic and skeet shoot before the two of us went out for dinner. Although I had grown up with shotguns and had one of my own since my 12th birthday, I could not hit anything. Louis did little better and was so nervous, he kept calling me, "Linda."

Dinner at a local restaurant was more enjoyable although it had its humorous if embarrassing moments as well. Arriving late, we had to take a table next to the band, a rather loud band which made it necessary for us to raise our voices to be heard. More than once, we kept right on talking above the music which was no longer playing. This garnered a few strange looks from neighboring tables but we pressed on aware our time was short and we had lots of ground to cover.

Louis talked at length of his military tour in Germany where, unlike most U.S. military personnel, he had lived and worked among German nationals. He had also become involved with the German collegiate ministry and wanted to return to work with university students.

Although I would later learn he was eager to return but did not want to return alone, which was why he began teaching me German phrases on our second date. He was a man on a mission, and it appeared to me early on he saw me as a part of that mission.

I was impressed and wondered if this could be the answer to my prayer of despair during my junior year when utterly disgusted with the dating scene, I had told God I was tired of fighting for my virtue and didn't want to be bothered with men until I met "the one."

However, there were things to consider. Louis was the son of a successful investment banker. His mother was the daughter of an old aristocratic Savannah family. Louis had been educated in private boarding schools in the Northeast where he had also attended college. My background was entirely different.

Because of the distance and our jobs, we only saw each other a half dozen times over the next nine months although we continued to write and talk on the phone periodically. Again, I met a man with a mission who cared for me, but this time I did not lose interest.

In time I would learn, after his junior year, he spent the summer traveling in Europe where on a rainy day in Geneva, he found a copy of C.S. Lewis's *That Hideous Strength* in a hotel wastepaper basket and read it through after which he began to wonder if there was something to this God thing after all. Although a professed agnostic during college, he had long been a seeker after truth.

He was well spoken and well educated. He could identify composers after hearing the first few bars of a symphony and various schools of art at a glance. His mother was a member of several St. Louis social clubs and dressed to the nines. She had a cleaning lady and a butler when she had large family gatherings.

His mother's family had entertained the president of the United States between the world wars and the home where she grew up was now a museum. Louis' great aunt was Juliette Low, founder of the Girl Scouts, whose English husband had been an intimate of the Prince of Wales.

I had only been out of the South once on a senior class trip and never outside of the U.S. Until the age of twelve, I lived in a house without plumbing, knew little of culture and the arts and was concerned that these differences just might prove to be insurmountable. The only thing we had in common was our mutual affection and faith in Christ. I was alternately elated I had found my prince charming and concerned that "too good to be true" often is. Louis, on the other hand, saw no obstacles.

He shared with me that when Becky and I had sung "Trust and Obey" at the January conference, a friend observing his interest in me asked if God was sending him any signals. He responded, "Only trust and obey" and that was what we needed to do now, trust and obey wherever God led.

I spent the summer of 1969 in Austin, Texas and Mexico on a short-term mission with 40 university students and young professionals from across the country. We all found summer jobs in the city and lived together in a rented fraternity house on the University of Texas campus. On weekends we had informational meetings on the Christian faith to which we invited students whom we had met during the week.

I found a job at the county hospital as a nurse's aide. My patients came from a world of poverty, drugs and crime that was entirely foreign to me. Most were terminal; either dying from cancer, drug overdose, gunshot wounds or having been brought in from local nursing homes to die. I prayed my way through each day. At the end of the summer, I felt I should have been awarded a second degree, this one in "The Realities of Life and Death in the Inner City."

We also spent two weeks visiting Wycliffe Bible translators working with indigenous tribes in remote areas of central Mexico. I was amazed at the commitment that led these missionaries to live in more primitive conditions in the 70s than I had lived in during the 50s on the farm in Alabama.

In early summer of 1969, Louis transferred to Norfolk, Virginia where he began a ministry to military personnel at the Naval Air Base. Being a history major, he also found a position for the fall term teaching middle school history. We continued to write and talk on the phone throughout the summer. When I returned to Columbus in late August, one of the families involved in the ministry with which Louis was affiliated, invited me for a long weekend.

Louis picked me up from the airport. After going out for dinner (no band this time), we went for a walk on the beach where he proposed, and I accepted. Thus, began the adventure of my life.

MARRIAGE AND THE MOVE TO TEXAS 1970

We were married in the summer of 1970 and moved to Texas for staff training. Our ministry assignment was the University of Texas at Arlington where we also enrolled as students; I to get my Texas teaching credentials in English and history and Louis to earn a master's in German Language and Literature with a view to returning to Germany.

Among the young couples in the weekly Bible Study we attended were Frank and Mary Alice Minirth. Some years later, Frank along with Paul Meier would co-found the Minirth Meier Clinics based in Dallas. A decade later, he would also play a significant role in our lives. Louis and I were young, in love and full of hope God would soon open a door for us in the German university ministry. There was only one problem. We still had very little in common other than our mutual affection and a commitment to serve the Lord. Also, we really didn't know each other. Although we had known each other for over a year, because of distance, we had only seen each other about a dozen times before the wedding.

Not only did we not know each other very well, I brought the "fall out" of sexual abuse to the marriage and Louis brought that of being an adult child of an alcoholic father. To survive, he became adept at dissociating himself from any suffering or problems going on around him. To him, they just didn't exist.

A couple of weeks into our marriage, Louis decided to change the points and plugs on the car. He had about an hour before we were scheduled to be at a meeting of the local staff trainees, so he thought he had time. The only problem was, he had never done this before; worse still, he didn't have the right tools. Removing the old parts wasn't so difficult but getting the new ones in place proved to be quite the challenge. Soon Louis was uttering expletives as parts slipped from his fingers and got lodged around the motor. My father had been a jack-of-all-trades and taught me well, so between us, we managed to get the car back together.

Although the car was finally running again, Louis had decreased significantly in my estimation. I never heard my father use profanity, nor had I known a man who couldn't handle tools. Worse still, I didn't know what to think of a prospective missionary who swore!

Not knowing how to express my concern, I became critical and judgmental. If Louis noticed it at all, he just ignored it as neither of us knew how to communicate or express our feelings constructively. As the tension grew, the only thing that kept us together was a determination not to separate. As confused as we were by our inability to communicate and get along, we were determined not to bring disgrace to the name of Christ by giving up and walking away, or to let anyone know how frustrated we were. All the other young couples in our group seemed perfectly compatible, and we were not about to admit that we weren't.

Thankfully things began to change when we found a good mechanic, and later enrolled at the University of Texas at Arlington. Each day after class we met in the student cafeteria for lunch and discussed the content of our courses for that day. As I shared the history lecture I had just attended, Louis drew maps of Hitler's advance across Europe, explaining the significant battles of that horrible war. He also knew details about the lives of players that weren't covered in the text. He told me the story of Corrie ten Boom, the Righteous Gentile, who like many other Christian families during the war, hid Jews in their homes in the Netherlands. Betrayed by neighbors, Corrie and her sister spent years in a Nazi concentration camp where her sister and father died. There was also the story of Dietrich Bonhoeffer and other Christians who were active in the German resistance and the Confessing Church which refused to bow to Nazi demands.

Louis had met Corrie ten Boom while stationed in Germany and was impressed by her commitment to reach Germans for Christ. The same Germans who had condemned her family to years of imprisonment. After the war, Corrie spoke at meetings throughout Germany and shared the hope of forgiveness of sins through Jesus' substitutionary death. While giving the invitation to receive Christ, Corrie was startled to see a former prison guard coming forward. He did not recognize Corrie but she knew him immediately as the guard who had beaten her sister unmercifully shortly before she died. Corrie later recounted it was the hardest thing she had ever been called on to do. But she knew God died for that man too.

Deeply impressed by her commitment, Louis hoped to be used of God himself in this land that had birthed not only Nazism but also Luther and the Protestant Reformation.

As we continued to review history, I discovered that Louis had also traveled throughout Europe and knew many of the areas of conflict first hand. I began to see my young husband through new eyes and came to respect him as the learned teacher and dedicated disciple of Christ that he was.

Finally, we had a common interest outside of the ministry, and we began to grow together as a couple, discussing those historical events. Ours was probably the only marriage saved by the grace of God and the history of World War II.

REFLECTION

Though well intended, my mentor suggested I had no need of counseling. Neither she nor I knew that buried hurts are buried alive and sooner or later will rise from the dead to cause more havoc. It takes a great deal of emotional energy to keep negative memories suppressed. The more energy required to deal with day-to-day stress such as caring for small children, adjusting to a new culture, or learning a foreign language, the more likely buried hurts are to rise to the conscious level as flashbacks making the individual feel as though they are back in time experiencing abuse all over again.

Christian missionaries, pastors and lay workers are doubly at risk. Already in Satan's crosshairs as he and his cohorts work to sabotage the work of the kingdom, the added stress of cultural adjustment and language study as well as the pressure of being accountable to supporters to produce spiritual fruit, can push the vulnerable over the edge.

Plagued by Pollyanna thinking, I concluded, if I was practicing the spiritual disciplines: having daily devotions, praying, doing Bible Study and sharing Christ with others, things would be "just fine." And they were for a while, a short while.

Looking back, I don't think I would have been successful at CRU staff training as I was too new to the faith and lacked the necessary spiritual disciplines and maturity. I also believe I was too insecure and emotionally unstable to take that step. "A man's heart plans his way, but God directs his steps" (Proverbs 16:9, NKJV). There have been times when the truth of that verse was a frustration, but mostly it has been a comfort when something I planned fell through. I always knew it was either not meant to be or God would use the disappointment for a higher purpose.

And then along came Louis Platt. I find it interesting the God of the universe meets us where we are and works through our foibles and insecurities to lead us along the path He has for us. This was clearly illustrated to me in how I met Louis and how that meeting perfectly answered my prayer that God would bring "the one" into my life without any initiation on my part. Only then would I know that the relationship was indeed from God.

Ever in pursuit of my father, drawn to men pursuing a cause, He led me to a godly young man with whom I would serve the Lord for the next 40 years. We were very different but became very similar. In areas of strength, we complemented each other well. Louis was goal oriented and could inadvertently offend in the pursuit of that goal. He was an intellectual, a master teacher with a doctorate and two master's degrees. Although college educated, my strength in the marriage was an intuitive ability to pick up on where people were emotionally and spiritually.

Louis was the epitome of the absent-minded professor. When the movie "Back to the Future" came out, scores of our friends commented on how similar Louis was to the character of the professor. He even looked like a younger version of Christopher Lloyd. Our saving grace was I had enough common sense for both of us. We made a good team.

I shudder to think how many individuals and couples suffer in silence even as we did because they fear admitting and seeking help for their woundedness. Again, "Don't tell. What will people think?" raised its ugly head. Sadly, it would be years before we sought the help we needed.

Thankfully today most missions and denominations have counseling services that were sadly missing in the 70s, 80s and 90s. In those days, if you were struggling on counseling resources available through member care for couples facing difficulties that are common to so many.

International speaker and Christian author of over 35 books, Mary Demuth, who as a five-year-old was gang-raped daily for a period of a year, is a help to many struggling with sexual intimacy in marriage. Her video http://www.marydemuth.com/i-was-raped-now-i-hate-sex-now-what provides insight in this area.

Paula Rinehart's book "Sex and the Soul of a Woman" is another excellent resource for support and guidance in this area.

RESPONSE

LIFE AFTER GRADUATION

1 Describe your first job after graduation? How was your situation similar or different to that of the author?

2 Do you see indications of dysfunctional coping mechanisms from childhood carried over into adulthood in the author's way of coping with the stress of the job?

3 The author indicates her mentor misapplied 2 Corinthians 5:17 to her situation regarding obtaining counseling for the effects of childhood sexual abuse, with the words, "If you want, you can pay a counselor to listen to your story, or you can tell God and be done with it."

▸ What are the dangers inherent in such an approach?

4 How would you explain the quote, "Buried hurts are buried alive only to resurface later"?

ENTER LOUIS PLATT 1969

5 The sovereignty of God being played out in our lives on a daily basis can be seen in how Glenda met Louis. God concerns Himself with all areas of our lives, is ever present and ever actively steering us in the direction of His will as we walk with Him (Proverbs 3:5-6).

▸ Can you perceive God's working in your life leading you to individuals whom you are to befriend, share the gospel with, encourage?

A DIFFERENT KIND OF RELATIONSHIP

6 Our first date as described in the text was a comedy of errors. Can you recall a similar situation in your life when an experience reminded you that God has a sense of humor?

7 Can you imagine such a courtship taking place today?

8 What kinds of conflict can you imagine arising as a result of the differences in their background? The abuse?

9 What kinds of challenges might arise from only having had a few dates before their engagement and marriage?

MARRIAGE AND THE MOVE TO TEXAS 1970

10 Can you think of a time when you measured a new leader against a past leader or your husband against your father or a former boyfriend? What is the inherent harm in such comparisons?

11 Consider when comparing two individuals, if you aren't comparing the weakness of one with the strength of another. How do the following verses relate to comparisons? Matthew 7:3-5; Romans 14:4; 2 Corinthians 10:12.

12 What strengths and weaknesses do you bring to relationships?

13 What negative coping mechanisms might one expect to bring to relationships from childhood abuse or neglect?

14 What dysfunctions might someone from an alcoholic family bring to a relationship?

15 What suggestions would you have for a couple with "nothing in common" except their "faith and mutual attraction?"

16 "The more energy required to deal with day-to-day stress, the more likely buried hurts are to rise to the conscious

level as flashbacks.

▸ Have you had the experience of seeing buried hurts rise to the surface?

17 What is wrong with this thought process?

▸ Plagued by Pollyanna thinking, I concluded, if I was practicing the spiritual disciplines: having daily devotions, praying, doing Bible Study and sharing Christ with others, things would be 'just fine.'"

18 According to the text, why might Christian missionaries, pastors and lay workers be doubly at risk?

19 The author's relationship with her father was one of pursuit. How did this show up in her dating relationships?

20 Describe your relationship with your parents. Do you share any of their strengths or dysfunctions?

▸ This question is not meant to reflect negatively on your parents, however parental relationships can be key in understanding our own dysfunctions. We are all wounded to one degree or another, but it is only when woundedness is recognized that it can be addressed.

21 The author writes, "I shudder to think how many individuals and couples suffer in silence even as we did because they fear admitting and seeking help for their woundedness."

▸ Can you identify with the author's struggles? Explain.

22 What resources are available to struggling singles, couples or families in the mission, church community where you serve?

CHAPTER 10
THE MOVE TO EUROPE

LIFE IN GERMANY 1974

After three and a half years of working in student ministry in Texas, we were invited to join the university ministry in Bonn, Germany. By then Louis had completed his M.A. in German, and I had completed two years of German language study. We finished raising support in November of '74, visited our families one last time, and in mid-December boarded a plane for Germany. Upon our arrival, we were met by a fellow staff member who welcomed us and gave a description of the student ministry and our responsibilities for the next weeks, namely get settled in our apartment and acclimated to our new surroundings.

As soon as we were somewhat settled, we went for a walk in the old town of Bonn. There is no more magical place than Germany during the holiday season. The town square is turned into a Christmas market with rustic wooden booths where spiced wine and Christmas cookies, as well as various toys and gifts are sold. The booths are hung with fresh garlands and gingerbread cookies of every shape and description. Colorfully decorated and wrapped in plastic, they sparkle among the garlands tempting every child who walks by. The crisp air is heavy with spice and the smell of hot sweet "Gluhwein."

Beautifully carved nativities and delicate glass and wooden Christmas ornaments are offered for sale in specialty booths. Everyone is out to see the sights. In the evening, strains of Bach's Christmas Oratory can be heard from the cathedral which dominates the city center.

Louis and I were invited to several Christmas parties, one of which was given by the students whom we would lead at the University of Bonn. They were a lively group of bright young people who often good-humoredly teased each other with wordplay or turn of phrase. Most of the students spoke English as they had studied it since grade school; however, I was committed to speaking only German. In the beginning, keeping up with their conversations was overwhelming, and in those first few months, I often went to bed with a throbbing headache. Despite the challenge, we were thrilled with the privilege of finally being on the mission field and the opportunity of making a contribution, small though it might be, toward bringing the gospel of Jesus Christ back to the land of Luther.

Although Louis was sufficiently proficient in the German language to give a short address at the New Year's Student Conference, setting up an apartment in a second language proved to be quiet the challenge. Neither of us had the vocabulary for purchasing curtain hooks, connectors for the washing machine or dozens of other household necessities, nor were those terms to be found in our German-English Dictionary. Registering our car alone took a dozen trips over the course of a week as Louis trekked to various offices spread all over town only to be told that he was, yet again at the wrong office, and needed to return to an already visited office for different documents which he would fill out in triplicate and then return.

Nevertheless, within a couple of weeks, curtains were hung, the kitchen installed, books on the shelves, plants in the windows, our car registered, and we were having students over for Bible study and other events.

Several of the girls expressed an interest in toile painting and soon my Thursday afternoons were occupied with teaching the girls decorative painting as I practiced my German.

Louis and I also enjoyed biking everywhere we went, especially along the Rhine or for a treat, an occasional afternoon coffee at the beautifully appointed Ritterhaus Café. But there were also stressors.

There was the pressure of language school. Four days a week I took the train south to Boppard for language study at the Goethe Institute. The train ran along the Rhine, past picture postcard villages unchanged through the centuries. Castles from the Middle Ages stood on the heights like sentinels keeping watch. However, beautiful though the setting was, three hours of train travel and four hours of German immersion class made for a tiring day.

The class was conducted entirely in German; an effective teaching method for rapid language acquisition, but it was also highly stressful. If I had a question, it had to be asked and answered in German. The only problem was after I managed to communicate my question, I rarely understood the answer. Also, the instructor, an older man spoke very little English and was hesitant to use the English he knew.

The simple act of going to the neighborhood grocery store was anything but simple. I had to ask for everything by name as it was all "behind the counter" out of reach. I meticulously made out my shopping list in German and hoped my pronunciation would be understandable. After a while, I became a known entity and the moment I began to speak, the housewives in line behind me, hearing my broken German would turn in sympathy to try to help me.

In addition, I was diligently trying to become a "German housewife," keeping the apartment up to German standards which meant spotless. I was also cooking with different ingredients, measurements and baking in centigrade. I quickly learned German baking powder was a tricky business and when misapplied could turn a coffee cake into a foul-tasting mess. There was also the pressure of leading a group of very bright German students in weekly Bible study with my limited language skills. Driven by perfectionistic tendencies, I cut myself no slack. Soon I was having to see a physical therapist to get some relief from my tight neck muscles, a clear reflection of my mental state.

Even though Louis was a student enrolled in theology classes at the university, there was also the pressure of being considered a "dangerous sect" by the general populace. The only recognized religious institutions in Germany were the Catholic and Lutheran churches.

Unfortunately, the latter had through the influence of liberal theology become more of a social institution than a religious one. In conversation with neighbors, we could devolve from an interesting young couple from the United States to members of a dangerous sect as soon as they learned we were not working under the auspices of the Lutheran or Catholic churches.

Shortly after our arrival, my mother was diagnosed with stage four cancer and would spend the next five years until her death in and out of treatment. Upon Mother's diagnosis, my father who suffered from bipolar disorder fell into a deep depression from which he was unable to extricate himself and was repeatedly hospitalized for electroshock therapy which sadly did not prove to be helpful.

Pulling himself together, at one point he decided to do some needed repairs on the roof. A misstep resulted in his losing his footing, falling to the ground, and breaking several vertebrae. Back surgeries followed, coupled with debilitating back pain which he would have for the rest of his life. My family was falling apart, and I was 5,000 miles away.

By this time, Louis and I had been married for ten years and for several years wanted to have children. Fertility treatment at best is stressful; treatment in a foreign country can be even more frustrating; however, it can also have its humorous side. One treatment consisted of sitting in a hot steaming bath of volcanic mud, the goal of which was to stimulate circulation which I was to monitor by checking my pulse every five minutes. After the prescribed 20 minutes of being submerged in the hot muddy water, my heart rate hadn't increased a bit. In irritation, I dumped the whole box of powder into the bath and turned the hot water back on. Twenty minutes later, my heart was pounding in my ears, and I was reaching for the cold water tap. Thus ended my venture into German fertility treatment, and eventually we moved on to the adoption process which brought its own set of stressors.

Meanwhile, each week around fifteen students from the University of Bonn came to our apartment for an investigative Bible study in the gospel of John. More than anything, we wanted those students to come to know Christ as their Savior and in turn, reach others for Christ. We prayed toward that end as did our support team back in the U.S.

The students began to invite their friends who asked other friends, and after months and months of Bible study and conversation, they began to come to faith in Christ. Some of these students would go on to become ministers in the state Catholic and Protestant churches, doctors, lawyers, teachers, professors and government officials, even one of eight German Supreme Court Judges.

I continue to have contact with many of our former students, individuals who are still actively involved in the ministry of reaching others for Christ.

This was something God chose to do despite our weakness and our struggles. That experience taught me never to think God cannot use me because I am struggling. If I am doing my best to walk with Him, He will use my life to help others in some way. We are never set aside unless we are being willfully disobedient.

TIME SORTS MOST THINGS OUT

In Matthew 6:25-33 Jesus tells us as long as we "seek first his kingdom" which, I believe, would be our ministry involvement and "his righteousness" which is our pursuit of spiritual maturity, He will take care of all our needs. However, at the end of this passage in verse 34, there is a caveat. He reminds us there will be trouble: "Each day has enough trouble of its own." Similarly, in John 16:33, Jesus reminds us, as long as we live in this world, we will experience difficulties: "In this world you will have trouble."

Tim Keller in his book, *Walking with God through Pain and Suffering*, points out the American goal of living a life of self-fulfillment and happiness as we pursue our dreams in no way prepares us to face life's inevitable suffering.[9] Similarly, according to international conference speaker and author Mary DeMuth, most Christians think living a disciplined Christian life will protect them from difficulty.

Very little if anything in our success-driven society prepares us for dealing with suffering. Mary insists this line of thinking is simply an American heresy. Believers outside of our privileged, first-world culture accept the truth of John 16:33, "In this world you will have trouble," and they strive to grow through those difficult experiences, even as we should. However, Western cultures emphasize escaping difficulties at all cost and learn little from the experience.[10] We tend to ignore the books of Job, Hebrews, 2 Timothy and 1 Peter among others, all of which deal with suffering and how we can benefit from it. Similarly in 2 Corinthians 1:8-9, "We do not want you to be uninformed.... We were under great pressure, far beyond our ability to endure, so that we despaired of life itself.... we felt we had received the sentence of death.... **But this happened that we might not rely on ourselves but on God, who raises the dead."**

Attractive though the "American Heresy" is, it doesn't line up with Scripture. How could it be otherwise when we have our own sin nature to contend with, as well as the sin nature of those around us? If that weren't enough, Satan and his army of demons whose goal is to kill, steal and destroy, has us in his crosshairs (John 10:10-29).

In addition, God, from time to time, in His wisdom chooses to test our faith. Faith untested remains weak. 1 Peter 4:12 tells us not to be surprised when these fiery trials come as though something strange is happening. In 1 Peter 1:7 we read that the testing of our faith is purifying, as gold is purified by fire. The message of Romans 5:1-5 is similar. When we trust God to guide us through times of testing, our faith is strengthened.

During difficulties, Jesus encourages us to be strong, believe in Him, and seek Him above all else. He also promises peace (John 14:27), spiritual productivity (Matthew 4:19), and His presence (Matthew 28:20b).

Difficult though life can be at times, most things do sort themselves out as we trust God, live a transparent life of commitment, practice the discipline and take comfort from the example of the suffering Christ. After six months of commuting three hours on the train for language study four days week, we found a language teacher, Irene Schroers, in Bonn just a short tram ride away who, although a strict taskmaster, was an excellent teacher.

Although she did not "believe in Jesus" as we did, she often helped Louis, of whom she was very fond, by proofreading his messages. One day when he arrived to have another message checked, she announced after proofreading his sermon on how Christ fulfilled prophesy (over 300 of them many written hundreds of years before His birth), she now "believed in Jesus." Knowing Frau Schroers as we did, we knew it was true, or she would never have claimed it.

In time, I grew accustomed to shopping several times a week, and with improved language skills, the local housewives no longer looked on in pain when I asked for items at the local grocers.

Sadly, my mother would not recover from cancer, but after two years of treatment, she did go into remission for a period of months during which she and my father visited us in Germany for two memorable weeks. Mother went to the open-air market with me and marveled at my ability to communicate and barter. She also marveled at my tiny kitchen and appliances, half the size of those in the U.S.

During their stay, we took a few days off and visited the Black Forest driving through miles and miles of farmland, much to my father's delight. Traveling back roads, we came to a vineyard being harvested. Mother wanted to stop and talk with the workers harvesting the grapes. We were a bit hesitant. After several years of living in Germany, we knew that Germans are not generally known for being open to spontaneous visits from strangers.

Nevertheless, Louis stopped the car and approached the farmer who surprised us with an invitation to observe the harvest and take a walk in the vineyard while he explained the process of winemaking. Upon our departure, we were given a bag of fresh grapes for the trip. My parents were delighted, and I learned a lesson: God is sometimes gracious in unexpected ways.

Several months after my parent's visit, we received a letter from my sister telling us that mother's cancer had returned with a vengeance and she was again on chemotherapy. I was terribly saddened by this news not only because Mother was terribly ill and having to once again endure the suffering of cancer treatment, but she had prayed diligently for years we would either have children or be able to adopt. I knew even if God answered her prayer, she was unlikely to live long enough to know them.

A short time later, we received a letter from Cheryl, one of the young professionals who had been an integral part of our U.S. student ministry. In passing, she mentioned she had a new roommate who was a social worker.

Although knowing it was a very long shot, nevertheless I wrote Cheryl, told her of our interest in adoption and asked if her roommate worked in that field or had any contacts that might be a resource for us as we pursued adoption.

About a week after posting the letter, we left for a New Year's retreat in southern Germany with our students. On the second day of the retreat, I received a phone call telling me I needed to return to the States immediately if I wanted to see my mother alive as she was seizing continually and the initial diagnosis was metastases to the brain.

We left the retreat and returned home to Bonn, arriving in the middle of a winter storm that dumped inches of ice and snow across the city. As we drove through deserted, ice-covered streets, I prayed my mother would live, and not only live, but live to see the grandbabies for whom she had prayed on our behalf.

Upon arriving back at our apartment, I hurriedly looked through the mail and found a large envelope from a Christian adoption agency. There was also a letter from Cheryl.

As I read, my eyes filled with tears of joy and anguish. On the day Cheryl received my letter of inquiry regarding adoption, her new roommate, Judy, had an interview at a Christian adoption agency. Judy took our letter of inquiry with her to the interview. She was hired that day as a social worker responsible for screening prospective adoptive parents. We were her first clients. She had enclosed a twenty-five-page document for us to complete and return as soon as possible.

As I packed for the States, Louis was on the phone trying to locate an airport which still had flights out despite the severe winter storm. In the end, he would drive me three hours to Amsterdam as the German airports were all iced in. However, there was one more obstacle. My soon to expire passport had to be renewed before I could leave the country as it was attached to our residence visa.

Louis called the American Embassy in Bonn, explained the circumstances to the young marine on after-hours duty and asked if there was any possibility of getting a passport renewed on the weekend. The young man replied that although the embassy was closed, understandably as it was Sunday, he would call the ambassador as soon as he got out of church and see what could be done. It seemed like a good sign, an ambassador who attended church. I returned to packing with renewed hope.

An hour later, we had a call from the embassy asking us to come in that afternoon for passport processing, and the next morning, after being up much of the night filling out adoption forms that required Louis' input, I was on a flight to New York. Weather-related delays resulted in missed connections, but I arrived in Huntsville safely Tuesday morning and went directly to my mother's hospital room where I found her sleeping peacefully.

While I was somewhere over the Atlantic, lab results revealed my mother's seizures were caused by a drug interaction which drained her body of potassium. It was not brain cancer. Mother was seizure free and would live to see another day. She remained, however, gravely ill as cancer had spread to her skeletal system resulting in terrible pain.

During the six weeks that followed, I took care of Mom and Dad, drove Mother to chemotherapy and her doctor's appointments. Her prognosis was not good, and Dad was again struggling with depression. I also stayed in touch with Judy, our social worker at the adoption agency. As soon as Louis arrived in the U.S., we were to travel to Oklahoma City for an initial interview. My mother was confident that this long prayed for grandchild was soon to arrive. I prayed she was right as I continued to fill out forms and pray.

Louis arrived back in the States for our scheduled furlough in mid-February. After a few days with my parents, we began our drive to Oklahoma City, again on ice-covered highways. Less than a mile from my parent's home, the driver in front of us suddenly braked, as did we in response, sending our car into a 360-degree turn coming to a stop on the edge of a steep embankment. Stunned, we sat there as cars whizzed by, gathered our wits and thanked God His hand of protection was on us.

Two days later, we arrived in Oklahoma City where we were warmly received at the adoption agency. However, we left discouraged as there were no infants available for adoption. Although we were not opposed to adopting an older child, we knew it would be too traumatic to submerge a newly adopted child into the German culture after our three-month home leave.

From Oklahoma, we returned to the Southeast to visit Louis' family in Savannah. It was there we received a call, a month later asking if we were ready to pick up our new baby boy!

When the call came through, a family friend happened to be present with his camera. Realizing this was an event worth recording, he ran through a roll of film as we laughed and cried our way through the conversation with the adoption agency.

The next day we drove to Atlanta, stopping at a strip mall along the way to pick up a few baby things to get us through the first few days. From Atlanta, we flew to Oklahoma City to pick up our baby, whom we named Jeremy Charles Platt after a relative on Louis' side of the family. Two years later, we returned to adopt a baby girl, Mary Elizabeth named for her grandmother.

My mother lived to see both children, hold them in her arms and thank God for His goodness to us.

Our last visit with Mom and Dad was when our little ones were three and eighteen months old. I returned from that visit with a heavy heart knowing I would not see my mother again in this life.

Her final months were especially difficult for all of us. I was scheduled to come home in February, around the time of her birthday, but her condition deteriorated quickly during the first part of December, and she died before I arrived.

I was heartbroken I had not been there, even more so later when a friend of mother's who was with her during her final days told me of her continually asking when I would arrive. Then she shared the following with me: "On the day before your mother died, she looked up at the hospital door and said, 'Why Glenda has come.'"

I listened in amazement as I realized, even though I was 5,000 miles away in Germany, Jesus in His mercy had me appear and perhaps comfort my dying mother just before she left this world.

Mother's death was bittersweet as both she and my father had suffered terribly during her last year of life, but she had lived to see the Lord gift us with two precious children in answer to her prayers.

By the middle of our second term, the hurdles that had seemed so insurmountable that first year, had been mostly resolved, some through a great deal of pain and suffering, others with joy. There was also the fruit in the lives of the students who witnessed our walk through the joys and the heartache.

THE PAST RESURFACES

In February of 1983, we were at the end of our second term and on the way home for an extended eighteen-month furlough during which Louis would complete his seminary degree at Dallas Theological Seminary.

Following his graduation, we returned to Germany where we would open a ministry to theology students at the University of Mainz. "Why," one might ask, "would theology students need someone to tell them about Jesus, especially in the homeland of Luther, the father of the Reformation?"

The answer is, simple. The land that birthed Luther, also birthed the roots of the postmodern movement through the works of Kant, Nietzsche, Heidegger and Schleiermacher. The result being, in many of Germany's great seminaries, the gospel of Jesus Christ is no longer taught.

Shortly after our return to Germany, our just turned five-year-old daughter through a complicated series of medical events, developed a severe allergic reaction to everything she ate. Her arms, legs, face and hands were covered with a burning, itching rash that turned to blisters. She slept fitfully and woke repeatedly during the night often screaming with pain. She was swollen with edema and had the appearance of having been scalded. We took her to every specialist in the area, none of whom could help. Finally, I took her to Johns Hopkins in Baltimore with the same results.

After months of very little sleep for either Liz or me, my daughter's symptoms began to recede and she was again able to sleep through the night. Life began to return to normal for everyone except me. It seemed I had reached a level of fatigue from which I could not recover.

Although it had been years since I had thought of him, one night I awoke with a start from a terrible nightmare during which the children, Louis and I were being pursued down endless corridors by

Nick, the relative who had molested me during my childhood. In the dream, I frantically pushed my family ahead of me as we raced down hallway after hallway in a huge glass building that went on forever. There was never an exit, just corridor after corridor. We were like rats being chased through a never-ending maze. Shaken to the core and heart pounding, I lay there wondering what it could possibly mean. It had been so long ago.

Despite the stress of our daughter's lingering illness and my own exhaustion, I continued taking care of the children, the house, shopping, preparing meals, even entertaining, but I felt as though I was walking a razor's edge where one false move would prove fatal. As the thoughts raging through my head became violent, I knew I had to seek help.

Louis and I had known Christian psychiatrist Frank Minirth and his wife, Mary Alice, since our early days in collegiate ministry in Texas. We had been in a couples' Bible study together long before Frank became a well-known Christian psychiatrist. During our last furlough, we had reconnected when I consulted Frank about periodic depression. Just prior to our departure, Frank gave us his number and said simply, "Call if you need help."

Realizing I desperately needed help, I called and was immediately put through. I began by saying, "Frank, I'm afraid I'm in trouble." After a few minutes spent in describing my symptoms, Frank responded, "Glenda, you need to get on a plane as soon as possible. A room will be ready for you at the clinic."

Several days later after making arrangements with friends who would help Louis care for the children, I was on that plane. A friend met me at the airport and drove me to the Dallas clinic where I checked myself in.

THE WRITING ON THE WALL

Looking back, I had clearly missed the obvious. Periodic bouts of depression were not uncommon, but I was always able to explain them away by saying, "I just need to spend more time in the Word" which in truth, would ameliorate the symptoms for a while.

I was clearly a type A workaholic and I knew it, even took pride in it, knowing it was a way to get lots of things accomplished; things that were important to me, my family and the student ministry. But I also realized the more fatigued I became, the less efficiently I worked and the less I accomplished. To this I responded with increased effort, worked harder, stayed up later and became more exhausted. It was a vicious cycle.

During counseling, I began to see I made it easy for others to expect more of me than I could reasonably deliver. I never responded negatively to a request, no matter how exhausted I was. If I saw a need, I assumed it was my responsibility to meet that need, often going to bed at night so tired that the effort of breathing was almost more than I could bring forth.

If life in Germany was difficult with a sick child and the local doctors suggested returning to the States to a drier climate, until God made that plain, we concluded we should remain in Germany. In retrospect, I wonder how much plainer it could have been. Yet, when you are emotionally and physically exhausted, logic often goes out the door.

After years of living this life to varying degrees, it seemed normal, even comfortable. I was laying down my life for the benefit of others. There were also the many students who had come to Christ and were serving Him. That must, I thought, be an indication I was serving the Lord, pleasing Him. Yet no matter how early I rose or how late I worked, I felt I had not done enough. I often reflected on John 14:27 and wondered why I rarely seemed to experience the peace of God as described in that verse. "Peace I leave with you; my peace I give you. I do not give to you as the world gives. Do not let your hearts be troubled and do not be afraid." Yet, I was fearful and troubled and very much in need of help which God provided in the form of strong Christian counselors and the continued practice of the Christian disciplines.

REFLECTION

I believe Satan, whose purpose is to kill, steal and destroy, gives special attention to those who serve or will one day serve in full-time Christian ministry. Don't be surprised if this is true in your life. Share your struggles with a trusted mentor or counselor. Join an accountability group. Satan knows the ultimate victory has been won through Christ's sacrificial death and resurrection, however, he is determined to derail and destroy the lives of as many believers as possible during the interim between now and Christ's return.

Looking back, it is clear to me that one mistake I made repeatedly was basing my decisions on what I felt was the "spiritual thing to do," instead of doing what my heart told me I needed to do. My mother was dying and asking for me. I needed to go home. I should have gone home. It would have been difficult. I would have traveled alone with two small children as Louis was in an intensive Hebrew course in Berlin. International travel is expensive, but had we applied to our home church, I am sure they would have helped with the cost. Traveling with two small children is challenging at best, but I could have managed. Nevertheless, I feel no guilt. The decision was made in good faith given the circumstances. The Lord intervened despite my poor judgment, for that I am eternally grateful and able to learn from my mistakes.

Unfortunately doing the "spiritual thing," motivated by that which would make me look good in the eyes of God and man, was still there in my thirties.

A friend who proofread the last few chapters asked, "Where was Louis when you were going through all this?"

"He was leading the university ministry and working on a doctorate," I replied, and could have added, "with my blessing."

From my skewed understanding of Scripture regarding the life of sacrifice to which Christians are called, I thought it was my duty to make sure Louis continued his studies and ministry undeterred by what was happening at home. My misguided understanding of Scripture meant I needed to sort this out on my own. He needed peace and quiet for his work and I did my best to ensure he had that time.

Having grown up with an alcoholic father and a co-dependent mother who tried desperately to protect her children from the effects of their father's addiction, as a child, Louis learned to shut himself off emotionally from the suffering going on around him. Sadly, that included the children and me. Although I felt this could not be right, I was so exhausted and confused in my thinking, I simply tried to survive as best I could.

After talking with Dr. Minirth on the phone, I felt maybe, just maybe there would be help for me, even possibly for both of us at the clinic.

During the four weeks that I spent at the Dallas clinic, I learned a great deal. First, I learned that it was possible to claim Philippians 4:13 (NKJV), "I can do all things through Christ who strengthens me," all the way to the psych ward, as that was what I had done.

Despite years of periodic depression and overwork in a desperate attempt to please the caricature of God I held, I had not sought the help I needed to deal with the long-term effects of the abuse nor had I known it was an issue. Finally, I was at the point where I could no longer ignore my need. Nick himself had risen from the depths of my psyche and I knew the past could no longer be ignored.

During the stressful period of our daughter's illness, I survived by shutting off my emotions. There are times when this is necessary to get control of an out of hand situation or make rational decisions in a crisis, but I survived like this for months on end.

I knew the Lord had led us to return to Germany so it had to mean that somehow we could get through this terribly difficult time. But I knew if I gave into my feelings, I would not be able to function, so I chose to think not feel, totally disassociating myself from my emotions in order to survive. I arrived in Dallas in an emotionally static state. I felt nothing other than a degree of relief that there I might find help and my children were safe.

Louis joined me the last week of my stay at the clinic. During that time of daily individual and couples counseling, Dr. Minirth shared with

Louis that his coping mechanism of shutting himself off emotionally was "killing his family." Not only were our daughter and I being affected but also our son, who was drowning in the German educational system. Dr. Minirth strongly encouraged Louis and me to return to Germany and begin the process of transitioning back to the States where we could receive consistent counseling, medical treatment for our daughter and get our son in an English-speaking school.

Although it would be another year before we both finally understood the necessity of this move, in the summer of 1988 we returned to the U.S. where we settled in the Dallas-Fort Worth area to work at our sending church, receive counseling and medical treatment for our daughter. There our son adjusted well and began to thrive in the U.S. educational system.

RESPONSE

LIFE IN GERMANY 1974

1 Can you recall a time when you were faced with one challenge on the heels of another? How did you get through that difficult period? Did you learn things that prepared you for the next series of challenges?

TIME SORTS MOST THINGS OUT

2 Many difficult periods are followed by a time of reprieve. Can you identify periods of reprieve in your past life and ministry?

3 Can you recall a difficult period through which you had to rely on the Lord in order to survive?

4 List character traits and activities that could be helpful when facing difficult times.

5 What role does your belief system play in surviving hard times?

6 Seeming coincidence often plays a role in God's directing our lives. Can you think of a time when a chance meeting or other coincidence resulted in a changed direction in your life? Explain.

7 Not all of our stories end happily. What resources do you draw on to get you through unhappy endings?

THE PAST RESURFACES

8 From your reading thus far, why do you think the past resurfaced as it did at just this time in the author's life?

THE WRITING ON THE WALL

9 What was the writing on the wall leading up to the emotional crisis that the author had missed?

10 How would you explain the difference between doing "the spiritual thing" and doing "the right thing?" Have you struggled in this area?

11 Can you explain the following statement? "During the four weeks that I spent at the Dallas clinic, I learned a great deal. First, I learned that it was possible to claim Philippians 4:13 (NKJV), 'I can do all things through Christ who strengthens me,' all the way to the psych ward, as that was what I had done."

12 Had you known the author during this period of her life, how could you have responded when she said, "From my skewed understanding of Scripture regarding the life of sacrifice to which Christians are called, I thought it was my duty to make sure my husband continued his studies and ministry undeterred by what was happening at home. My misguided understanding of Scripture meant I needed to sort this out on my own. He needed peace and quiet for his

work and the student ministry. I did my best to ensure he had that time"?

13 How would you have counseled the author's husband in light of the following? "Louis grew up with an alcoholic father and a co-dependent mother who tried desperately to protect her children from the effects of their father's addiction. From an early age, Louis learned to shut himself off emotionally from the suffering going on around him."

14 The author writes, "During the stressful period of our daughter's illness, I survived by shutting off my emotions. There are times when this is necessary to get control of an out of hand situation or make rational decisions in a crisis, but I survived like this for months, if not years."

‣ This coping mechanism is called dissociation. Can you think of a time when you may have employed this form of coping?

15 Do you agree with the assertion by Tim Keller from his book, *Walking with God through Pain and Suffering,* where Keller states the American goal of living a life of self-fulfillment and happiness as we pursue our dreams in no way prepares us to face life's inevitable suffering?[11] Explain your position.

16 What reasons can you give for believers experiencing difficulty? Consider the following verses: John 10:10-29; 1 Peter 4:12, 1:7; Romans 5:1-5; 2 Corinthians 1:8-9.

17 Summarize the resources you draw on during difficult times.

CHAPTER 11
EFFECTS OF CHILDHOOD ABUSE AND NEGLECT

A DISTORTED VIEW OF GOD, SELF, AND RELATIONSHIP WITH OTHERS

Neglect and abuse rarely end with the abusive incidents. They affect how we view ourselves, our relationships with others and most importantly, our view of God.

A DISTORTED VIEW OF GOD

After the abuse began, I concluded God either did not love me or was too busy with other things to see what was happening in my life. My mother's understanding of God as a righteous judge who didn't have time for the everyday troubles of mortals, colored not only her view of God but mine as well.

Knowing that God and my parents were good, I concluded the fault must lie with me. I wasn't worth protecting. The solution was obvious. I would simply have to show them all, God included, I was worthy of their love and protection. At the same time, it didn't seem right. From Sunday school, I knew God was supposed to love "all the little children" and parents were supposed to protect their children. As a result of the inconsistency between the teaching I received at church and my life experience, I grew increasingly distrustful and resentful toward God and my parents. This resulted in a loss of confidence in my parents' love and commitment to protect me. Also, my view of God was rapidly devolving from that of a loving Father to that of a distant, impossible to please, deity who at best was tolerant of me but never pleased.

A DISTORTED VIEW OF SELF

Having experienced sexual harm as a small child, I concluded early on I must be at fault or bad things wouldn't happen to me. Over time, I came to see myself as damaged goods, incapable of pleasing anyone, especially my father and God. Although I never verbalized these beliefs, nor was I even aware of them for many years, they were there coloring my decisions, interactions and ability to experience the love and acceptance of God, my parents and others.

As a result, I became consumed with proving I was worthy of being loved, developed a type A personality and as an adult, became a workaholic with perfectionist tendencies.

RELATIONSHIP WITH OTHERS

This need to prove my worthiness spilled over into my relationships with others. However, despite my efforts, it seemed as though nothing I did, no accomplishment I achieved was acknowledged by anyone. By middle school, I was becoming increasingly resentful and depressed; convinced if I were to survive, I would have to learn to depend on myself and no one else.

Not recognizing my father's love for me, my formative years were spent in pursuit of his affection. During my teen and early adult years, I was only interested in young men who were not really interested in me. If they were interested, in my distorted way of thinking, they weren't worth pursuing. Sadly, the pursuit and rejection of these young men felt familiar and somehow comfortable, a mirror of my relationship with my father. Yet, at the same time, the pursuit was enticing; a challenge to be overcome.

In addition, I seemed to attract friends who were even more dysfunctional than I. Having known suffering first hand, I wanted to alleviate the suffering of those around me. I did this by taking on the responsibility of meeting the needs of others, often needs they should have met themselves.

Unfortunately, I took responsibility for meeting those needs with little regard for my own, became overextended, exhausted, and upon occasion, angry and resentful toward those whom I sought to serve. Not only were they not taking care of themselves, but they weren't appreciative of my efforts to take care of them either.

Real problems arise when the individual being "helped" becomes dependent on the help being given, all the while knowing they should be caring for their own needs. This results in feelings of guilt and resentment toward the well-intended helper, who in the final analysis, was primarily "helping" out of a sense of guilt or in order to feel better about themselves as in my case. Thus, codependence is born and begins to wreak havoc.

CHANGING DISTORTED VIEWS OF SELF, GOD AND RELATIONSHIPS WITH OTHERS

Time spent in the Word, prayer, Bible study, listening prayer, support groups, counseling, reflective writing and honest conversations with likeminded believers, are powerful tools for changing distorted views. Fundamental change of these distorted views must occur for healing to take place. However, change rarely comes quickly.

A NEW VIEW OF SELF

I must decide, sometimes daily, if I am going to adhere to the view of myself as seen through childhood distortions, or if I will accept what God says about me as clearly stated in Scripture. Will I believe Satan's lie that I am damaged goods, unusable in the kingdom of God or believe what God says about me? "You are precious and honored in my sight . . . I will give people in exchange for your life" (Isaiah 43:4a, c).

When the loop about my being damaged goods begins to play, I counter it with truth from the Scriptures. This is a part of the sanctification process described in Romans 12:1-2 where we are told to "be transformed by the renewing of your mind," which includes new ways of thinking.

As I learned from a Vietnam veteran friend who suffers from PTSD, recent brain science has discovered that it is possible to reprogram the brain by speaking truth aloud during the seconds following a negative thought. Repeatedly countering negative thoughts with truth can create new neural pathways which can gradually replace old ones.

I am valued

In John 3:16 and John 5:24, we are told God valued us enough to send Christ to die for us so we might be forgiven for our misdeeds. John 1:12 says as believers in the Lord Jesus Christ, we have peace with God and have become His children, members of His household. Ephesians 1:4-5 says God chose us as His children before the foundation of the world. These acts by the Creator reflect our worth in His eyes.

My Eternal Destiny is Secured

In Ephesians 1:13 we are told we are sealed in Christ with the Holy Spirit of promise. In reference to our secure position in the household of God, Jesus said in John 10:29, "My Father, who has given them to me, is greater than all; no one can snatch them out of my Father's hand." Our security rests on that which God has done and is doing, not on our efforts.

I Am Not Powerless

Paul prays that we would know the incomparable power that is available to us in Christ. This is the same power which raised Jesus from the dead and seated Him at the right hand of God and us in Him; so loved and honored are we in the Son (Ephesians 1:18-20). This is also the same power that enabled Jesus to carry out His life and ministry here on earth, the same power that is available to us.

I Am Created to Contribute Toward the Work of the Kingdom

In Ephesians 2:10 we read we are God's masterpiece, created in Christ Jesus so we can do the good works that God planned for us to do long before we were born; quite possibly, even back when He chose us as His children before the foundation of the earth (Ephesians 1:4). Not only does God have a job description for us, He also provides job training though the experiences He either brings or allows into our life. At salvation, He further equips us to do our job by giving us spiritual gifts specific to the job as well as guidance through the indwelling Holy Spirit (Ephesians 2:10, 4:11-13; 1 Peter 4:10-11; Ephesians 4:11-13; 1 Corinthians 12:8-11; Romans 12:6-8).

I Am Capable of Change

Thoughts are powerful change agents for good or evil. "For as he thinks in his heart," Proverbs 23:7 (NKJV) tells us, "so is he." When I catch myself thinking negative thoughts, I refocus on what God says is true. It's only possible to think about one thing at a time. We decide what we will think and, in many ways, what we will "be" as determined by those thoughts.

I Am Positionally Perfect, Experientially Maturing

2 Corinthians 5:17 (NKJV) says that "old things have passed away; behold, all things have become new." That is absolutely true, *positionally*. As God sees us, we are not only the person He created and equipped to fulfill specific roles in the kingdom here on earth, but He also sees us as perfect in Christ, clothed in Christ's righteousness, freed from all vestiges of sin.

One aspect of our job in this life is to work with God through the power of the Holy Spirit toward *experiential* maturity or sanctification in Christ. The practice of the spiritual disciplines plays a key role in sanctification. 2 Timothy 2:15 says, "Do your best to present yourself to God as one approved, a worker who does not need to be ashamed and who correctly handles the word of truth" (see Chapter 14).

Focus on the Positive

Does all of this discourage me? Only if I'm focused on what "I'm not," instead of what "I am" in Christ. Focusing on the Lord, His love for me and His power working through me to accomplish the good works that He has planned for me, energizes me and gives me hope. Even if I don't know "the plan," He knows it and promises to complete that "good work" which He began in me before Jesus returns (Philippians 1:6). It really isn't all on me. He, through the power of the Holy Spirit, works in us "to will and to act in order to fulfill his good purpose" (Philippians 2:13) and He will complete it.

We are sons and daughters of the God of heaven, the Creator of the universe. I am an important member of the family, a contributing member working in the family firm. My contribution to the kingdom is so important that God planned my job description long before I was born. Preparation for my job in the kingdom is ongoing as I grow in faith and trust. My life is a series of journeys. Each completed journey prepares me for the next.

Considering all of the above, how can we not see ourselves as valued and valuable for the kingdom of God? Although my life was affected by abuse and neglect, it is not defined by that abuse. My life is defined by my relationship to the King of Kings. I am His beloved daughter.

A NEW VIEW OF GOD THE FATHER

Again I must decide, "Will I believe the Scriptures or Satan's lies based on past experiences?" Eve believed Satan's lie that God was withholding good from her by forbidding fruit from the tree of knowledge of good and evil. If we listen to Satan's lies we too, will be deceived into thinking that God is withholding good from us; that He does not have our best interests at heart. This lie is as old as the story of the fall. Perhaps even as old as Satan's fall for he too must have doubted God's love and plan for his life or he would not have desired to raise his "throne above the stars of God" to sit "on the utmost heights" to make himself "like the Most High" (Isaiah 14:13-14).

Evidence of God's Love: Christ's Death

We are so precious in His sight that He sent His Son from the hallowed halls of heaven to live among sinful men, to be rejected, scorned, vilified and brutally crucified as a common criminal by the very ones He came to save. God then turned His back on His beloved obedient-to-death Son. How the heart of God must have broken as that wrenching cry erupted from the soul of His Son, "My God, my God why have you forsaken me?" (Matthew 27:45-46b).

Had the answer been given, it would have been as equally heartbreaking, "I have turned my back on you, my Son, for the sake of these, these who have rejected you, spat upon you, scorned you and brutally crucified you. It is for them and others like them I have turned my back on you so they too, have the opportunity to become my beloved children."

Even as I write this, my heart screams, "Where is the logic in that? No sane person in the civilized world would sacrifice their son's life for someone else's misdeeds. They would be prosecuted to the furthest extent of the law. No one does this!" Only God and God in Jesus would do this to welcome us into His family.

Tim Keller in his book, *Galatians For You*, writes we should keep the gospel ever before our eyes for it is when we look at what Jesus did for us that we understand God's love and sin loses its allure. However, it must be a continual reviewing of His love and sacrifice, for sin is a continual temptation. [12]

Evidence of God's Love: We Are Given Responsibility

Second Corinthians 5:17-21 tells us that our sins are gone, we are reconciled to God and given the ministry of reconciliation. It has been said that God doesn't just "save us from something," He "saves us to something;" the ministry of reconciliation. Furthermore, He uses our experiences both good and bad to prepare us for that ministry. Nothing that we have experienced or suffered is lost. God will use it for good as we walk with Him (Romans 8:28; Ephesians 1:11).

God Redeems the Negative Things in Our Lives for Good

Isaiah 43:4 (NKJV) states, "I will give men for you, and people for your life." This verse says to me that God is using all my life, even the heartbreaking parts for good. One of the glorious parts of God's power and sovereignty is that He takes those terrible parts of our lives and redeems them so that they can be used to serve others as well as benefit ourselves.

Similarly, the crucifixion could have been seen as a total victory for Satan. Indeed, Satan may well have thought he had won. However, Jesus rose from the dead and as C.S. Lewis described it in The Chronicles of Narnia, history began working backwards. Death was overcome. God, the Father worked it for good for the salvation and redemption of humankind as well as all of nature which will be perfectly restored in the new heaven and earth (Romans 8:22-24).

Furthermore, in Jeremiah 29:11 we read, "'I know the plans I have for you,' declares the LORD, 'plans to prosper you and not to harm you, plans to give you hope and a future.'" What better hope is there than to know that all that happens to us can be reversed, reinvented, turned inside out and upside down for the purpose of good? (Romans 8:28; Ephesians 1:11).

Psalm 27:13 (NASB) says, "I would have despaired unless I had believed that I would see the goodness of the LORD in the land of the living." This promise is for the here and now. There will be respite. Things will get better. Our loved one may still die of cancer, our children may remain distant from the Lord, but there will be respite in our soul as we cling to Jesus.

Jeremiah 31:3b-4 has been a wonderful encouragement to me through the difficulties of life: "I have loved you with an everlasting love; I have drawn you with unfailing kindness. I will build you up again . . . and . . . you will go out to dance with the joyful."

These verses and others have been a comfort and inspiration to me as I have seen joy returning to my life.

A NEW VIEW OF MY RELATIONSHIP WITH OTHERS

As a young Christian, my interactions with other believers sometimes degenerated into thinly veiled, self-adulating conversation about the latest book I'd read by a trending Christian author or an interesting message that I had heard, the purpose of which was to impress others with how spiritual I was and how worthy I was to be their friend. Clearly my understanding of the meaning and purpose of fellowship in the body of Christ was skewed at best.

My understanding of evangelism was equally off base. I felt it was my responsibility to share the gospel with everyone I met. For a then quiet, shy introvert, it was a heavy burden to bear not only for myself but also for those whom I attempted to evangelize.

In time I learned a totally different view of Christian fellowship as well as evangelism. However, change did not come rapidly. It was and continues to be a gradual process of identifying and dealing with dysfunctional coping mechanisms, many of which began during childhood.

CHANGE COMES THROUGH SPIRITUAL GROWTH

Although spiritual growth is a work of the Holy Spirit, it also requires work on our part. Sometimes very hard work. When I find myself falling back into the old way of thinking that I am simply damaged goods and useless in the kingdom, I have a choice. I can stay there or confess my sin of not believing the truth of what God says about me in Scripture and take positive steps forward such as the following:

- Pray asking God if this low point is the result of some unconfessed sin in my life. If the Holy Spirit brings something to mind, then I confess it, thank Him for His forgiveness and move on. If not, then I ask Him to remove the feelings of discouragement by the power of the Holy Spirit (Romans 8:13). Often, within moments, it is gone which tells me it may well have been a spiritual attack.
- Get in touch with my mentor or counselor and ask for prayer or guidance.
- Review verses that have been an encouragement to me in the past.
- Review the fruits of the Spirit and ask the Lord what He would have me focus on today (Galatians 5:22-23).
- Remembering how God has worked on my behalf in the past can also be a powerful tool for refocusing my thoughts. Throughout Scripture, believers were charged to remember past acts of God on their behalf. Many of the Old Testament celebrations commemorated past deliverance through mighty acts of God.
- Reviewing portions of Scripture referencing our adoption into the family of God and being sealed with the Holy Spirit of promise into that family can also be helpful. Our position in the family of God is in no way dependent on our performance. It is the Holy Spirit who secures our salvation.
- Many times during the week, I will look back on the crucifixion, on what Jesus did for me as a reminder of my value in the eyes of God. That He valued me enough to give me not only a position in the family but responsibility in the kingdom of God here on earth, lifts my spirit and opens my eyes to everyday opportunities to serve Him through acts of kindness to others whether sharing the gospel or offering help to someone in need.

REFLECTION

I don't know when I began to recognize the dissonance in my thinking regarding God. I was deep into it by the time I was falling asleep clutching the hem of my mother's gown in the hope that if we died in our sleep, I would not be left behind.

Later, as an adult, I professed to believe in God, the loving Father, yet I could not believe He loved me. Felt sorry for me maybe, but love? No!

Just as my thinking was clouded regarding God's love for me, it was also clouded regarding my father's love for me. Of course, he loved me. He sacrificed terribly for our family. You don't do that for someone you don't love. My thinking was so tainted by my experience, I could perceive neither God's nor my father's love.

The parallel between my perception of my father who in my eyes was "impossible to please" no matter how hard I tried and God, eventually became obvious, even to me. However, how to change that misconception would be long in coming, yet come it would.

RESPONSE

A DISTORTED VIEW OF SELF, GOD AND RELATIONSHIP WITH OTHERS

1 Where do you observe the quote below in the author's relationships with her family of origin, with her husband and children, and her relationships with others in the body?

▸ "Neglect and abuse rarely end with the abusive incidents. They affect how we view ourselves, our relationships with others and most importantly, our view of God."

2 How did the author deal with her felt need to prove her worthiness to others?

3 Do you resonate with any of the following quotes from the text? Explain.

▸ "Not recognizing my father's love for me, my formative years were spent in pursuit of his affection."

▸ "During my teen and early adult years, I was only interested in young men who were not really interested in me. If they were interested, in my distorted way of thinking, they weren't worth pursuing. Sadly, the pursuit and rejection of these young men felt familiar and somehow comfortable, a mirror of my relationship with my father. At the same time, the pursuit was enticing; a challenge to be overcome."

▸ "I took responsibility for meeting the needs of others with little regard for my own, became overextended, exhausted, and upon occasion, angry and resentful toward those whom I sought to serve. Not only were they not taking care of themselves, but they weren't appreciative of my efforts to take care of them either."

▸ "Real problems arise when the individual being "helped" becomes dependent on the help being given, all the while knowing they should be caring for their own needs. This often results in feelings of guilt and resentment toward the well-intended helper, who in the final analysis, was primarily 'helping' out of a sense of guilt or in order to feel better about themselves.... Thus codependence is born."

CHANGING DISTORTED VIEWS OF SELF, GOD AND RELATIONSHIPS WITH OTHERS

4 Have you seen a correlation between time spent in spiritual disciplines and your sense of well-being?

A NEW VIEW OF SELF

5 Does the following ring true with you? If so, in what way?

▸ "I must decide, sometimes daily, if I am going to adhere to the view of myself as seen through childhood distortions, or if I will accept what God says about me as clearly stated in Scripture, 'You are precious and honored in my sight' (Isaiah 43:4a)."

6 Romans 12:1-2 tells us "to be transformed by the renewing of your mind."

▸ What are you doing in the areas of spiritual disciplines to bring about this transformation? Even small baby steps practiced consistently can make a difference.

7 "Repeatedly countering negative thoughts with truth can create new neural pathways which can gradually replace old ones."

▸ Are you countering negative intrusive thoughts with truth from Scripture?

I am Valued

8 How does Christ's sacrificial death reflect our value in the eyes of God? Consider John 1:12, 5:24; Ephesians 1:4-5, 2:12-13.

My Eternal Destiny is Secured

9 What does Ephesians 1:13 and John 10:27-29 reveal about the certainty of your eternal destiny once you believe in Christ as your Savior and Lord and seek to follow Him? On whom is your eternal security dependent?

I Am Not Powerless

10 We have access to the same power that raised Jesus from the dead and seated Him at the right hand of God and us in Him (Ephesians 1:18-20). This is also the same power that

enabled Jesus to carry out His life and ministry here on earth.

▸ What are some practical ways in which you can access this power for your daily life?

I Am Created to Contribute Toward the Work of the Kingdom

11 In Ephesians 2:10 we read we are God's masterpiece, created in Christ Jesus to do good works that God planed for us to do even before we were born (Ephesians 1:4). God not only gives us work to do in His kingdom, but He equips us to do that work through spiritual gifts.

▸ When you consider the desire of your heart and the gifts you have received, what good works do you think God has for you to do?

▸ Which gifts has God gifted you with for work in His kingdom? (Romans 12:6-8; 1 Corinthians 12:8-11; Ephesians 2:10, 4:11-13; 1 Peter 4:10-11).

I Am Capable of Change

12 "For as he thinks in his heart," Proverbs 23:7 (NKJV) tells us, "so is he." When I catch myself thinking negative thoughts, I refocus on what God says is true. It's only possible to think about one thing at a time. We decide what we will think and, in many ways, what we will "be" as determined by those thoughts.

▸ Which intrusive thoughts do you do battle with? Which strategies do you employ for change?

I Am Positionally Perfect, Experientially Maturing

13 Second Corinthians 5:17 (NKJV) says that "old things have passed away; behold, all things have become new." That is true, *positionally* which means God sees us, not only as the

person He created and equipped us to be but also as perfect in Christ.

▸ However, a major part of our "job" in this life is to grow into mature believers as we practice the spiritual disciplines and learn to walk with Jesus on a daily basis. This growing process is called *experiential* or *practical sanctification.*

▸ Consider Galatians 2:20, 2 Timothy 2:15 and Romans 6:6, 12-13 which speak of both positional and experiential sanctification.

▸ After prayerfully reflecting on the above verses, describe next steps that you need to take in this maturing process.

FOCUS ON THE POSITIVE

14 When things go badly, we can still focus on the positive.

▸ Read the following verses and list all the positive aspects that can be a comfort to us during difficult times: Philippians 1:6, 2:13; Romans 8:28; 2 Corinthians 1:8-9; Isaiah 43:1-3a.

A NEW VIEW OF GOD THE FATHER

15 Eve believed Satan's lie that God was withholding good from her by forbidding fruit from the tree of knowledge of good and evil.

▸ In which areas of your life are you most tempted to think God is withholding good from you? How does this affect your trust relationship with God?

Evidence of God's Love: Christ's Death

16 "Tim Keller in his book, *Galatians For You,* writes we should keep the gospel ever before our eyes for it is when we look

at what Jesus did for us that we understand God's love, and sin loses its allure." [13]

▸ How might one make this continual reviewing of Christ's love and sacrifice a daily practice?

Evidence of God's Love: We Are Given Responsibility

17 Second Corinthians 5:17-21 tells us that our sins are gone, we are reconciled to God and given the ministry of reconciliation. Furthermore, He uses our experiences both positive and negative to prepare us for that ministry.

▸ Make a list of positive as well as difficult experiences that God has allowed in your life. As you reflect on these experiences, ask God to show you how He has and is using them for good to equip you for ministry.

God Redeems the Negative Things in Our Lives for Good

18 The crucifixion could have been seen as a victory for Satan. However, through Christ's sacrificial death and resurrection, redemption was made available for humankind as well as all of nature which will be perfectly restored in the new heaven and earth (Romans 8:22-24). Explain.

▸ Can you think of something that felt like a death experience you have seen God redeem?

A NEW VIEW OF MY RELATIONSHIP WITH OTHERS

19 Do you, like the author, sometimes find yourself trying to impress other believers with how spiritually mature you are in Christ?

CHANGE COMES THROUGH SPIRITUAL GROWTH

20 Spend some time reflecting on your life of late. In which areas do you see opportunities for growth?

▸ Ask the Lord to pinpoint an area where He would like to help you grow during the next months.

▸ Ask the Lord to help you develop a plan for moving forward in this area. Write it out. Share it with a friend who will pray with you and hold you accountable.

PART II
INEFFECTIVE STRATEGIES

Through decades of Christian ministry, serving as a single woman, a pastor's wife, in home missions, and on the mission fields of Europe, I have had the privilege of knowing many Christian workers from numerous parachurch groups, missions and denominational organizations.

All of them have several things in common. They desire to serve the Lord, see individuals come to Christ, disciple them in small groups and teach them to disciple others to do the same. All of this with the goal of building the body of Christ, the church universal.

With such noble goals, it is surprising that one of the main reasons for missionaries leaving the ministry is conflict among team members. Sadly, it is similar among Christian workers in home missions.[14,15]

For many, the struggles that lead to their departure are carried alone as few want to risk sharing difficulties with leadership. Knowing that such complaints could be interpreted as emotional immaturity on their part, or a lack of spirituality, many just endure rather than speak honestly about the challenges they are facing.

Sadly these conflicts can often be traced to unresolved childhood issues and dysfunctional coping mechanisms learned at an early age. One of the most common effects of unresolved issues is a sense of insignificance or low self-esteem. Ironically this can also present as pride, judgmentalism, rigidity and a lack of openness as walls of self-defense are constructed.

Low self-esteem can also result in an inability to recognize or accept affirmation, codependent behaviors, workaholic tendencies, over sensitivity to perceived slights or taking on the offenses of others.

Adult survivors of childhood trauma from abuse or neglect can also become overly controlling with perfectionist tendencies, frequently second guessing themselves and others, rather than taking people at face value. Sadly, unless these issues are recognized and dealt with, personal, family and ministry relationships can suffer, and diminished fruitfulness may be the price paid.

This is not to say that God cannot use us in our imperfect state. We can rejoice that He can and glories in doing so. In 2 Corinthians 12:9a, we read in reference to Paul's thorn in the flesh, "But he [Christ] said to me [Paul], 'My grace is sufficient for you, for my power is made perfect in weakness.'" Indeed, He can use us more effectively as we become more aware of our need.

However, it is only to the extent we recognize and bring our areas of weakness, sin and brokenness to the Lord for healing that we can begin to be made whole in these areas. Furthermore, it is only to the extent we live transparently as we go through this healing process that God can use our own brokenness to bring healing to others in similar situations.

When we hide our struggles behind a mask of spiritual or intellectual superiority or simply go into hiding as opposed to sharing our struggles with mature, trusted individuals, or counselors (James 5:16), we encourage others to hide their struggles as well, and the brokenness continues.

The following chapters contain a description of dysfunctional coping mechanisms (also called defense mechanisms), the roots of which were often formed in childhood and carried over into adulthood.

RESPONSE

1. With such noble goals in common, what might be the source of missionaries' struggle to get along with each other, or that matter, any of us?

2. Do you recognize this tendency in your own life as a missionary or layperson committed to working in the church?

3. With whom can you share your concerns regarding a lack of unity on your team?

4. "It is only to the extent we recognize and bring our areas of weakness, sin and brokenness to the Lord for healing that we can begin to be made whole. Likewise, it is to the extent we live transparently as we go through this healing process that God can use our own brokenness to bring healing to others in similar situations."

   ▸ Where do you experience this level of openness and mutual growth or the lack thereof? What can you do to contribute toward healthy change?

CHAPTER 12
DYSFUNCTIONAL COPING MECHANISMS

DENIAL AND DEFENSIVENESS

Denial

For many years, I told no one of the past harm that had occurred. I simply told myself it had happened to many, and I needed to get over it and move on. However, buried hurts cannot heal. Instead they fester and affect our lives in myriad ways as we develop dysfunctional coping mechanisms in an attempt to convince ourselves that we are fine. It's the other person who has a problem. Only when these hurts are brought out into the light of God's truth can healing begin.

John 8:31b-32 quotes Jesus as saying to His followers, "If you hold to my teaching, you are really my disciples. Then you will know the truth, and the truth will set you free." Other translations of "to be set free" indicate "you will be liberated."

As a young Christian, I attempted to share with my mentor about the sexual harm I had experienced. She asked me not to share but rather suggested I claim 2 Corinthians 5:17b which says, "The old has gone, the new is here!"

Believing that to be true, and at the same time wanting her approval, I accepted her counsel and "moved on." The only problem was the baggage of abuse moved on with me.

Later when I became engaged, I wondered if the abuse would affect my relationship with my soon-to-be husband. However, because I was walking with the Lord, having my quiet time and memorizing Scripture, I concluded I should be able to move into marriage without any ill effects from my years of abuse. Unfortunately, this thinking isn't unusual among individuals with abuse issues and it would be years before we sought the help we needed to have a healthy marriage. I kept thinking, "If we just went to this seminar or read that book, surely things would be better." I was always looking for the "quick fix" instead of realizing the solution as well as the problem lay in my past. Denial is one of the most debilitating dysfunctional coping mechanisms. Without recognition of the root problem, there can be no lasting healing.

Those who struggle with denial often wear a mask of self-righteousness, pretending everything is "just fine" when nothing could be further from the truth. This attitude sadly often culminates in a downward spiral ending with either a breakdown or nervous collapse from an inability to live up to legalistic standards, as it did with me. Others choose to break away from the faith as they can no longer deal with the strain of hiding their feelings of failure in front of fellow believers.

Either is a sad event that does not have to occur. For a more in-depth explanation of the above, see Dr. David A. Seamands's book *Healing for Damaged Emotions.*[16]

Defensiveness

Because individuals who have experienced abuse or neglect as children often struggle with feelings of inferiority or insecurity, this makes it very difficult for them to accept constructive criticism or critique as it feels like a frontal assault. Already convinced they are damaged goods, their reaction can appear to be a prideful rejection of any suggestions made. They can also respond with a counter attack. Such an event is sometimes followed by withdrawal and days of depression during which various counter arguments, which will never be delivered, are rehearsed ad nauseam.

At other times, defensive walls of indignation rise from behind which imaginary volleys of "Who do they think they are?" are hurled as they reassure themselves they are guiltless parties—"It's the others who are at fault."

I know. I've wasted lots of time in these fruitless endeavors. Meanwhile, I've learned to ask what personal need I am looking to people to fulfill that only God can meet. Then I confess that area of sin, remember what the risen Christ has done out of His love for me, and learn what I can gain from the critique given by asking the Lord what He would have to say to me in this area. Accept it. Act on it and press forward.

SELF-DEPRECATION AND SELF-CONDEMNATION

Self-Deprecation

Some individuals with low self-esteem may unknowingly adopt a self-deprecating attitude, consciously or unconsciously thinking if they grovel first, they will generate sympathy rather than be rejected or judged.

I can remember once in my twenties a friend telling me I really should stop apologizing for "breathing." He pointed out I apologized continually. My response was, of course, "I'm sorry!" at which point we both burst into laughter. I was beginning to get the point.

I was eternally apologizing or alternately playing the helpless damsel when I thought it would serve my purposes as I sought the "father" who would love me and take care of me. Yet when I felt pressured or criticized, I could also defend myself with an angry outburst.

Scripture tells us we are so valued that we have been adopted into the family of God, and Jesus has made us accepted in the beloved (Ephesians 1:5-6). What this means is God sees the essence of our being, how He created us to be and how we will be once Christ returns. He sees beyond our brokenness and sin to who we really are in Him.

To think of ourselves as less than valued sons and daughters of the Father is to disregard Christ's saving work on our behalf.

Self-Condemnation

Self-condemnation is often the result of a prevailing sense of guilt and insecurity. David Seamands in his book, *Healing Damaged Emotions,* speaks of the "tyranny of the oughts." "Should I have said that?" "Why did I say that?" "Should I have just remained silent?" "What should I have said instead?"[17]

Today I generally conclude if I meant well and no one was offended, I'm not going to waste time and energy second-guessing myself.

Romans 8:1 reminds us "there is no condemnation for those who are in Christ Jesus." When I slip back into those old habits, I simply remind myself God is big enough to handle my well-intended mistakes and I move on. Sometimes more quickly than others.

PERFECTIONISM AND CONTEMPT

Perfectionism

Adult survivors of childhood abuse and neglect can become depressed and angry with themselves for not living up to their own legalistic standards of perfection. Even when they do measure up, there is no real sense of accomplishment as the bar always magically rises to a higher level. Anger toward God often follows as He, from their distorted point of view, demands more than they can possibly deliver.

Upon the rare occasion when a perfectionist does measure up, they can be prideful, obnoxious braggarts. Only those individuals with low self-esteem feel the need to point out their accomplishments to others. I have had the dubious privilege of reminding myself of this upon numerous occasions. "Let someone else praise you . . . and not your own lips" (Proverbs 27:2).

When I first read about perfectionism I thought that cannot be me. Just walk through my house. There are stacks of books everywhere. But that isn't what's meant. Perfectionism is requiring more of yourself than you can reasonably deliver. That was and sometimes still is me.

Contempt or Judgmentalism

Not only do adult survivors of abuse or neglect often expect perfection of themselves, but of everyone else as well. Holding others to a standard of perfection can place an enormous strain on relationships. Why should I hold others to a standard that I cannot attain? Jesus condemned the Pharisees for doing this very thing when they laid heavy burdens on men's shoulders that they themselves were not willing to carry (Matthew 23:4).

When I become critical or contemptuous of others, because they "don't measure up," Romans 14:4 often comes to mind: "Who are you to judge someone else's servant? To their own master, servants stand or fall. And they will stand, for the Lord is able to make them stand." Similarly Romans 14:13 says, "Therefore let us stop passing judgment on one another. Instead, make up your mind not to put any stumbling block or obstacle in the way of a brother or sister."

Countering wrong thinking with truth from the Scriptures is an effective response to judgmentalism, contempt and a myriad other sins

SELF-SUFFICIENCY OR INDEPENDENCE AND WORKAHOLISM

Self-Sufficiency or Independence

Adult survivors of childhood neglect and abuse can become overly self-sufficient. As a child having seen I could not rely on the protection of others, I developed the perspective I could only depend on myself. This happened so gradually I was not aware it was a conscious decision.

Sadly, this unhealthy form of independence can lead to an inability to trust others on a deeper level and hinder the development of a trust relationship with God. It is also contrary to the functioning of the body of Christ (Ecclesiastes 4:9) and is a straight path to burn out which was where I eventually found myself.

First Corinthians 12:12-31, Romans 12:4-5 and 1 Peter 4:10 speak clearly of the interworking and interdependence of the body of Christ. From a biblical point of view, it is a turning from trusting God for protection to trusting myself, which is in effect, a form of idolatry (Proverbs 3:5-6).

Workaholism

Perfectionism and self-sufficiency can lead to workaholism. I found that I could not even make a decent showing of meeting my standard of perfection unless I worked late into the night on a regular basis. An unhealthy need to prove what a good Christian I was led to a life of over commitment and exhaustion.

Although I would upon occasion delegate responsibility to others, the work was rarely done to my satisfaction. When this occurred, I would often finish the job myself as I held a mental tirade about the incompetence and lack of responsibility of others.

If God the Father took a day of rest, I certainly need one, even though to this day I find it hard to take time off for rest and relaxation.

PASSIVE-AGGRESSIVE BEHAVIOR, REBELLION AND RATIONALIZATION

Passive-Aggressive Behavior

Passive-aggressive behavior is a subtle expression of hostility which can be characterized by any of the following: procrastination, controlling or resistant behaviors such as task avoidance, or sullen compliance.

An example would be an individual who doesn't want to do a task eventually complies but does it in such a way as to make sure everyone knows it is compliance under duress. Another example would be an individual who repeatedly arrives late for meetings they consider redundant. However, to say so could jeopardize their job so they resort to passive-aggressive behaviors.

A helpful article by Berit Brogaard D.M. Sci. Ph.D. on this topic is "*5* Signs That You're Dealing with a Passive-Aggressive Person and How to Respond Effectively" was posted in *Psychology Today.* [18]

Whereas the article contains practical suggestions, Matthew 5:23-24 tells us we are to reconcile with those whom we have offended or who have offended us, and we are to do it right away without delay. Reconciliation is so important it takes precedent over worship (Ephesians 4:26; Matthew 18:15). Don't be satisfied with "effective responses" alone. Make reconciliation your goal.

Rebellion

The opposite of passive-aggressive behavior is open rebellion. During almost 20 years of teaching in the juvenile justice system, I observed some children will develop a rebellious, prideful stance or an "I don't care" attitude, whereas, inside they care very much. Thinking such as, "You don't like my behavior, fine. I'll show you I don't need you. You can't tell me anything!" is not uncommon.

As adults we rarely verbalize such immature thoughts, but that doesn't keep us from thinking them, acting them out in passive-aggressive ways, and having our emotional energy sapped by them. They can also lead to outright rebellion such as divorcing which is an open statement of, "I do not need you." Scripture is very clear regarding God's view of rebellion as being like the sin of witchcraft (1 Samuel 15:23).

Rationalization

The American Psychological Association defines rationalization as "the act of justifying discreditable actions after the event."[19]

This defense mechanism is often used to explain or defend bad behavior by placing the blame at someone else's door. It goes something like this, "You're right, I did lose my temper, but it was you who started it by saying...." And the fight is on, but to what end? Nobody wins.

The roots of this behavior often lie in defense mechanisms developed during childhood. For example, a child who learns to control his parents through tantrums, may as an adult try to control his family through angry outbursts, then rationalize someone was pushing his/her buttons which caused the explosion.

Proverbs 21:2-4 points out self-righteousness and rationalization as sin.

LYING

Lying and Embellishment

Many who struggle with childhood feelings of inadequacy or not measuring up, will also struggle with lying. Desperate to appear successful, they manufacture interesting stories they hope will be believed and earn them respect in the eyes of others.

Interestingly the relative who abused me was known at his workplace as "Lying Nick." Since abusers in most cases were abused themselves as children, I have often wondered what happened to Nick to set him on the course that proved destructive for so many children. Even so, past experience in no way justifies present behavior.

I too struggled with lying and embellishment and still catch myself exaggerating, even to this day, then having to retract and tell it straight (Leviticus 19:11).

As a child and even into young adulthood, it was chronic. I lied when I didn't need to lie, even when it was obvious I was lying. My mother's treasured scarf and red velvet rose with the crystal dewdrop, one of the few nice things she owned, was found outside after a rainstorm. I was the only one who played with it. Yet, I lied.

PROJECTION

Projection or the Inability to Perceive Reality

When life is based on assumptions that are untrue such as God cannot love me or bad things would not have happened to me, perceiving reality can be difficult. Other people's motives are often questioned for no reason. Baseless negative assumptions or projections are made. (See Matthew 12:1-5 for an account of the Pharisees questioning Jesus about the Sabbath.)

For example, often at conferences I will enter a room where I know no one, only to find that everyone is talking in small groups. Rather than assume they cannot possibly be interested in me which is projecting my negative thoughts onto these unsuspecting individuals who don't even know I'm in the room, I can ask the Lord for guidance regarding which group I should join, approach that cluster and simply ask if I may join them and take it from there.

When I project my negative thoughts on others, it affects my ability to relate naturally. I come across as being guarded. This guardedness observed by others affects their response to me, which in turn, makes me feel even more insecure. I assume they are thinking negatively of me, when I started it the first place with my own negative projections.

In a recent article entitled "To Have a Friend: Overcome the Common Way Women Sabotage a Potential Friendship," writer and counselor Paula Rinehart provides a name for countering this dysfunction. It's called "taking back projections."[20]

Over the years, I have also learned not to enter a room or go to a meeting without praying, "Lord, lead me to someone whom I can encourage or someone who can encourage me." That prayer rarely goes unanswered.

I love the C.S. Lewis quote, "Humility is not thinking less of yourself, but thinking of yourself less."

SEEKING VALIDATION

Seeking Validation Through Transference

Transference is a validation seeking coping mechanism characterized by the redirection of childhood emotions from one person or object to another, often the transfer of feelings for a parent to a counselor.[21]

In a recent conversation with a friend who has invested many years on the field shepherding missionaries, she described validation as follows:

> "All children are born with a need for a close, affirming relationship with their parents. When it is missing, children of both genders will seek it all their lives. To experience validation or to feel valued is the God-given need of every little girl and boy. For a girl, this begins with a need to be valued

> by her father. If a young girl sees that her father loves and values her mother, the message is clear that women are valued. The effect is the same when a father cuddles his daughter, affirms her, makes her feel worthy. Through these experiences, she learns that she is valued and feels secure in his love. When this nurturing is missing, she will spend her whole life looking for it, searching for it, crying out for it in her soul."

A tragic result of a lack of validation can be transference to predators. This occurs when a young child is attracted to a pedophile who reminds them of a significant person in their life whose affection they were never able to obtain.

Transference, however, is not limited to children. When I finally sought help and met my counselor for the first time, I wanted to turn and flee. I felt drawn to this man whom I had never met and repulsed by him all at the same time, but I was clueless as to why.

Somehow, I got through the first counseling session and on the drive home, talked about my reaction with my husband. As we prayed and I reflected on what just happened, it soon became clear to me that the counselor reminded me of Nick; same build, same coloring, same hair, same outgoing personality. Those characteristics were a trigger taking me back to my childhood and the emotional conflict I faced. At the same time, he reminded me of my father. Undoubtedly the similarities between Nick and my father's appearance contributed to Nick's power over me as a child.

Fortunately, counselors are trained to deal with transference, and when I shared my reaction with my counselor during our next session, I gained insight into how to respond to those triggers which are shared at the end of this chapter.

Young women who are attracted to older caring men are often seeking their father and sadly fall into intimate relationships without understanding why.

Transference, however, can also be to places or situations that trigger feelings of unease or panic.

One hot summer day as my late husband Louis and I were driving through a small East Texas town en route to a conference, I scanned the storefronts looking for a place where we could get something cold to drink. Suddenly before me stood a grocery store straight out of the early 50s. My chest tightened. I had difficulty breathing. I wondered if I was having a heart attack.

Then I realized the storefront was identical to the one where Nick took his children and me for ice cream. Just inside the sagging double screen doors would be a large red rectangular cooler with Coca-Cola written on the front in fancy script. Another silver cooler with sliding glass doors on top would be standing next to it filled with popsicles and ice cream bars. There I was again where I had stood 30 years before peering over the top of the ice cream cooler hoping Nick would buy me ice cream too. Once I understood the cause of my panic, I was OK. The fear was gone.

Another example of transference can be experiencing discomfort when someone gives an innocent hug or even a pat on the arm or back. If caught off guard, that can still feel strange to me although I can now receive such gestures with grace and no longer silently scream, "Don't touch me."

Responding to Transference

- If the transference is to a counselor, share it immediately with him or her. They are trained to help clients understand transference and counter it.
- Share it with a good friend, spouse or mentor.
- Examine ways in which the two individuals are alike and different.
- Pray asking the Lord to enter the situation and enable you to understand what is happening, what you can learn from it and how you can best respond.

SEEKING VALIDATION THROUGH PEOPLE PLEASING

A people pleaser is someone whose life revolves around taking care of the needs of others. This dysfunction is typically rooted in fear of rejection or failure stemming from childhood relationships in which love and acceptance were conditional.[22]

Although people pleasers can be highly productive in their careers, burnout is ever a danger as they seldom practice self-care. Codependence and passive-aggressive behaviors can also result from people pleasing behaviors.

Having the attention and gaining the affection of my father was so important to me that I remember as a young child making mental lists of things I could do to gain his approval.

In high school and college, I was desperate to be part of the in-crowd. To be accepted, I was expected to freely participate in one-night stands. Fortunately, on that front, I decided the price was just too high to pay. I simply refused.

Later when I was being discipled by a parachurch group, I memorized my verses and did over and beyond the expected, not for the sake of growing closer to the Lord but to gain respect and acceptance in the eyes of my leaders.

When I worked as a nanny, I did my work 200 percent. There was never anything for the parents to complain about, yet inside I felt resentment that they didn't appreciate that 200 percent, and I never felt I measured up to their expectations.

Not once did it occur to me the reason lay within me and had nothing to do with my host family's expectations. Had I discussed these frustrations with them, much misunderstanding on my part might have been avoided.

Scripture is clear about the danger of people pleasing. Proverbs tells us, "Fear of man will prove to be a snare, but whoever trusts in the LORD is kept safe" (Proverbs 29:25). In addition, the apostle Paul in Galatians 1:10b says of himself, "If I were still trying to please people, I would not be a servant of Christ."

SEEKING VALIDATION THROUGH CODEPENDENCE

In the past when I thought of codependency, I thought of spouses of individuals with chemical dependency. I didn't think of myself. That is until I read Melody Beattie's book, *Codependent No More.* The author described individuals who were so obsessed with caring for others that they neglected their own needs.[23]

Could that be me? I wondered. *Weren't my acts of service for others, acts of Christian charity?* As I continued to read, I concluded, *Maybe they were, maybe they weren't.*

It all had to do with motivation. *Was I serving to pump up my sagging self-esteem and make others think more highly of me, or was I helping because it was the right thing to do at that time?* [24]

As I read further, I thought, *Was my goal the happiness of those around me? Did I take things personally and become defensive? Did I struggle with guilt, shame and fear? Did I fear being who I was, whoever that was, as I wasn't at all sure what I thought or felt much of the time? I was too preoccupied with trying to figure out what others were thinking, feeling or needing, so I could make them feel better. Did I take on the responsibility of others, enabling them to live irresponsibly? Did I help where help wasn't needed? Did I try to fix things that didn't need fixing? Did I do so much for others that I began to resent them not doing those things for themselves? Did I lose sleep trying to figure out how to fix other people without even once thinking I might be the one who needed fixing?*[25]

The answer to all was, "Yes," a resounding, "Yes!" As I looked back over the list of characteristics, several things stood out to me. Although I was a committed Christian, public school teacher and minister's wife, I never really felt good about myself. There was always some area of my life I was concerned about, usually something beyond my control.

For example, one of my students might not be doing well in school and blame me even though no homework was handed in and test scores were low. I would lay awake at night trying to figure out how to motivate that student to bring up his grades, lest my supervisor call me on the carpet for having a failing student.

Or I might have finally risked sharing something personal at a Bible study only to be met with an embarrassed silence which shouted, "We don't want to know that about you, and we aren't telling you anything personal about us!" On the other hand, it could have been something as benign as someone at church or school not speaking to me or bringing up a contraposition to something I shared in a discussion, all of which would leave me feeling inadequate.

People who grew up in a state of fight, flight or freeze often have difficulty relaxing, and find themselves jumping at any problem that "needs" solving. Often referred to as being a "Crisis Junky," this is a form of codependency and needs to be recognized and treated as such.

By the end of the fourth chapter of *Codependent No More*, I knew the problem was my miserable view of myself, and I knew the source; years of childhood abuse, but I didn't know what to do about it. I would pray through verses such as Psalm 27:1, "The Lord is my light and my salvation—whom shall I fear?" and my heart would respond, "I fear everyone and everything."

As I continued reading, I realized I felt happiest when there was a crisis to solve because it made me feel important. I who felt I was the lowest of the low, could be a hero, step in and help solve a problem. This realization made me ill, but I also knew that once I knew what the problem was, I could begin to change.

I started on my knees praying, "Lord Jesus, I don't want to live like this. I am tired of being the universal mother, taking care of everyone, depressed because I can't do it all and continually exhausted." That prayer marked the beginning of a new direction.

These are the principles that have and are helping me change:

- Stop being reactive, bouncing from one crisis to another. When there is a crisis, my immediate response is, "Let's take care of this." The problem is, I may be depriving someone of an opportunity to take responsibility or to learn from their mistakes.

- Regarding relationships, I need to be very clear in my own mind about what I want from a relationship and what I can bring to it. This needs to be communicated; otherwise, it is too easy to fall back into old patterns of taking care of everyone except myself.

- My spiritual gifts are serving and compassion. However, the shadow side of these gifts is codependence. By weighing situations and making a conscious decision to seek God's direction before jumping in to serve, I am learning to avoid this pitfall and finding new freedom in the Lord.

- Stop trying to control the universe or more specifically, everyone I love. Besides, the more I preach, the less they hear.[26]

INTELLECTUALIZATION

Intellectualization has been defined as avoiding emotions by focusing on facts and logic.[27] This was my practice when our daughter became terribly ill at age five. I just refused to feel. I had a sick child who needed constant attention, and I didn't have time to give in to my emotions. As a result, I stuffed them until I was on the verge of losing touch with reality.

Another form of intellectualization is thinking, "If I can just understand why this is happening, it won't hurt so much." When my late husband was diagnosed with a deadly disease and died 15 months later, I kept thinking, "If I could just make sense of this. If I could see purpose in it, I could more easily accept his sudden illness and death." However, I eventually realized some things cannot be understood. They simply must be accepted.

"Trust in the LORD with all your heart and lean not on your own understanding" (Proverbs 3:5).

REGRESSION

Regression is defined as a reversion to behaviors of an earlier period in life during times of duress. Adults who were abused or neglected as small children are often searching for a "parent" who will protect them and take care of them.

I have observed that I tend to revert to coping mechanisms adopted as a child when I am disappointed in someone dear to me. I pull back and remind myself, "I can do just fine without their help."

Rather than share my hurt, I withdraw emotionally. This is a terribly dysfunctional way of handling hurt and disappointment. Spending time in prayer seeking to understand if my expectations are realistic and then speaking the truth in love after things have calmed down is often helpful.

When trauma or hurt occurs at a young age, the individual can become emotionally "stuck" at that age, expressing anger like a small child and even throwing temper tantrums. When that happens, it's time to go back to that age and see what got them stuck there.

In conclusion, Susan Krauss Whitbourne authored an article entitled "The Essential Guide to Defense Mechanisms," published in *Psychology Today.* The article lists the ten most common dysfunctional coping mechanisms. It is impossible to address your own defense mechanisms unless you know what they are.[28]

An extensive list of defense mechanisms is presented in an article entitled "Coping Mechanisms." The list is interactive and includes positive as well as negative coping mechanisms with examples. *http://changingminds.org/explanations/behaviors/coping/coping.htm* .

RESPONSE

DENIAL AND DEFENSIVENESS

Denial

1 Why do you think denial would be an issue with childhood trauma victims?

2 How does John 8:31b-32 speak to the area of denial: "If you hold to my teaching, you are really my disciples. Then you will know the truth, and the truth will set you free"?

3 Why might some people feel so uncomfortable when anything regarding abuse is shared, no matter how discretely?

4 Have you had the experience of being told by a well-meaning individual that you need to put childhood trauma behind you and move on? If so, how did their response affect you?

5 Why would denial be one of the most frustrating dysfunctional coping mechanisms for a therapist?

6 Have you found the following to be true in your life? "Those who struggle with denial often wear a mask of self-righteousness, pretending everything is 'just fine' when nothing could be further from the truth."

7 Why do you think this would be the case? What affect would this have on healing woundedness?

Defensiveness

8 Already struggling with feelings of inferiority, survivors of childhood trauma find it difficult to accept constructive criticism or critique as it feels like a frontal assault.

▸ Has this been your experience? If so how do you respond knowing that there can be an element of truth in critique even if it feels unjust?

9 Tim Keller, author of *Walking with God through Pain and Suffering*, suggests that when we feel hurt, we should ask ourselves what personal need we are looking to people to fulfill that only God can meet. How might this be helpful?[29]

SELF-DEPRECATION AND SELF-CONDEMNATION

10 Scripture tells us we are so valued that we have been adopted into the family of God and are accepted in the beloved (Ephesians 1:5-6; Romans 8:1).

▸ In light of the above, are we not disregarding the saving/sanctifying work of Christ when we engage in self-deprecation and condemnation? Explain.

11 Self-condemnation is often the result of a prevailing sense of guilt and insecurity. David Seamands in his book, *Healing Damaged Emotions*, speaks of the "tyranny of the oughts" exemplified by thinking, "I ought to do this, I should have done that."

▸ In what situations are you inclined to terrorize yourself with the "tyranny of the oughts?"[30]

▸ How do you counter this inclination? What does Romans 8:1 have to say to this?

PERFECTIONISM AND CONTEMPT

12 Is perfectionism, meaning "requiring more of yourself than you can reasonably deliver," an issue in your life. If so, in what way?

13 Do you sometimes hold others to a standard that you cannot attain (Matthew 23:4)?

14 What should our attitude be toward judging the behavior of others (Romans 14:4, 13)?

SELF-SUFFICIENCY OR INDEPENDENCE AND WORKAHOLISM

15 Many who experience trauma related to abuse and neglect develop the perspective that they can rely only on themselves. Workaholism follows as no one can be trusted to follow through.

▸ Does this resonate with your experience?

16 What affect might this have on the interworking and interdependence of the body of Christ and trust in God the Father (1 Corinthians 12:12-31; Romans 12:4-5; 1 Peter 4:10)?

▸ In addition, putting our trust in anything other than God is a form of idolatry. Can you share an example of this from your life?

PASSIVE-AGGRESSIVE BEHAVIOR, REBELLION AND RATIONALIZATION

17 Passive-aggressive behavior is a subtle expression of hostility characterized by: procrastination, controlling or resistant behaviors such as task avoidance, or sullen compliance, all of which flies in the face of Matthew 5:23-24 and 18:15.

▸ Does any of this ring true in your life?

▸ How do you counter it? See Matthew 5:23, 24; Colossians 3:13; Matthew 18:15-17.

18 The opposite of passive-aggressive behavior is open rebellion. Scripture is very clear regarding God's view of rebellion as being like the sin of witchcraft (1 Samuel 15:23).

▸ Is open rebellion an issue in your life?

▸ How are you dealing with it?

19 The American Psychological Association defines rationalization as "the act of justifying discreditable actions after the event (generally by placing the blame at someone else's door)."[31]

▸ Any resonance here (Proverb 21:2)? Explain your method of addressing this issue.

20 Why might lying be an issue for a child experiencing trauma and struggling with issues of inferiority?

PROJECTION OR THE INABILITY TO PERCEIVE REALITY

21 When life is based on false assumption, perceiving reality can be difficult.

▸ Are there areas in your life where perceiving reality might be difficult? Perhaps in groundless questioning of people's motives or general distrust? Explain.

SEEKING VALIDATION THROUGH TRANSFERENCE

22 Transference is a validation seeking coping mechanism characterized by the redirection of childhood emotions from one person or object to another.[32]

▸ Have you experienced transference from a parent or other individual whose affection you sought to someone else? A stranger? A predator? A counselor? A father figure? A place? Explain.

SEEKING VALIDATION THROUGH PEOPLE PLEASING

23 A people pleaser is someone whose life revolves around taking care of the needs of others. This dysfunction is typically rooted in fear of rejection or failure stemming from childhood relationships in which love and acceptance were conditional.[33]

▸ Has this coping mechanism been an issue in your life? Explain.

SEEKING VALIDATION THROUGH CODEPENDENCE

24 The author writes, "Codependence has to do with motivation. *Do I serve others to pump up my sagging self-esteem and make them think more highly of me, or do I get involved because it is the right thing to do at that time?*"[34]

▸ Is codependence an issue in your life? How do you determine the difference between God leading you to get involved and your simply being an enabler?

INTELLECTUALIZATION

25 One form of intellectualization is thinking, "If I can just understand why this is happening, it won't hurt so much. However, I eventually realized some things cannot be understood. They simply must be accepted."

▸ Have you struggled with understanding that which isn't understandable from our finite perspective? Explain.

▸ How did you finally come to peace (Isaiah 55:8-9)?

▸ How does Proverbs 3:5 speak to intellectualization.

"Trust in the LORD with all your heart and lean not on your own understanding. In all your ways acknowledge Him..." (Proverbs 3:5).

REGRESSION

26 Regression is defined as a reversion to behaviors of an earlier period during times of duress.[35]

▸ Individuals who experienced trauma at a young age can get stuck there emotionally and during periods of stress revert to coping mechanisms implemented at that age. Examples might include childish temper tantrums, sulking or acting helpless. List examples from your life. How do you counter them

PART III
STRATEGIES THAT WORK

HEALING PREREQUISITE

In John 5:6 Jesus asked the lame man sitting by the pool of Bethesda, "Do you want to be healed?" Those who heard must have thought, "Jesus, are you crazy? He's been lame for 38 years. Of course, he wants to be healed." But did he?

In my mid-thirties when I finally sought counseling for the abuse I had experienced as a small child, I remember the surge of relief that washed over me when my counselor said, "The emotional struggles that you are experiencing are directly related to the abuse you experienced as a child. Given the harm, they are understandable." Having thought all those years that my struggles had to be related to some deep character flaw or mental illness, I felt like shouting from the rooftops, "I'm not crazy. There is a reason for all these years of depression."

For the first time in my life, someone understood. That reassurance enveloped me like a warm blanket. But then, almost immediately, the Lord spoke to my heart, "But, do you want to be healed?"

At first, I was shocked by the question. Then as I thought about it, I realized I had been comfortable in my dysfunction. Being a martyr from doing too much for others had given me a sense of pride and superiority. That realization sickened me and my answer to the Lord was clear, "Yes, I want to be healed. Where do I begin?" The answer was immediate, "Start with forgiveness."

RESPONSE

HEALING PREREQUISITE

1. Have you given serious thought to the question, "Do you want to be healed from your emotional woundedness?"

    - How do you answer that question?

2. What steps have you taken to move toward healing?

3. What steps do you still need to take?

CHAPTER 13
EFFECTIVE STRATEGIES FOR HEALING

FORGIVENESS: A MAJOR STEP IN HEALING

Forgiveness can seem impossible. How can someone be forgiven who refused to acknowledge wrongdoing? How could I forgive Nick who did this to me, to my husband, to my children and all with whom I come in contact, for all are affected by that abuse?

Forgiveness, however, is something that God does through us when we ask that of Him. It is not a feeling that we conjure up. It is an act of obedience. God says forgive other people when they sin against you. But He doesn't stop there. He says that our forgiveness is dependent upon our forgiving others (Matthew 6:14-15).

Carrying unforgiveness breeds a victim mentality and can easily lead to a root of bitterness which can mar all of our relationships even further and stunt spiritual growth (Hebrews 12:15). It has been said that a lack of forgiveness is like drinking poison and expecting the other person to die. It poisons us, poisons our outlook on life, our present and our future.

I told God that I felt like the whole thing was unfair and I didn't feel like forgiving anyone. However, I certainly wanted to be forgiven of my own sins so I would do the best I could, and God would have to do the rest.

I then asked God to work that forgiveness in my heart and I made a list of all the people I needed to forgive. My name was at the top of the list. Among other things, I needed to forgive the child who was my former self for not "telling," for not avoiding contact with Nick at all cost, but mainly for not getting help sooner than I did as an adult. I also needed to forgive my husband for not seeking help for both of us. I needed to forgive the perpetrator Nick, Cousin Josie for not protecting me or informing my parents, and I needed to forgive my parents for their lack of vigilance. However, most of all I had to "forgive" God for allowing the abuse to happen in the first place.

Whereas I know **God does not need forgiveness as He does not sin**, for years I struggled with, "How could God let this happen, not only to me but to all the other innocent, unprotected children in the world?" Theologians have struggled with this question for millennia, and I know it is unlikely I will bring any new insight to the discussion. I only know that God in His wisdom chose to give mankind freedom of choice. An inescapable implication of freedom of choice is the freedom to choose to do evil. If individuals have freedom to choose, some will choose evil.

Finally I could pray, "Lord I forgive myself for not seeking help sooner and thinking that I could handle the fallout from abuse on my own. I forgive my parents for not protecting me, Cousin Josie for remaining silent and Nick, difficult though it is, I forgive him too, and I pray for the other victims that they too might experience relief from the suffering these acts have brought into their lives."

Then I continued through the list and verbally forgave each person listed there. I even said the words, "Lord, I forgive you for allowing this to happen," even though He needed no forgiveness as all He allows comes from a heart of love. Then I left the rest to Him.

Sometime later when I thought back on that event, it occurred to me instead of feeling resentment toward Nick who had been the source of so much loss and suffering, I began to wonder what happened in his childhood to produce such unmitigated abuse of little children. I found myself feeling sad for the small child who had been Nick and who had never been freed.

In Ephesians 1:11 God is referred to as the one who "works out everything in conformity with the purpose of his will." This text does not say that everything is His will, it says He takes what happens and works it out so that it will contribute toward His purposes. The more familiar Romans 8:28 says the same thing, "And we know that in all things God works for the good of those who love him, who have been called according to his purpose." For me and many others, this has been and may continue to be a long, arduous journey; however, good will result in the end. We have His promise. He does work all things for good for those who are called according to His purpose. The implication of the next verse (verse 29) together with Romans 8:28 is God will use these terrible events to conform us to the image of Christ.

Job never knew why he suffered. Even when God answered him, He didn't tell him why the suffering had occurred. We may never know either, but we do know that God can take the vilest of circumstances and use them for His purposes. Satan meant the abuse to destroy. God is using it to work healing in my life and the lives of others.

UNDERSTANDING THE ROLE OF JESUS AND THE HOLY SPIRIT

Hebrews 4:15 tells us, "For we do not have a high priest who is unable to empathize with our weaknesses, but we have one who has been tempted in every way, just as we are—yet he did not sin."

Jesus our high priest knows every hurt, every insecurity and every loss, including those caused by abuse and neglect. He understands fully because He suffered every humiliation thinkable from being vilified by the Pharisees to being crucified and left to hang on a cross while His mockers looked on in jeering triumph.

As our high priest, He provided the final sacrifice for our sins (Hebrews 2:17). He also bore the fallout from all of our pain and trauma and not only ours, but that of the whole world. Then He sat down at the right hand of God where He intercedes for us (Romans 8:34).

Out of His understanding of our suffering and the burdens we carry, He sent the Holy Spirit as our comforter and guide (John 15:26, 14:16-18).

The Holy Spirit helps us in our areas of weakness (Romans 8:26) which includes all our fears, insecurities and misconceptions regarding God, ourselves and others.

The awareness that believers suffer from such areas of weakness unrelated to sin is not a new concept. John Fletcher, a contemporary of John Wesley, wrote in the mid-1600s concerning parishioners who "bind heavy burdens on themselves of their own making [perfectionism] and when they cannot bear them, they are tormented with guilt." Wesley, himself wrote of those who, "continually condemn themselves without cause [self-deprecation, condemnation, self-contempt] imagining things to be sinful where Scripture nowhere condemns it, supposing other things to be their duty [codependence, perfectionism, workaholism and people pleasing] where Scripture nowhere enjoins it." Thankfully in these and in other areas of dysfunction, we have the aid of the Holy Spirit.[36]

When Jesus told His disciples of His impending departure, He also told them He would not leave them comfortless but would send a comforter from the Father, the Holy Spirit, the Advocate, the Spirit of truth (John 15:26, 14:17). In John 16:13, the Spirit is referred to as the one who will guide us into all truth. Can anything be more comforting, or more frightening, than knowing the Holy Spirit will reveal to us truth about ourselves? However, the Spirit doesn't stop there. He will also guide us into how to deal with that truth regarding our own sin and weakness, not revealing more than we can handle at any given time. His revelation is given in measure according to where we are emotionally and spiritually (John 16:12).

Individuals who have experienced abuse and neglect often struggle with perceiving reality. They tend to second-guess their decisions as well as those of others. Relying on the Holy Spirit for guidance "into all truth," subjective though it may sound, can add peace and confidence that would otherwise be sadly missing. See Rusty Rustenbach's *Listening and Healing Prayer,*[37] as well as Dallas Willard's *Hearing God: Developing a Conversational Relationship with God.*[38]

In addition, the Spirit also helps us in our areas of weakness and prays on our behalf when we are so distraught that we cannot formulate words (Romans 8:26). In verse 27 we are told that the Spirit prays for us "in accordance with the will of God."

David Seamands illuminates Romans 8:26 through a word study of *paraclete,* the Greek word for Holy Spirit. *Para* means "alongside," and *kaleo* means "to call." A paraphrase could be: "I will send you one whom you can call upon who will come alongside and help you with your infirmities and weaknesses."[39]

The Greek word for *help* in Romans 8:26 is a combination of three words *sun-* "along with or together," *anti*-"on the opposite side" and *lumbano*-"to take hold of." Taken together *sunantilumbano* means "to take hold of together with us on the other side." We have a helper, the Holy Spirit, who will come alongside and help us carry, sort out and deal with our burdens. [40]

THE ROLE OF SPIRITUAL DISCIPLINES

As a young Christian and for many years afterward, the practice of spiritual disciplines was merely another attempt on my part to gain standing in the eyes of God and my spiritual mentors.

Contrary to my early understanding, the real purpose of spiritual disciplines is to draw near to God, learn of His character and love, get to know Him deeply, and become more like Christ. James 4:8a tells us, "Come near to God and he will come near to you."

The better we know God, the more we experience His love and presence, the faster we heal, the stronger we become, the deeper our faith grows, and the more Christlike we become. Consider Romans 8:28-29 and 2 Corinthians 3:16-18. That being said, don't expect hot house fruit. Spiritual growth takes time. Healing takes time.

RESPONSE

FORGIVENESS: A MAJOR STEP IN HEALING

1 Review the section on forgiveness noticing what forgiveness is and isn't.

▸ What steps have you already taken toward forgiving those responsible for neglect and/or abuse during your childhood?

2 Ask the Lord for guidance in making a list of those whom you still need to forgive.

▸ Go through the list with the Lord asking Him to work forgiveness in your heart for each person, then as you can, say the words: "I forgive ___________for _________, filling in the blanks"

▸ Don't expect to feel warm fuzzies toward the person you are forgiving. Remember forgiveness is something God works in us. It isn't about how we feel toward them; it isn't about letting them off the hook. Your relationship with those who mistreated you may not change outwardly. You may still need to protect yourself from the forgiven individual and in time, you may need to confront them. This is about gaining freedom through forgiveness. It is about being obedient (Matthew 6:14; Luke 17:3-4). It is about asking God to work forgiveness in your heart.

UNDERSTANDING THE ROLE OF JESUS AND THE HOLY SPIRIT

3 Have you received Jesus' gift of redemption provided through His sacrificial death (Hebrew 9:12)? Before we can forgive others, we must seek forgiveness from Jesus. Not that we were complicit in any abuse perpetrated against us, but we all sin in various other ways and need forgiveness.

4 Hebrews 4:15-16 tells us that Jesus sympathizes fully with our weakness for He has been tempted just as we have been, yet without sin. This God/Man, Jesus, can understand and help with any problems or concerns that we bring to Him. Furthermore, He tells us to bring these issues to Him without hesitation and we will receive help.

▸ How do you respond to having direct access to Jesus and His promise that we will receive grace to help in time of need?

5 What do the following verses tell you about the role of the Holy Spirit: Romans 8:26; John 14:16-18, 16:5-15?

THE ROLE OF SPIRITUAL DISCIPLINES

6 Although spiritual growth is a work of the Holy Spirit, it also requires work on our part. Describe this required "work on our part" as it relates to the spiritual disciplines.

CHAPTER 14
SPIRITUAL DISCIPLINES

DAILY DEVOTIONS

Whereas being a part of a vibrant church fellowship of local believers is essential, it isn't enough. Do you want to grow your faith? Romans 10:17 tells us our faith grows through exposure to the Word of God. Although this includes hearing exposition of the Word, personal reading, study and Scripture memory are essential as well if we are to be equipped to minister deeply in the lives of others. This requires setting priorities and investing time and effort. For mothers of young children, it also requires grabbing those minutes as you can.

One young missionary mom of four homeschooled children began incorporating a daily "Quiet Time" in her children's schedule. When it was time for her daily devotions, she reminded her children that it was time for them to read or play quietly for the next half hour. Immediately, they scrambled to find their favorite book or game as they settled down in various corners.

When I was the caregiver for my late husband who at the time was terminally ill, I would grab a few minutes to read until I found a verse that spoke to my heart. Being exhausted from sorrow, stress and lack of sleep, I could never remember the verse that had spoken to me, but desperately needing it, I left the Bible open on the counter with the verse marked, and glanced at it as a reminder as I passed by. No matter how difficult the circumstances, a way can be found to spend at least a few minutes of time in the Word on a regular basis.

I find that I gain more from my time in reading the Word if I underline those portions that speak to me, then journal my thoughts in a document or journal. Periodically, I read through past journal entries looking for trends that indicate how God is leading me or has been working in my heart over time.

One of my personal goals is to have a well-marked Bible to leave to each of my children and grandchildren. I want them to know years from now, perhaps generations from now, the meaning that the Word of God had in my life and can have in theirs.

The study of God's Word is essential if we are to grow to maturity. If there isn't a Bible study in your local church, Bible Study Fellowship is in most cities across America and in many foreign countries. If you can't find a study, recruit a friend and start one yourself. You will learn even more if you prepare and lead it yourself. Second Timothy 2:15 reminds us of the importance of studying God's Word so that we can teach it accurately, "Do your best to present yourself to God as one approved, a worker . . . who correctly handles the word of truth." This only comes through regular intake of the Word of God.

Studying the Word of God on a regular basis and applying it to your life will begin to generate healing, give perspective and bring peace. Innumerable times I have observed in my own life as well as in the lives of others, a direct correlation between the amount of time spent in the Word and the present level of peace as opposed to anxiety. This makes sense as Psalm 119:165a tells us, "Great peace have those who love your law" and Jeremiah 15:16 tells us that the Word of God brings joy and delight to our hearts.

Because there are so many excellent books written on the subject of spiritual disciplines and spiritual formation, I have only included cursory coverage on the topic of personal devotions. Foster and Griffin's, *Spiritual Classics*, is a good place to begin (see Reading List for other suggestions). However, the main thing is get started, just you and your Bible and a computer document or notebook for your journal. Whenever possible, have your devotions the same time and place every day. Keep a notepad at hand to write down things that pop into your mind that you must take care of later. This will help you stay focused.

Enjoy your time alone with the Lord. Begin by asking the Lord to speak to your heart, remind you of any unconfessed sin, and then calm your heart. Read the Word and take notes on anything that stands out to you. Share your joys and burdens with the Lord but don't stop there. Share what you have learned with someone else and offer to read the Word with them as well.

LISTENING AND HEALING PRAYER

The Scriptures tell us to pray without ceasing, to pray for government leaders, for those in spiritual leadership, for our enemies and for anything that concerns us (1 Thessalonians 5:17; 1 Timothy 2:1-2, 3:1-16; Philippians 1:19; Matthew 5:44). We are to offer up prayers of praise, adoration and thanksgiving, supplication and confession (1 Chronicles 16:23-31; Philippians 4:6; James 5:16; Colossians 3:16-21; 1 John 1:9). Why? Because God needs the attention? No, because we need the reminder that He is ever present, all powerful, in control, and concerned about that which concerns us. He also answers those prayers: "Yes, no, or silence," which I have often found means, "Wait!"

When we bring concerns before the Lord focusing our minds on His power and care for us as well as His resources for working the worst of circumstances into something good, it changes us. Even in the midst of pain and suffering, we can experience joy and peace (John 14:27). Yet that joy and peace can be short lived unless we consistently practice the disciplines (1 Thessalonians 5:17).

Although it is crucial that we pour our hearts out before God with all of our frustrations, fears and pain, do not let yourself get stuck in a negative loop bewailing circumstances you or others are facing. Thank God that although you see no potential for good, you know it is there as He has allowed the trials to come and promises to use them for good (Ephesians 1:11, 2 Corinthians 1:8-9).

After thanking God that He will indeed use these negative circumstances for good, focus on praying through Scripture. Pray through one of the prayers of Jesus, Psalms or the prayers of Paul found in the epistles. They are all wonderful models for prayer. If ever at a loss as to what you can pray for yourself or someone else, pray Paul's prayers (Ephesians 1:3, 17-19, 3:16-19; 2 Corinthians 13:7; Philippians 1:9-11; Romans 15:5-6; 1 Thessalonians 3:9-10, 5:23-24). Nothing pulls me out of despondency like praying through Scripture.

Another form of prayer that has been used for healing in the lives of many including myself, has been the practice of Listening and Healing Prayer as described in Rusty Rustenbach's book of the same title.[41] It is a user-friendly comprehensive guide to conversing with God and even more importantly being still before God and listening. Dallas Willard's *Hearing God* can also be a helpful resource.

Although Listening Prayer can be subjective, consulting with a spiritual leader who knows you well and makes sure that your answers are aligned with Scripture will serve as protection. The practice of these biblical principles has been life changing for me.

FELLOWSHIP IN THE BODY OF CHRIST

Hebrews 10:24-25, a cornerstone for defining Christian fellowship, reads as follows, "And let us consider how we may spur one another on toward love and good deeds, not giving up meeting together, as some are in the habit of doing, but encouraging one another—and all the more as you see the Day [of Christ's return] approaching."

Wuest in *Word Studies in the Greek New Testament* translates this passage as, "Let us constantly be giving careful attention to one another for the purpose of stimulating one another to love and good works."[42]

Putting this into practice would include prayerful preparation as well as conversation centered around sharing the Word, prayer and personal needs. Inviting Christian friends over for dinner and a game isn't Christian fellowship. Granted the former assumes a certain level of openness and commitment, but if all of what we define as fellowship is tailgate parties with friends from church, we've missed something. There is indeed place for the latter, but it should be balanced with times of thoughtful, purposeful conversation about spiritual issues and personal struggles.

The fellowship of those He was leaving behind was paramount in the mind of Christ the night before He died for He knew that their survival in the faith and the spread of the gospel depended on it. At the Last Supper, He shared the following with His disciples: "A new command I give you: Love one another. As I have loved you, so you must love one another. By this everyone will know that you are my disciples, if you love one another" (John 13:34-35).

It is interesting that the command to "love one another" is in the present active subjunctive which means, continuous action. We are to keep on loving one another. According to the lexicon, the subjunctive mood indicates doubt. Jesus knew we would fail but wanted us to keep on keeping on.

On the other hand, the verb form used in "as I have loved you," referring to Christ, is aorist active indicative, meaning action occurred and completed in the past. I love the beauty of this contrast. Jesus loved us completely in the past. It was completed then. Nothing will ever change His love for us. He doesn't have to keep on working on loving us. We have to keep on working on loving Him and each other.

Also, on the night before Christ died, He prayed fervently to the Father for the unity of the body. His words were: "I in them and you in me—so that they may be brought to complete unity. Then the world will know that you sent me and have loved them even as you have loved me" (John 17:23).

Note according to this verse, one reason this unity is so critical is that it is a witness to the world that Jesus is the Messiah. The spread of the gospel is dependent on our love for one another. This was also included in the Last Supper Discourse cited above, "Then the world will know that you sent me." Both references document Christ's final instructions to His disciples on the night before He died. They are of paramount importance and as such, are continually under attack by Satan whose goal is to destroy our witness to the world that Jesus is the Messiah (John 10:10).

Furthermore, Romans 12:10b encourages us to "honor one another above ourselves" rather than seeking honor for ourselves. When we are insecure in who we are in Christ, we tend to use our fellowship time to seek recognition for ourselves; to impress others with how spiritual we are. How fitting that the body of Christ should have as its goal honoring others; whereas, in this world and too often in the body itself, it is all about self-adulation.

In contrast, we are to speak the truth in love, walk in love, walk in the light, walk in unity, and share what we are learning in our spiritual walk with others in the body (Ephesians 5:2, Colossians 3:16-17 Philippians 2:1-4;1 John:1:7, James 5:16).

We are to devote ourselves "to the apostles' teaching and to fellowship, to the breaking of bread and to prayer" (Acts 2:42). We are to bear one another's burdens and "do good to all people" (Galatians 6:2, 10). However, this doesn't just happen each time we have a potluck. It requires a commitment to Christian fellowship. Again, consider Hebrews 10:24-25, which points out the need for us to give thought or to consider how we can encourage one another, or "how we may spur one another on" to "love and good deeds." This is a powerful witness to the world that Jesus is the Messiah, the Savior of the world.

Sadly, this is a far cry from the spaghetti feed that we often call fellowship. It isn't that which Christ brought before His disciples at the Lord's Supper and fervently prayed for the night before He died, and it isn't that which will result in a strong witness to the world that Jesus is the Messiah.

Over time my own view of Christian fellowship changed from a venue for displaying my spirituality to an opportunity to learn from others. I was full of questions: "What is the Lord speaking to you about these days? What are you learning in your walk with the Lord?" Some people were taken aback. But some, seeing the intent of my heart, were glad to answer my questions and feed my soul. As I grew in the Lord, my focus turned outward and I prayed, "Lord lead me to someone I can encourage in their walk with You and to someone who can encourage me." I continue that prayer to this day, and invariably He does.

THE IMPORTANCE OF SPIRITUAL GIFTS

The nurturing of the body of Christ in Christian fellowship is so important that God through the Holy Spirit gave each believer unique gifts for the purpose of building up or strengthening the body toward the goal of full maturity in Christ.

Although the following is a list of church offices, gifts are implied. In Ephesians 4:11-13, we read, "So Christ himself gave the apostles, the prophets, the evangelists, the pastors and teachers, to equip his people for works of service, so that the body of Christ may be built up until we all reach unity in the faith and in the knowledge of the Son of God and become mature, attaining to the whole measure of the fullness of Christ."

Romans 12:6-8 gives one list of spiritual gifts which includes prophesy, serving, teaching, encouragement, giving, leading and mercy. First Corinthians 12:8-10 adds the following: words of wisdom, words of knowledge, faith, gifts of healing, effecting of miracles, distinguishing between spirits, tongues, and the interpretation of tongues. First Corinthians 12:7 reminds us of the purpose of spiritual gifts. They are for the common good, for the building up of the body of Christ.

Also, 1 Corinthians 14:1 exhorts us to pursue the gift of prophesy. Although the gift of prophesy like the other gifts listed in 1 Corinthians 12 can be given individually by the Spirit of God (1 Corinthians 12:7-11), we are told that we can acquire the gift of prophesy and that we are to pursue it. But what exactly is this gift that we are commanded to pursue? In verse 3 of 1 Corinthians 14 NKJV, Paul says that the person who prophesies "edifies, exhorts and comforts" others in the body of Christ.

The basis of exercising the gift of prophesy is a growing knowledge of the Word of God for it is through the sharing of the Word that people are edified, exhorted and receive comfort.

What exactly is the meaning of edification, exhortation and comfort? A simple definition of edification is to build others up or strengthen them in the faith. Romans 10:17 tells us, "Consequently, faith comes from hearing the message, and the message is heard through the word about Christ." If we are to edify one another, we must have a growing knowledge of the Word of God which only comes from reading, study, memorization and hearing the Word taught and discussing what we are learning with mature believers.

Exhortation has been defined "to encourage to the point of action." As believers indwelt by the Spirit of God, we often know the truth upon which we need to act but need a push in the right direction to get started. As directed by the Spirit, speaking the truth in love is also a form of exhortation. "As iron sharpens iron, so one person sharpens another" (Proverbs 27:17).

However, comfort for believers is rooted in being heard. No one wants answers until they know they have been really heard. Then we can point them to the truth of Scripture.

In short, we are to use the gifts that God has given us through the Holy Spirit for the building up of the body of Christ. We are also to seek the gift of prophesy by studying God's Word and sharing it with others in the body as the Spirit directs for their edification, exhortation and comfort but first, we must actively listen to the thoughts and concerns of those whom we seek to help, otherwise our words, no matter how wise, will fall on deaf ears. These are not responsibilities reserved for pastors or counselors but are given to us all for the building up of the body of Christ.

ACCOUNTABILITY

Everyone needs a mentor with whom they can practice James 5:16, "Therefore confess your sins to each other and pray for each other so that you may be healed. The prayer of a righteous person is powerful and effective." This is a command, a command for our own good.

There is something about confessing or verbalizing struggles that often gives clarity and insight. For a problem to be solved, it must be identified. As believers in Christ, we have the guidance of the Holy Spirit as He guides us into all truth (John 16:13). That truth we are told in 2 Peter 1:3 is sufficient for life and godliness. However, there is also a need for someone to hold us accountable.

Ecclesiastes 4:9-10 tells us, "Two are better than one, because they have a good return for their labor: If either of them falls down, one can help the other up. But pity anyone who falls and has no one to help them up."

James 5:19b-20 continues this line of thought, "If one of you should wander from the truth and someone should bring that person back, remember this: "Whoever turns a sinner from the error of their way will save them from death and cover over a multitude of sins."

Individuals who have grown up believing lies, especially need someone who will help them identify those lies and counter them with truth. Believing lies can result in all sorts of errors, many of which have previously been identified as dysfunctional coping mechanisms.

This person in whom we confide needs to be chosen carefully. It must be someone who is trustworthy and mature in the Lord. They should also be of the same gender whenever possible. Timothy had Paul, David had Johnathan, the disciples had Jesus and each other. Who is your mentor?

SHARING MY FAITH

Sharing my faith was also an area I had to rethink. Having the misconception I could avoid disappointing God by sharing the gospel as often as possible, evangelism became a burden to me as well as to those with whom I shared.

As I studied the sovereignty of God, I began to realize if I asked, God would lead me to individuals whose hearts He had prepared.

Many times, I have seen that evangelism not supported by prayer will fail. It isn't enough to share the gospel with someone every day or every time we sit next to someone on a plane. We need to preface those events with prayer and preparation, "Lord, lead me to someone whose heart you have prepared and give me the words to share."

Having "the words to share" presupposes time spent in the Word, learning a simple gospel presentation and having "Jesus Stories" of God's work in my own life to share.

The first prerequisite, however, to sharing the gospel is listening to their story. On a plane or train, a simple question such as, "Are you headed home?" will often open the door to a conversation where one question leads to another until God opens a door of opportunity and I am able to share some aspect of my faith.

On a recent flight, I found myself sitting next to an associate professor of philosophy from a local state university. After several minutes of conversation initiated by the above question, he asked, "Are you going home to Seattle?"

In response, I was able to share that at one time, Seattle had been my home, but I had spent the last three years on the mission field. He shared that he was from a Christian background but had turned away from faith during his university studies. He talked at length, however, of his frustration with his students who had no real purpose or plan for their future. I silently prayed that God would guide our conversation and shared from my life as things came to mind. In the end, I asked if I could send him a copy of one of my favorite books, *The Reason for God*, by Tim Keller. Without hesitation, he immediately gave me his mailing address as well as his email address. At that point, I knew that God had gone before and prepared this young man's heart.

DISCIPLESHIP

Many volumes have been written by learned scholars on this topic. There is little hope that I will add anything new. However, keep in mind that Jesus' call to believers today is the same as that to His disciples 2,000 years ago in Matthew 4:19, "'Come, follow me,' Jesus said, 'and I will send you out to fish for people.'" His call to total commitment remains the same today as it was then. "Whoever wants to be my disciple must deny themselves and take up their cross and follow me. For whoever wants to save their life will lose it, but whoever loses their life for me will find it" (Matthew 16:24b-25). "Very truly I tell you, unless a kernel of wheat falls to the ground and dies, it remains only a single seed. But if it dies, it produces many seeds" (John 12:24).

We are to live a life of sacrifice and commitment, walking in a manner worthy of the Lord to please Him in all we do, providing an example for others to follow (Matthew 28:19-20; Colossians 1:10; 2 Timothy 2:2). We can only do this by the power of the Holy Spirit living within us as we walk in the light as He is in the light, confessing our sin, and again starting afresh (1 John 1:5-9).

Matthew 28:18b-20 (see also 2 Timothy 2:2) contains our job description. Jesus said, "All authority in heaven and on earth has been given to me. Therefore go and make disciples of all nations, baptizing them in the name of the Father and of the Son and of the Holy Spirit, and teaching them to obey everything I have commanded you. And surely I am with you always, to the very end of the age."

The Great Commission contains one verb and three participles. The verb "go' is second person plural. This is to be a community effort. One pastor translated it, "Y'all go." The three participles tell us what we are to do: make disciples, baptize them and teach them to obey all I have commanded you.

We cannot teach His commands unless we are actively reading and studying His Word and applying it to our lives. This requires time and discipline. For example, Paul says to his spiritual son, Timothy, "You then, my son, be strong in the grace that is in Christ Jesus. And the things you have heard me say in the presence of many witnesses entrust to reliable people who will also be qualified to teach others" (2 Timothy 2:1-2), which is followed by, "Do your best to present yourself to God as one approved, a worker who does not need to be ashamed and who correctly handles the word of truth" (2 Timothy 2:15).

Again, this is not possible unless we invest the time and discipline required to become daily students of the Word, and then step out in faith asking God to lead us to those whom He has prepared for us to disciple. Do not be surprised when those He leads you to disciple have a past similar to yours. Second Corinthians 1:3-4 clearly states that God comforts us in our difficulties so that we can comfort others with the same comfort we have received.

We disciple others with the backing of Christ who has been given all authority in heaven and earth, who will be with us to the end of the earth (Matthew 28:18-20). That is powerful! That gives us purpose as long as we draw breath. Furthermore, remember God wastes nothing. What we have learned from our life experiences not only strengthens us but equips us to help others.

AN ATTITUDE OF GRATITUDE AND PRAISE

Gratitude unlocks the fullness of life. It turns what we have into enough, and more. It turns denial into acceptance, chaos into order, confusion into clarity. It can turn a meal into a feast, a house into a home, a stranger into a friend (Melody Beattie).[43]

Gratitude and praise go together as an attitude of gratitude leads to praise. The Old and New Testaments are replete with admonitions to praise the Lord. A derivative of the words: praise, rejoice, bless the Lord and thankfulness appears nearly 900 times in the Old and New Testaments. The Lord clearly places a high priority on praise and gratitude. In contrast, salvation is mentioned 121 times.

Psalm 22:3 (KJV) says that God inhabits the praise of His people. I remember a house church meeting in a Paris suburb when during a time of praise, I looked up at the ceiling where I saw in my mind's eye hovering angels singing God's praise. It looked like the ceiling of the Sistine Chapel. It felt like I was standing at heaven's portal. God truly does inhabit the praise of His people.

In Psalm 134:1, there is a particular injunction to servants of the Lord and ministers to praise the name of the Lord, "Praise the LORD, all you servants of the LORD who minister by night in the house of the LORD."

Charles Spurgeon further explores the meaning of this verse in *The Treasury of David*, "Bless him for permitting you to serve him, fitting you to serve him and accepting your service. To be a servant of Jehovah is an incalculable honor, a blessing beyond all estimate." [44]

Paul describes rejoicing as a "safeguard" for us (Philippians 3:1). When we rejoice in the Lord, who He is and what He has done, our focus is on Him, His sovereignty, His character, and not on our problems. The problems remain, but they are seen through the lens of His possibilities and promise to "work all things for good" as we walk in His will. Praise lifts not only our vision but also our hearts. Tensions ease and stress seeps away.

I find the best way to praise God is by praying through Scripture. Psalms 34 and 145 through the end of the book are great psalms which are my "go to" passages for praise. However, my very favorite praise passage is God's answer to Job's complaint in Job 38:1-41. It's not a passage to pray through as much as it is a passage to read aloud and let your heart soar to the cadence of God's glory and power. But, the very best passages to pray through are the ones that leap from the page and speak to your heart during your times of devotion before the Lord.

When challenges or problems arise, it is easy to replay them repeatedly as we look for that elusive solution. Praise takes us out of that loop and gives our minds and souls a break even if it doesn't solve the problem. It also takes us out of the right side of our brain so we can think logically about possible solutions. [45]

When I am with someone whose soul is terribly burdened by a load impossible to bear, I ask if I may pray with them, specifically focusing prayer on God's love, understanding, presence and power to do that which we cannot. This often brings more comfort than all the words I could say.

Although it requires effort, we can develop an attitude of gratitude, thanking God that His plan is to work out everything according to the purpose of His will (Ephesians 1:11). Nothing that we experience is lost if we look to the Lord to reframe it for His purposes. He has also promised to complete the good work that He has begun in us before Christ returns (Philippians 1:6). That alone is cause for gratitude and praise.

RESPONSE

DAILY DISCIPLINES

1 Where are you strong in the area of Spiritual Disciplines?

2 Where do you need to work in order to continually apply 2 Timothy 2:15?

3 What practical steps will you take to accomplish this?

FELLOWSHIP IN THE BODY OF CHRIST

4 And let us consider how we may spur one another on toward love and good deeds, not giving up meeting together, as some are in the habit of doing, but encouraging one another—and all the more as you see the Day [of Christ's return] approaching." Hebrews 10:24-25

▸ Wuest in *Word Studies in the Greek New Testament* translates this passage as, "Let us constantly be giving careful attention to one another for the purpose of stimulating one another to love and good works."[46]

▸ How does fellowship as you experience it in your area of ministry compare to Hebrews 10:24-25?

▸ What are the strengths of the fellowship you experience?

▸ In what areas might it need further strengthening to more fully conform to Hebrews 10:24-25?

5 Is the fellowship in your ministry reflective of Christ's teaching on love and unity taught the night before He died (John 13:34-35)? Also consider Paul's teaching on devotion, love and honor in the body (Romans 12:10). How does your fellowship compare?

6 Is the fellowship in which you are involved characterized by speaking the truth in love, walking in love, light, unity and sharing what we are learning in our spiritual walk with others in the body (Ephesians 5:2, 19; Colossians 3:16-21; Philippians 2:1-2; 1 John:1:7; Acts 2:42)?

▸ If not, what one thing can you do to contribute to change?

THE IMPORTANCE OF SPIRITUAL GIFTS

7 In addition to the gifts given to each believer for the building up of the body of Christ (see Chapter 12), we are told to pursue the gift of prophesy which is based on a growing knowledge of the Word of God, for it is through the sharing of the Word that people are edified, exhorted and receive comfort (1 Corinthians 14:1).

▸ Where would you need to begin in the pursuit of the gift of prophesy?

▸ What exactly is the meaning of edification, exhortation and comfort in this context?

ACCOUNTABILITY

8 Who is your mentor? With whom do you practice James 5:16, "Therefore confess your sins to each other and pray

for each other so that you may be healed. The prayer of a righteous person is powerful and effective"? This is a command, a command for our own good.

9 For growth to occur, areas of need must be identified. In this, we have the guidance of the Holy Spirit as He guides us into all truth (John 16:13). That truth we are told in 2 Peter 1:3 is sufficient for life and godliness. However, there is also a need for someone to hold us accountable.

▸ If you are without a mentor, what steps can you take to locate one?

10 Who are you mentoring or discipling?

SHARING MY FAITH

11 Does the following resonate with you? "Being convinced I could only please God by sharing the gospel at every opportunity, evangelism became a burden to me as well as to those with whom I attempted to share." Explain.

▸ As I studied the sovereignty of God, I began to realize if I asked, He would lead me to individuals with prepared hearts. As I prayed for guidance, I began to see fruit and experience a lot less stress related to sharing my faith.

DISCIPLESHIP

12 Christ's call to a life of commitment and sacrifice is the same as it was 2,000 years ago: "Whoever wants to be my disciple must deny themselves and take up their cross and follow me" (Matthew 16:24b).

▸ These are hard sayings, yet they are a part of the call to discipleship. Where is the Holy Spirit prompting you to deepen your commitment as His disciple?

13 Matthew 28:18b-20 and 2 Timothy 2:15 contain our job description. Jesus said, "All authority in heaven and earth has been given me. Therefore go and make disciples of all na-

tions, baptizing them in the name of the Father and of the Son and of the Holy Spirit, and teaching them to obey everything I have commanded you. And surely I am with you always, to the very end of the age."

▸ List how you are already contributing toward the Great Commission in the area of "teaching them to obey all I have commanded you." Do not overlook the ministry within your own four walls.

▸ Make another list and pray about how you might extend your contribution in time.

▸ Consider opportunities within reach, i.e., other parents at sports events, colleagues at work.

14 What is the prerequisite to "teaching them" given in 2 Timothy 2:1-2, 15?

15 The Great Commission (Matthew 28:18b-20) contains one verb and three participles. The verb "go' is second person plural. This is to be a community effort requiring teamwork. The three participles tell us what we are to do: make disciples, baptize them and teach them to obey all I have commanded you.

▸ What resources are we promised as we go in community to obey this command?

▸ What personal preparation is needed?

AN ATTITUDE OF GRATITUDE AND PRAISE

16 Many of the Old Testament celebrations and festivals were to commemorate a deliverance or blessing from the Lord.

▸ Make a list of your own blessings and times of deliverance from the Lord to use for prayers of praise.

17 How can you apply Ephesians 1:11, Romans 8:28 and 1 Corinthians 10:13 when there is seemingly nothing for which you can praise God?

18 How might "rejoicing" be a safeguard for us (Philippians 3:1-2)?

19 List or underline all the things for which one could be grateful listed in Psalm 34. Pray through the list. Notice how focusing on God's love and care lifts your heart.

CHAPTER 15
PRACTICAL STEPS TOWARD HEALING

TELL YOUR STORY

In his book, *Opening Up: The Healing Power of Confiding in Others*, James Pennebaker head of the department of psychology at the University of Texas, writes that his decades of research indicate that "actively holding back or inhibiting our thoughts and feelings can be hard work... which over time diminishes the body's immune function, heart and vascular health as well as the efficient working of the brain and nervous system often resulting in major and minor illnesses."[47]

Getting your story our into the light of day is crucial for your physical, mental and spiritual healing. Begin by just telling your story. Tell it to your spouse or a trusted friend. Share it in a support group. As you speak, not only will healing begin, you will gain understanding into how your own story has affected your relationship with God, others and yourself. You will also begin to see connections between your story and those of others.

It is often through verbalizing our struggles that the underlying issues which need addressing come to the fore. You will also begin to see effects of abuse and neglect that continue in your life today. If you are a verbal thinker, sharing your story will give insight into where you are in the healing process and how to address the defense mechanisms that have developed because of past harm.

Sharing your story can be easier if you first write it down. If you aren't a writer, bullet points listed chronologically can help get you started. The next chapter, "Writing to Heal," may also be of help as well as the questions for response at the end of the chapter.

Secondly, if you sense a need, find a professional who can guide you on your journey. Local churches often have a list of trusted Christian counselors whom they recommend. However, purpose in your heart before that first appointment, be brutally honest about any past harm or issues with which you are struggling. Current issues may or may not be related to childhood harm, but share them. Your counselor can help you evaluate how best to tackle the issues. Consider making a list of bullet points to guide your discussion. Much time and money can be saved if you go prepared to speak the unbridled truth during that first interview.

Thirdly visit different support groups in your area until you find one that meets your needs. Celebrate Recovery is a Christian version of Alcoholics Anonymous which has groups that address issues of co-dependency as well as other defense mechanisms. Many churches also offer small groups for adult survivors of childhood abuse and neglect.

I learned a great deal from a Celebrate Recovery group for co-dependents that I attended for a year. As I listened to the stories being shared, I could not only see myself but also where my co-dependence could lead. I was also encouraged as I saw my story help others. James 5:16a says, "Therefore confess your sins to each another and pray for each other so that you may be healed." Some commentaries indicate that the meaning of "confess your sins" encompasses "confess your weaknesses, your woundedness" to one another that you may be healed.

Get started. Share with a trusted friend. If you feel led to do so, find a Christian counselor and a support group. All of this will take time, but get started. Then once you have those resources lined up, be honest and don't hold back. Those who share honestly and listen carefully benefit most.

WRITING TO HEAL

Writing for many is a precursor to speaking "your truth;" that which needs to be gotten out into the light of day for healing. Getting thoughts down on paper, examining them to see if they express what you are thinking often not only brings personal clarity and understanding but makes it easier to share what's on your heart.

God used writing in my life to redeem a childhood lost to abuse and shame. In the past when I was asked about my growing up years, I would quickly give some blithe answer about growing up in the country, running barefoot through the cool grass on a hot summer's day, chasing the farm animals, while all the time thinking, "You don't want to know!"

Periodically I had thought writing it all down might enable me to finally be done with it, and perhaps regain some part of my lost childhood, but each time I sat down to write, I couldn't get beyond the first paragraph which I had written decades before. The words refused to come.

Finally, I decided to use the process I had used teaching autobiographical writing in public school:

- List bullet points of memories in no particular order as they come to mind. The important thing being to get them down on paper.
- Organize the list chronologically.
- Expand each memory, adding details.
- Further expand each memory into a paragraph, adding additional information as it comes to mind.
- Combine paragraphs into chapters as details surface.

This is the writing method I used in writing the biographical section of this book.

Writing thoughts down on paper provides distance needed to look at things objectively. Writing can also provide opportunity to recall positive experiences that have become overshadowed by the negative. At times, a thread of God's redeeming work can be observed running through the story.

When I began writing, all I could remember was the abuse and resultant trauma. However, as I wrote, I began to recall serendipitous moments that were like balm to my soul, bringing a smile and at times outright laughter.

As previously mentioned, Dr. James W. Pennebaker has done extensive research at Stanford and the University of Texas related to the health benefits of trauma disclosure through writing. He has been recognized by the American Psychological Association as a top researcher in the field of writing to heal. Based on these studies as well as my own experience and that of others, I believe there is help to be had from simply writing your story. Even more, share your story with a spiritually mature friend or counselor, someone who can reflect it back to you, ask questions and encourage you to write and share further. Getting that story out into the light of day is the first step in healing.

DEVELOPING POSITIVE COPING MECHANISMS

C.R. Snyder in his book entitled Coping: *The Psychology of What Works*, suggests the following steps for developing positive coping mechanisms to replace negative ones.[49]

1. Immediate problem solving: Addressing the problem at hand

If I react badly, I need to apologize and ask for forgiveness, see what I can learn from the incident and move on instead of berating myself for being a "bad Christian" or denying I did anything wrong. I need to live in the present and deal with the present (1 John 1:7-9).

2. Root-cause solving: Addressing the underlying cause

Seek help in dealing with past experiences that could be at the root of current problems. Are you controlling because you were not protected during childhood? Are you super sensitive to suggestions or constructive criticism because you couldn't do anything right as a child (James 5:16; Proverbs 27:6, 17)? Don't use the past as an excuse to continue bad behavior, but do recognize the connection and seek help.

3. Benefit-finding: Look for ways to benefit from your challenges, past and present

I am keenly aware that the experiences from my childhood, although I would never have chosen them, have resulted in insight and empathy for others that I would not have otherwise had. God has promised to bring good out of the bad things that happen but sometimes we need to look for it if we are to recognize it (Romans 8:28).

Look for the following:

- Spiritual growth: Seeking to find opportunities for spiritual and emotional growth.
- Look for patterns of dysfunction in your life.
- Recurring behaviors such as angry outbursts or defensive responses can also be indicative of unresolved issues from the past. Ask trusted friends if they have observed patterns of dysfunction.

In summary, positive coping means seeing problems as growth opportunities, accepting personal responsibility without self-condemnation, asking for forgiveness, then developing a plan that addresses the issues and working that plan with a trusted mentor or counselor.[50]

HEALING CAME SLOWLY AND CONTINUES TODAY

Tim Keller in his book, *Galatians for You*, suggests that we cannot overcome our weaknesses by merely "trying harder." Instead, we must realize at the bottom of our struggles lies our desire to maintain control of our lives through our own efforts or defense mechanisms. Keller refers to these tactics as an effort to save ourselves from pain or discomfort. We are simply looking to something other than God for protection and fulfillment.[51]

When I realize I am getting stressed, it helps if I ask myself, "What am I looking to this person or situation to give me that only God can?" Then I confess it and see what I can do to deal with the situation at hand (John 1:9).[52]

Psalm 18:16-19 says, "He reached down from on high and took hold of me; he drew me out of deep waters.... He brought me out into a spacious place; he rescued me because he delighted in me." The Lord continues to extend the promise of daily deliverance as I am tempted to fall back into old patterns of negative thinking.

THE DAILY BATTLE

The following pages chronical ineffective coping or defense mechanisms and how to counter them in everyday life.

Case in point: Control.

I tend to be a fearful person, fearing that which I cannot control; fear of the future, fear for myself and especially for my family.

I speak the truth: I have a choice. I can "listen" to God's promises to never leave me or forsake me, no matter what happens, or I can live in fear of harm. There is no guarantee evil will not occur. Nowhere in the Bible is that promised. Psalm 34:19 tells us "many are the afflictions of the righteous," however, we do have the promise that when we go through the waters and the fire, He will be with us (Isaiah 43:2). Note it does not say "if" you go through the waters and fire, it says "when."

Case in Point: Perfectionism.

It's 5 o'clock and I wanted to have dinner in the oven by now but arrived home late. As I pull ingredients from the cabinet and refrigerator, I can feel my stress level rising.

I speak the truth: I know at that point, it is time to stop and ask, "Is this about making dinner or about being the perfect wife and homemaker?" Obviously the latter. Worst case scenario, we can eat canned soup.

Whether I have dinner on time or not in no way affects my value as a child of God or my value in the eyes of my husband. I speak the truth. I don't need to be perfect. I am "accepted in the Beloved" (Ephesians 1:5-7, NKJV).

Second Corinthians 10:12 speaks of how unwise it is to compare ourselves with others. It is equally unwise to compare ourselves with some lofty standard. The result will either be discouragement if we don't measure up or pride if we do which are sin on both counts.

Case in point: People Pleasing.

Example 1
I don't like Chinese food. To me it seems overcooked, over salted and starchy, but my husband loves it.

I speak the truth: One evening as we were going out to dinner, he asked where I would like to go. I answered, "Anywhere but Chinese. I really don't like Chinese food." Solution reached: my husband eats Chinese when he goes to lunch.

Trivial though it may sound, this was a big step for me. It opened the door for me to express my preferences rather than trying to second-guess what would make everyone else happy.

It's OK to ask for what you want. You won't get it all the time, but you certainly won't if you don't speak up.

Example 2
I cannot watch SiFi or anything violent. My TV viewing is limited to Masterpiece Theater and BBC Drama. My husband loves SiFi. If I watch it, I don't sleep well. I have learned to accept it and read a good book instead.

I speak the truth: It's OK. I really don't have to be all things to all people. I also know it is from having been exposed to too much violence as a small child in the form of films depicting WW II as well as having been given too much information regarding suicidal ideations in our family. I need to operate within the boundaries of what works for me. "By the grace of God I am what I am" (1 Corinthians 15:10a).

Case in point: Codependence.

I am ultimately only responsible for myself, not for the welfare of the whole world. When I take on responsibility for helping someone or solving a problem they should be solving themselves, I will soon feel overwhelmed, can't sleep, know I am overextended and must reevaluate my involvement and act accordingly.

I speak the truth: I am only responsible for myself. God is responsible for His other children. They are also responsible for themselves. I will help in any way God directs, otherwise, I will not. "Trust in the LORD with all your heart, and lean not on your own understanding; in all your ways acknowledge Him, and **He shall direct your paths**" (Proverbs 3:5-6 NKJV; James 1:5).

Case in point: Transference.

Example 1
Upon occasion I have had the experience of being uncomfortable around someone from the moment we met. Only later would I realize the individual in their appearance or way of relating, reminded me of one of the main players in my childhood.

I speak the truth: In John 7:24 we are told not to judge by appearances but rather to be kind and compassionate (Zechariah 7:9). When relating to these individuals who seem to show up in my life from time to time, I must remind myself, yet again, I am not six years old and have no reason to assume negative intent on their part.

Example 2
In the past I found myself being strangely drawn to tall men with dark hair. My late husband, Louis, and I made a pact early in our marriage. If we were ever attracted to another individual of the opposite sex, we would confide in each other immediately. Louis was reassuring and supportive, although I hadn't a clue as to what was going on until years later when I realized it only happened when the men in some way resembled my father or Nick who also resembled my father in coloring and build.

I speak the truth: Given my childhood experiences, this is understandable; however, I am no longer that child seeking her father. In addition, I claim 2 Corinthians 10:5b, "We take captive every thought to make it obedient to Christ." I also remind myself that I have a heavenly father who is watching over me, caring for me. I no longer need an earthly father.

When there has been a sexual relationship with someone outside of marriage, even if it was not consensual, it is often helpful to pray with a mature believer asking for any and all spiritual ties, sometimes referred to as soul ties, with that individual to be broken.

I have found Neil T. Anderson's book, *The Bondage Breaker*, helpful in addressing the influence of past ties. Ephesians 6:12 (NASB) tells us, "Our struggle is not against flesh and blood, but against the rulers, against the powers, against the world forces of this darkness, against the spiritual forces of wickedness in the heavenly places."[53]

Case in point: Depression.

When I begin feeling depressed or out of sorts, having eliminated all the usual causes such as lack of sleep, recent disappointment, etc., I monitor my thoughts. Am I problem focused or solution focused? When I focus on God, the real God who loves me and gave Himself for me, not the caricature of God I carried around in my head for many years, things come into perspective. I have objectivity, can evaluate the situation and devise a plan for moving forward. If no solution is foreseeable, I simply lay the whole thing at the foot of the cross and leave it there. God has dealt with bigger challenges than any I will lay down before Him.

I speak the truth: "I would have despaired unless I had believed that I would see the goodness of the LORD in the land of the living" (Psalm 27:13 NASB). In the end, it is God's grace that keeps us sane in this crazy world.

If depression lasts more than a few days and is recurrent, professional help must be sought. Time in the Word and prayer will not counter a brain chemical imbalance. Do not try to address this on your own. Seek medical help. In my early thirties, I ignored these symptoms to my own detriment and that of our family and ministry.

Case in point: Independence, Perfectionism, Martyr or Doormat, and Regression.

Having a tendency toward people pleasing, I can become overextended to the point of exhaustion, irritability and being a pain to live with. Having taken on too much, it is easy for me to expect others to step in and help me out, "After all, I help them all the time!"

That request for help may or may not be forthcoming. They actually may have healthy boundaries. If I don't receive help or don't receive it in what I consider a timely manner, I get impatient and do it myself, staying up late and overworking. Besides, didn't I learn as a child that I could depend on no one?

I speak the truth: Lord, I have gotten myself into an absolute state by not seeking your guidance in the responsibilities I accept. Forgive me for going my own way and trying to be the universal mother. Thank you that nothing really matters except walking with You and living in harmony with those around me (Matthew 6:33). Amen.

LEAVING THE PAST BEHIND

From a practical kingdom point of view, the real tragedy of child abuse and neglect in addition to the physical and mental anguish, is the loss of self, security in the Lord's love and spiritual productivity through the effects of abuse taken into adulthood.

For many years, I saw God as a righteous, distant, disapproving deity unlikely to ever be satisfied with any of my accomplishments; a mirror image of my perception of my earthly father.

My giving lip service to the belief that God was a loving Father stood in direct contrast to my inability to understand how a loving Father would allow such unmitigated evil to occur in my life. This led to the conclusion that I was simply not worthy of His protection.

"Of course, bad things happen to me," I concluded, "my parents didn't protect me as a child, neither did God, why should He now?" Although often not acknowledged or recognized for what it was, this belief hung like a dark cloud on the horizon ready to move in during times of discouragement or uncertainty.

This began to change in my thirties when an insightful counselor suggested that rather than focusing on God as my Father, I should try thinking of Jesus as a loving brother who was there carrying me through those horrible periods of my life. It would be years before I recognized God as my loving Father.

Unfortunately, the few times I tried to speak with someone about my emotional and spiritual struggles, I was told I should be careful about what I shared, or I could damage my husband's ministry and advancement opportunities. Sadly, it was an emotional breakdown resulting in part from a lack of guidance and support that eventually brought us home from the mission field.

In time, change did come, although gradually as I continued in the Word, primarily through reading Psalms and other portions of Scripture that spoke of God's love for me, His child. Further progress was made when I participated in a support group for abuse victims. As I listened to the stories of others, I sadly realized I was not such an anomaly. Time spent in inpatient was necessary for several weeks after the emotional breakdown in Germany. That was followed up with months of counseling and years of reading the Word that helped to change my thinking. Several books I found especially helpful are listed in the Reading List.

In time, I *began* to see myself as God's precious child, loved, cherished and gifted. I *also began* to see God as my all-powerful, loving Father who has my best interests at heart. I *began* to see my relationship with others in the body of Christ as a relationship of equals, working together to support each other as we build His kingdom here on earth. I say, *"I began...."* because it was only the beginning, I continue to learn and grow in these areas today.

Should you find yourself in a similar situation, don't look back and say, "I should have gotten help years ago, then I would have had a more fruitful ministry for Christ, now it's too late."

It isn't too late.

It may be had we sought counseling earlier, our ministry would have been more fruitful; however, I do know God honored our obedience to Him and our desire to serve Him as best we knew how at that point. As a result, there are many church leaders and lay ministers serving Christ throughout Germany, the Southwest and the Pacific Northwest who trace their spiritual roots back to time spent in Bible study with us, wounded though we were.

I also am convinced that when we do the best we can with the resources we have, God gives extra grace. Believing God would use us, even as I struggled to believe God loved me, takes a special kind of grace which He honored in the lives of men and women. His Word did not return void.

In the spring of 2016 at a reunion of the students to whom Louis and I had ministered in the 70s and 80s, Wolf Christian, the then director of The Navigators in Germany who was also a former student in our ministry, sat next to me at the dinner table. At the end of our celebratory meal, he said, "Glenda look around you," as he gestured toward the assembled group of former students. "These," he continued, "are the fruits of your labor." Tears of gratitude flowed down my face. May the Lord be praised for His faithfulness during difficult times.

In the intervening years, things have changed a great deal. Most mission organizations now have member care and pastoral care staff who shepherd singles, couples and families, providing a neutral safe place where struggling individuals and couples can obtain help from qualified counselors and coaches. Supervisory staff are also becoming more aware of the need to provide emotional support and encouragement to their ministry staff. Avail yourself of these resources.

Yet for many women and men as well, in full time or lay ministry, it sometimes continues to be easier to endure the suffering of living with an unrealistic, unreachable standard of perfection as they seek the approval of a caricature of a loving Father instilled in their minds from a dysfunctional childhood, rather than admit they need help. Unfortunately the fear of embarrassment should coworkers "find out" or of bringing harm to their ministry, keeps them silent. Do not fall prey to this lie of Satan as I did for many years! Step out in faith and share your struggles with your supervisor or member care staff. That's what they are there for. That is their role.

Sometimes I wonder who I would have been had the abuse never occurred. While I may never know the answer to that question, I do know I have a heart for the hurting and a great understanding for those who suffer. I also have the experience to tell them, "Don't become comfortable in your role as a victim. Recognize what has happened. Mourn your loss, but then by God's grace, forgive the perpetrator. Reclaim your life, day by day, as you trust Him who works all things for good, for those who are called according to His will (Romans 8:28). Then reach out to others who are suffering." Therein lies our ultimate healing.

In conclusion, know this, if you were parented by mortals, you will have baggage! If you parent mortals, they will have baggage! Use the tools and resources God has given to counter the negative coping mechanisms developed early on and enjoy the life He has given living it to His glory "knowing Heaven, once attained, will work backwards and turn even the agony (of all we have experienced here on earth) into a glory"[54] (2 Corinthians 4:17).

Although my life was affected by abuse and neglect, it is not defined by that abuse. My life is defined by my relationship to the King of Kings. I am his beloved daughter.

You turned my wailing into dancing;
you removed my sackcloth and clothed me with joy,
that my heart may sing your praises and not be silent.
Lord my God, I will praise you forever.
Psalm 30:11-12

RESPONSE

TELL YOUR STORY

1. Do you have a story of childhood trauma?

2. Have you shared this story with anyone? What was their response?

3. Please know if you share your story with those who have unresolved issues of childhood trauma, their response may be less than enthusiastic. But also know that hearing your story may be the first step in moving them toward dealing with their own issues.

▸ Why do you think these individuals often respond negatively?

WRITING TO HEAL

4 Writing for many is a precursor to speaking "your truth." Getting thoughts down on paper can provide distance needed to look at things objectively. It can also provide opportunity to recall positive experiences that have become overshadowed by the negative. Often a thread of God's redeeming work can also be observed throughout the story.

5 Use the method below to write a rough draft of your story.

▸ List bullet points of memories in no particular order as they come to mind. The important thing is to get them down on paper.

▸ Forget grammar, spelling and style, just write as thoughts come to mind.

▸ Organize the list chronologically.

▸ Expand each memory, adding details.

▸ Further expand each memory into a paragraph, adding additional information as it comes to mind.

▸ Combine related paragraphs into chapters as details surface.

Reread what you have written asking the Lord to bring to mind additional events that would contribute to healing. Incorporate the memories into your story.

6 Share your story with a counselor or someone you trust who can reflect it back to you, ask questions and give suggestions for your continued journey. This will encourage you to write and share further. Getting that story out into the light of day is a big step toward healing.

DEVELOPING POSITIVE COPING MECHANISMS

C.R. Snyder in his book, Coping: The Psychology of What Works, as referenced in Chapter 15 of this text, suggests practical steps for developing positive coping mechanisms. Review that section before answering the following questions:

▸ Why do you think Snyder starts with "Immediate Problem Solving: Addressing the Problem at Hand"?

▸ Explain how you would go about Snyder's second step: Root-cause solving which is addressing the underlying cause (James 5:16; Proverbs 27:6, 17; John 8:32).[55]

▸ Benefit-finding: Look for ways to benefit from your challenges, past and present (Romans 8:28). Make a list.

▸ Spiritual growth: List possible ways of turning the problem into an opportunity for spiritual growth.

▸ Also consider asking trusted friends if they have observed patterns of dysfunction in your life. Take their observations before the Lord asking for insight and a plan to deal with them.

In summary, positive coping means seeing problems as growth opportunities, accepting personal responsibility without self-condemnation, then developing a plan that addresses the issues and working that plan.

HEALING CAME SLOWLY AND CONTINUES TODAY

7 Tim Keller in *Galatians for You*, states, "We cannot overcome our weaknesses by 'trying harder.' Instead, we must realize...at the bottom of our struggle lies our desire to maintain control of our lives through our own efforts [defense mechanisms]. We do this in an effort to save ourselves from pain. We are ... looking to something other than God for protection and fulfillment."[56]

▸ Can you pinpoint an area in your life where this may be true? Take it to the Lord and ask what He would have you do. Discuss it with your spiritual leader, mentor or counselor. Look up related Scripture that will be a support.

THE DAILY BATTLE

8 Review "Dysfunctional Coping Mechanisms" Chapter 12 of the text, then do the following exercise:

▸ Make a list of the Dysfunctional Coping Mechanisms listed in Chapter 12 that you utilize in your daily life.

▸ Spend some time thinking about specific situations where you employ the dysfunctional coping mechanisms that you listed.

▸ Using the format in Chapter 15 of the text under the sub heading "The Daily Battle," individually analyze the situations where you utilize dysfunctional coping mechanisms that came to mind and describe them under "Analyze (Case in point)."

Case in point: *Describe a situation in which you personally utilize a specific defense mechanism.*

▸ Next under "Speak the Truth," describe how you can counter the defense mechanism used with truth from the Scripture. Again, follow examples from "The Daily Battle" Chapter 15 in the text.

Speak the Truth: *Remind yourself of truth from God's Word that will help you counter the specific defense mechanism you are addressing.*

LEAVING THE PAST BEHIND

9 Set aside some time to prayerfully look back over Part III, Chapter 13—"Effective Strategies for Healing," Chapter 14—"Spiritual Disciplines," and Chapter 15—"Practical

Steps toward Healing" asking God to make you aware of any steps that you still need to take to move forward in the process of *Leaving the Past Behind and Moving Forward with Hope and Courage.*

▸ Write down any steps that He brings to mind. Share them with someone who will encourage you to follow through and hold you accountable. We all need support in this area.

10 Spend time in quiet reflection, asking God how He can redeem the woundedness that you have experienced and use it for ministry in the lives of others. Then praise Him for His redeeming grace that wastes nothing that we have experienced.

Praise be to the God and Father of our Lord Jesus Christ,
the Father of compassion and the God of all comfort,
who comforts us in all our troubles,
so that we can comfort those in any trouble
with the comfort we ourselves receive from God.
2 Corinthians 1:3-4

APPENDIX
GIFTS FROM MY PARENTS

Among my mother's gifts to me was an interest in the pursuit of God. Although she had to wear thick reading glasses and use a magnifying glass as she held the Bible within inches of her face, she did her best to read the Bible to my sister and me. Her favorite passages were from the gospels which she would read until her eyes ached with strain.

I will forever be influenced by her determination to never assume she could not accomplish a task without first trying. Whether it was reading a book, or upholstering a couch with an old bedspread, she never backed down. Years later on the mission field, I would do the same. Our old faded sofa gained years of new life under that orange and yellow striped bedspread turned upholstery fabric.

As there was little construction work to be had in our area, Papa often had to work away from home. This meant the farm work, care of the animals, milking, birthing, all of it fell to mother.

Her willingness to do whatever it took to care for and provide for her family whether it meant repairing a fence in the middle of the night or straining to read the Bible to her young girls, makes her a guiding light in my life.

Mixed in with the difficult times runs a golden thread of rich times of learning from the two wonderful people who were my parents. They used all the resources they had to raise my sister and me. I am very grateful for their love and care despite their own hardship and suffering. I first became aware of my father's love of books when at age five I noticed the five inch thick, burnt orange volume of Webster's Dictionary lying on our rickety homemade bookshelf. It must have been a new acquisition as there were few other books besides the dictionary and the Bible on the shelf and I could hardly have missed it lying next to my two Little Golden Books, *Santa's Workshop* and *Cinderella* and a few secondhand paperbacks of Papa's. At that time, our entire library in addition to the titles above consisted of an old copy of *Lost Horizons* and few Zane Grey paperbacks. But all that would soon change once Papa discovered the People's Book Club and new books began arriving each month. However, none of those books would ever compare to that grand orange dictionary.

In the middle there was a section containing colored illustrations of innumerable species from the plant and animal kingdom. Once discovered, I could often be found pouring over those illustrations of strange creatures and insect eating plants with some alarm as I wondered if there was a little girl eating plant as well.

Papa loved those illustrations too and would sometimes comment on one or the other. A few years later, we would become the proud owners of the first set of encyclopedias in our neighborhood. Immediately I found Volume A and looked up animals, then plants where to my delight I found even more illustrations. When Papa wasn't so tired he had to go to bed right after supper, I would often see him sitting in a straight back chair or on the old recovered couch reading one of the volumes.

If ever there was a dirt farmer, construction worker, renaissance man, it was my father, encyclopedia educated. From years of reading in many different areas, he could talk with anyone on just about any topic that wasn't purely academic. I just wish I had inherited his memory as well as his love of learning.

He was a wonderful conversationalist and armchair philosopher with a keen sense of justice. I remember one summer he hired a local man, Jed, from the African American community to help with the work on the farm that he was no longer able to do alone. When it came time for the noon meal, Papa said to Jed, "Dinner is ready, we'll wash up at the well, then go on in."

Jed stopped short and said, "No, Mista Louis, that wouldn't be right."

Papa responded, "Jed, any man good enough to work on my place is good enough to sit at my table."

Papa's sense of justice would influence my actions for years to come from riding in the back of the bus in the 60s to teaching inner-city minority kids for over a decade and a half.

Once after an evening spent discussing American History of the 1700s, my late husband, Louis, who had several advanced degrees, including a master's degree in history, remarked that my father had a much better grasp of early American history than he did.

Papa's love for history was also passed on to me influencing my studies at the university as well as my returning to Europe in my 60s to teach history at an international school. During our years in Europe, I listened with great interest to firsthand accounts of life during WW II and visited numerous historical sites. It was easy. They were everywhere.

READING LIST

Akin, Paul, "The Number One Reason Missionaries Go Home," May 25, 2017. Accessed October 15, 2017. https://www.imb.org/2017/05/25/number-one-reasons missionaries-go-home/.

Anderson, Neil T., *The Bondage Breake*r (Eugene, Oregon: Harvest House Publishers, 2000).

Babbel, Susanne, "Who Are the Perpetrators of Child Abuse?" *Psychology Today,* May 2011. Accessed November 2018. https://www.psychologytoday.com/us/blog/somatic-psychology/201105/who-are-the-perpetrators-child-abuse.

van der Kolk, Bassel, "Post-Traumatic Stress Disorder and the Nature of Trauma," *Dialogues* in Clinical Neuroscience, NXBI-NIH. Mar: 2(1):7-22. 2. Accessed November 23, 2017. https://www.ncbi.nlm.nih.gov/pmc/articles/PMC3181584/.

Beattie, Melody, *Codependent No More: How to Stop Controlling Others and Start Caring for Yourself* (Center City, Minnesota: Hazelden Foundation, 1992).

The Language of Letting Go: Hazelden Mediation Series (Center City, Minnesota: Hazelden Publishing, 1990).

Bremner, J.D., "Traumatic Stress: Effects on the Brai*n," Dialogues in Clinical Neuroscience* - NCBI - NIH. Accessed September 27, 2017. https://www.ncbi.nlm.nih.gov/pmc/articles/PMC3181836/.

Britain Lorey, *It's MY Body: A Book to Teach Young Children How to Resist Uncomfortable Touch, Children's Safety Series and Abuse Prevention,* January 1, 1982. https://www.amazon.com/Its-Body-Uncomfortable-Childrens.../dp/0943990033.

Brogaard, Berit, "Five Signs That You're Dealing with a Passive Aggressive Person and How to Respond Effectively," *Psychology Today,* November 2016. Accessed August 14, 2018. https://www.psychologytoday.com/blog/the-superhuman-mind/201611/5-signs-youre-dealing-passive-agcgressive-person.

Colman, Andrew M., *The Oxford Dictionary of Psychology* (3ed.) (Oxford: Oxford University Press, 2008).

Johnson, Joni E., "Female Animal Abusers," *Psychology Today*, July 2012, Accessed August 18, 2018. https://www.psychologytoday.com/us/blog/the-human-equation/201207/female-animal-abusers.

Keller, Tim, *Galatians for You*. (United Kingdom: The Good Book Company, 2013).

Walking with God through Pain and Suffering (New York: Penguin Random House LLC, 2013).

Klemm, William R., "Thwart Stress Effects of Memory," *Psychology Today*, December 2016. Accessed June 12, 2018. https://www.psychologytoday.com/us/blog/memory-medic/201612/thwart-stress-effects-memory.

Lerner, Harriet, *The Dance of Anger: A Woman's Guide to Changing the Patterns of Intimate Relationships* (New York: William Morrow & Co, an Imprint of Harper Collins Publishers, 2014).

Lewis, C.S., *The Great Divorce* (New York: Harper Collins Publishers, 1973).

Murray, Bridget, "Writing to Heal," *Journal of the American Psychological Society*, June 2002.

Pagato, Sherry, "Are You a People Pleaser?" *Psychology Today*, October 2012. Accessed August 18, 2018. https://www.psychologytoday.com/us/blog/shrink/201210/are you-people-pleaser.

Pennebaker, James W., "Emotion Disclosure and Health," *The American Psychological Association*, 2018, January 20, 2018. Accessed July 13, 2018. http://www.apa.org/pubs/books/4318401.aspx?tab=3.

Opening Up: The Healing Power of Confiding in Others (New York: Avon Books, 1991).

Reinhart, Paula, *Sex and the Soul of a Woman* (Grand Rapids: Zondervan, 2010). "To Have a Friend: Overcome the Most Common Way Women Sabotage a Potential Friendship." Accessed September 20, 2018. http://www.paularinehart.com/blog/2017/1/18/to-have-a-friend

Rusty Rustenbach, *A Guide for Listening and Inner-Healing Prayer: Meeting God in the Broken Places* (Colorado Springs, Nav Press, 2011).

Schaefer, Frauke C. and Schaefer, Charles A., eds. *Trauma and Resilience: Effectively Supporting Those Who Serve God* (Chapel Hill, North Carolina, August 2012).

Seamands, David A., *Healing for Damaged Emotions* (Colorado Springs, Colorado: David C. Cook, 1981).

Snyder, C.R., ed. *Coping: The Psychology of What Works* (New York: Oxford University Press, 1999).

Spurgeon, C.H., *Treasury of David.* Accessed September 18, 2018. https://www.blueletterbible.org/Comm/spurgeon_charles/tod/ps134.cfm?a=612001.

Stanley, Charles, "The Benefits of Praise," *In Touch Magazine*, January 26, 2015. Accessed March 18, 2018. https://www.intouch.org/read/magazine/daily-devotions/150126-the-benefits-of-praise.

Straker, David, *Dictionary of Psychology* Accessed August 14,2018. www.changingminds.org/explanations/behaviors/coping/intellectualization.htm.

Taylor, William D., *Too Valuable to Lose: Exploring the Causes and Cures of Missionary Attrition*, Globalization of Missions Series, 1997. Accessed September 21, 2017. http://www.worldevangelicals.org/resources/rfiles/res3_168_link_1292517737.pdf.

Thorpe, Catherine, *The Healing Timeline* (Bellevue, WA: Timeline Press, 2009).

Whitbourne, Susan Krauss, "The Essential Guide to Defense Mechanisms," *Psychology Today*, Sep 6, 2017. Accessed January 14, 2018. https://www.psychologytoday.com/us/blog/fulfillment-any-age/201110/the-essential-guide-defense-mechanisms.

Whitney, Donald S., *Spiritual Disciplines for the Christian Life*, Updated 20th Century Edition (Colorado Springs, Nav Press, 2014).

Willard, Dallas, *Hearing God: Developing a Conversational Relationship with God* (Downers Grove, IL: InterVarsity Press, 2012).
The Spirit of the Disciplines: Understanding How God Changes Lives (New York: Harper Collins, 1991).

Wuest, Kenneth S., *Wuest's Word Studies: From the Greek New Testament,* Volume II (Grand Rapids, Michigan: B. Eerdmans Publishing Company, 1973).

ABOUT THE AUTHOR

Glenda Platt Alvord

An adventuress from childhood, it was not surprising that Glenda left home at 16 to attend a high school that would better prepare her for college. Nor would it have been surprising that she traveled to Lesvos, Greece at age 70 to minister to Syrian refugees.

Her role models were her parents who eked a living from unproductive farm land while her father supplemented the family income working construction despite severe back injury. Both parents wanted more for their girls and sacrificed dearly to pay tuition at Auburn University where Glenda would be the first in her family to graduate.

Following graduation and a stint teaching middle schoolers, Glenda and her new husband, Louis Platt, traveled to Germany with the Navigator's Collegiate Ministry where they would serve for a decade and a half at the universities of Bonn and Mainz.

When their daughter's ill health and Glenda's emotional state brought them home from Europe, Louis served as associate pastor at West Side Presbyterian Church in Seattle and Glenda taught language arts and writing to encarcerated youth for Seattle Public Schools.

After Louis' death in 2010, Glenda remarried in 2012 and returned to the mission field in Kandern, Germany with husband, Herb Alvord, where they worked at Black Forest Academy and became involved with Greater Europe Mission as shepherds for young missionary families. This traveling ministry took them from Ireland to Bulgaria where they delighted in being grandparents to missionary kids and providing encouragement to their parents.

Glenda currently lives in the Pacific Northwest from which she travels to Europe several times a year where she continues to walk alongside young missionary women and their families. She can be reached at leavingthepastbehindblog.@wordpress.com or by email at leaving.the.past.behind.blog@gmail.com.

ENDNOTES

1. Bassel van der Kolk, M.D., *"Posttraumatic Stress Disorder and the Nature of* Trauma," *Dialogues in Clinical Neuroscience*, NXBI-NIH. Mar: 2(1):7-22. 22, https://www.ncbi.nlm.nih.gov/pmc/articles/PMC3181584/.

2. Susanne Babbel Ph.D., MFT, "Who Are the Perpetrators of Child Abuse?" *Psychology Today,* May 2011, https://www.psychologytoday.com/us/blog/somatic-psychology/201105/who-are-the-perpetrators-child-abuse.

3. William R. Klemm, Ph.D., "Thwart Stress Effects of Memory," *Psychology Today,* December 2016. https://www.psychologytoday.com/us/blog/memory-medic/201612/thwart-stress-effects-memory.

4. Joni E. Johnson Psy.D., "Female Animal Abusers," *Psychology Today*, July 2012, https://www.psychologytoday.com/us/blog/the-human-equation/201207/female-animal-abusers

5. Bridget Murray, "Writing to Heal," J*ournal of the American Psychological Society,* June 2002, 25.

6. J.D. Bremner, "Traumatic Stress: Effects on the brain," *Dialogues in Clinical Neuroscience* - NCBI - NIH. https://www.ncbi.nlm.nih.gov/pmc/articles/PMC3181836/

7. Lorey Britain, *It's MY Body: A Book to Teach Young Children How to Resist Uncomfortable Touch, Children's Safety Series and Abuse Prevention*, https://www.amazon.com/Its-Body-Uncomfortable-Childrens.../dp/0943990033.

8. Eds. Frauke C. Schaefer, M.D., Charles A. Schaefer, Ph.D., *Trauma and Resilience: Effectively Supporting Those Who Serve God* (Chapel Hill, North Carolina, August 2012), 84.

9. Timothy Keller, *Walking with God through Pain and Suffering* (New York: Penguin Random House LLC, 2013), 26-27.

10 Mary DeMuth, Writer's Conference, Burtigny, Switzerland, October 2016.

11. Keller, *Walking with God through Pain and Suffering,* 26-27.

12. Timothy Keller, *Galatians for You* (Epsom, England: The Good Book Company, 2013), 69.

13. Ibid.

14. Paul Akin, *The Number One Reason Missionaries Go Home*, May 25, 2017. https://www.imb.org/2017/05/25/number-one-reason-missionaries-go-home/.

15. William D. Taylor, *Too Valuable to Lose: Exploring the Causes and Cures of Missionary Attrition*, Globalization of Missions Series, http://www.worldevangelicals.org/resources/rfiles/res3_168_link_1292517737.pdf.

16. David A. Seamands, *Healing for Damaged Emotions: Recovering from the Memories That Cause Our Pain* (Colorado Springs: David C. Cook, 1981), 79-82.

17 Ibid, 27-29.

18. Berit Brogaard, D.M. Sci. Ph.D., *5 Signs That You're Dealing with a Passive Aggressive Person and How to Respond Effectively, Psychology Today*, November 2016, https://www.psychologytoday.com/blog/the-superhuman-mind/201611/5-signs-youre-dealing-passive-agcgressive-person.

19. Andrew M. Colman, PhD, *The Oxford Dictionary of Psychology* (Oxford: Oxford University Press, 2019), 637.

20. http://www.paularinehart.com/blog/2017/1/18/to-have-a-friend.

21. www.merriamwebster.com/dictionary.

22. Sherry Pagato, Ph.D., *Are You a People Pleaser?, Psychology Today*, October 2012, https://www.psychologytoday.com/us/blog/shrink/201210/are-you-people-pleaser

23 Melody Beattie, *Codependent No More: How to Stop Controlling Others and Start Caring for Yourself* (Center City, Minnesota: Hazelden Publishing, 1992), 98.

24. Beattie, *Codependent No More*, 120.

25. Ibid., 122.

26. Ibid., 156.

27. changingminds.org/explanations/behaviors/coping/intellectualization.htm.

28. Susan Krauss Whitbourne Ph. D., The Essential Guide to Defense Mechanisms, Psychology Today, Sep 6, 2017. https://www.psychologytoday.com/us/blog/fulfillment-any-age/201110/the-essential-guide-defense-mechanisms.

29. Ibid.

30. Seamands, *Healing for Damaged Emotions*, 79-80.

31. Andrew M. Colman, Ph.D., *The Oxford Dictionary of Psychology* (Oxford: Oxford University Press, 2019), 637. http://www.oxfordreference.com/abstract/10.1093/acref/9780199534067.001.0001/acref-9780199534067-e-7077?rskey=LdWUUV&result=7341.

32. Ibid.

33. Pagato, *Are You a People Pleaser?*

34. Beattie, *Codependent No More*, 120.

35. Andrew M. Colman, PhD, *The Oxford Dictionary of Psychology* online version. (Oxford: Oxford University Press, 2019). http://www.oxfordreference.com/abstract/10.1093/acref/9780199534067.001.0001/acref-9780199534067-e-7077?rskey=LdWUUV&result=7341.

36. Seamands, *Healing for Damaged Emotions*, 79.

37. Rusty Rustenbach, *A Guide for Listening and Inner-Healing Prayer: Meeting God in the Broken Places* (Colorado Springs, Nav Press, 2011).

38. Willard, Dallas, *Hearing God: Developing a Conversational Relationship with God* (Downers Grove, IL: InterVarsity Press, 2012).

39. Seamands, *Healing for Damaged Emotions*, 79.

40. Ibid, 136.

41. Rustenbach, *A Guide for Listening and Inner-Healing Prayer*, 51-62.

42. Kenneth S. Wuest, *Wuest's Word Studies: From the Greek New Testament* (Grand Rapids, Michigan: Wm. B. Eerdmans Publishing Company, 1973) 182.

43. Melodie Beattie, *The Language of Letting Go*: Hazelden Mediation Series (Center City, Minnesota: Hazelden Publishing, 1990), 197.

44. C.H. Spurgeon, *Treasury of David,* Commentary on Psalm 134. https://www.blueletterbible.org/Comm/spurgeon_charles/tod/ps134.cfm?a.=612001.

45. Charles Stanley, "The Benefits of Praise," *In Touch Magazine*, January 26, 2015. https://www.intouch.org/read/magazine/daily-devotions/150126-the-benefits-of-praise.

46. Kenneth S. Wuest, *Wuest's Word Studies: From the Greek New Testament,* Volume II. (Grand Rapids, Michigan: Wm. B. Eerdmans Publishing Company, 1973), 182.

47. James W. Pennebaker, *Emotion Disclosure and Health,* The American Psychological Association, 2018. http://www.apa.org/pubs/books/4318401.aspx?tab=3.

48. Ibid.

49. C.R. Snyder Ed., *Coping: The Psychology of What Works* (Oxford University Press, 1999). http://changingminds.org/explanations/behaviors/coping/positive_coping.htm.

50. Ibid.

51. Keller, *Galatians for You*, 69.

52. Ibid.

53. Neil Anderson, *The Bondage Breaker* (Eugene, Oregon: Harvest House Publishers, 2000), 199-253.

54. C.S. Lewis, *The Great Divorce* (New York: Harper Collins Publishers, 1973), 64.

55. Snyder, Coping: *The Psychology of What Works* http://changingminds.org/explanations/behaviors/coping/positive_coping.htm.

56. Keller, *Galatians for You*, 69.

AFTERWORD

After 14 years of university ministry in Germany, we returned to the States in the fall of 1988. Thanks to the support of friends, family and ministry supporters, the transition back was easier than expected. Through continued counseling we learned new ways of communicating and supporting one another. The change of climate, as the German doctors predicted, did wonders for our daughter's allergies and she was soon healthy again.

Louis ministered at our home church in Arlington, Texas while he completed his doctoral studies. I involved myself with the children and their busy lives of sports, church and school activities. A Bible study for survivors of childhood abuse taught by a good friend was a tremendous help during that first year back. There were of course times of discouragement and depression however they became increasingly shorter in duration.

In the winter of 1992 Louis was called to West Side Presbyterian Church in Seattle as Associate Minister of Discipleship and Outreach where he continues to be remembered for his shepherd's heart and wise counsel gained from the school of experience. The Saturday morning men's Bible Study and small groups that he began continues to flourish. He was a master of church history and his classes on the subject are still spoken of today. Shortly before he died in 2010 a parishioner wrote on his blog, "Louis, you spent years teaching us how to live. Now you are showing us how to die."

In 1994 I began teaching language arts for Seattle Public schools where I would continue until the year after Louis died. Those were productive years during which I was honored by King County Commissioner, Ron Sims for increasing reading scores of incarcerated youth at King County Detention Center. An article in the local Seattle newspaper highlighting that success was carried nation-wide by the AP. Almost immediately I began receiving phone calls from language arts teachers across the country many of whom successfully adopted my methods of teaching reading specifically to incarcerated youth.

In 2011 I met Herb Alvord, a Baptist minister with a heart for missions. A year later we were married and shortly after went to the mission field where we initially worked at Black Forest Academy, then with Greater Europe Mission walking alongside young missionary couples. In 2017 Herb was diagnosed with Non Hodgkin Lymphoma and died 15 months later.

I continue the work with Greater Europe Mission walking alongside young missionary families and singles, traveling to Europe several times a year.

I have been blessed with a joyful life of ministry born out of experiences that could only come from walking with the Lord through difficult times.

"He reached down from on high and took hold of me; he drew me out of deep waters. He rescued me..." and sent me out "to dance with the joyful."

Psalm 18:16, Jeremiah 31:3,4

Glenda Platt Alvord
Seattle, Washington

Made in the USA
Columbia, SC
08 September 2019